This book is dedicated to the RSPCA and Freedom Food, the RSPCA's nationwide farm animal assurance and food labelling scheme, that follows animals' wellbeing from birth to slaughter. Freedom Food focuses solely on improving the welfare of farm animals reared for food, so all members of the Freedom Food scheme meet the RSPCA's strict welfare standards.

Together we both strongly and passionately believe that what the RSPCA does is outstanding both for the welfare of animals and for the future of this country. British farmers produce some of the finest quality meats, off the best land, from native breeds which can and should continue to improve things for both the animal and the consumer, with the animal always coming first.

'As a farmer and butcher it is my duty to provide my animals with good husbandry, then I can provide my customers with quality items and a clear conscience.'
Tim Wilson

'As a food writer it is my passion to search out provenance ingredients. When it comes to meat this means it must have been looked after well, naturally fed, considerately slaughtered, dry aged and purchased from a reputable butcher in order for me to truly enjoy my work in the kitchen.'
Fran Warde

'It is clear that the Ginger Pig have their hearts and minds in good animal husbandry and are excelling at demystifying where food comes from. I am delighted we were able to recognise them in the RSPCA Good Business Awards 2010 and wish them every success for the future.'
David Bowles, Director of Communications, RSPCA

GINGER PIG
MEAT BOOK

TIM WILSON & FRAN WARDE

Photography by Kristin Perers

MITCHELL BEAZLEY

Contents

THE GINGER PIG

Tim with Brisket, a Grand Bassett Griffon Vendeen.

This book is a meat manual for the inquisitive domestic cook. The word 'provenance' is thrown about a lot these days with regards to the food we eat, and with very good reason, as it means 'to know the origin, source, birthplace, roots, pedigree and derivation'. All these things are vital for us to know about every piece of meat we buy.

You'll find out how meat changes through the seasons and what is best to cook at each time of the year. You'll also learn about the different cuts of meat and what they should be used for in your kitchen. We hope to empower you to have an educated conversation with your local butcher and feel that you can shop for meat with knowledge and enjoyment.

One of my greatest pleasures is helping people to understand British farming: where meat comes from and how it should be farmed. Small rural farming enterprises are dying out, and need to be supported because they form the foundation of the countryside. Good farmers look after their stock well – it is their greatest asset – and give the butcher excellent meat.

Farming has created our countryside: the cottages, fields, hedgerows, stock, green fields and birds. If we want to keep all this beauty, we need to buy British meat and produce.

My business, The Ginger Pig, has enabled me to keep an upland farm with livestock, give employment to skilled stockmen and butchers and, while doing this, increase the numbers of native British breeds. I would like to see more businesses follow a model of animals being reared and sold by one owner, who is then more responsible for the wellbeing of his stock.

Throughout this book, Fran and I show you the hard work and skill that goes into producing quality meat. We also describe the best breeds (all native British breeds; my passion), how they should be farmed and fed to deliver the very best meat and most importantly, how they should be cooked. I just want to add one short note to hearten and encourage all those who want to farm sustainably and with great care for their animals. At the start of The Ginger Pig I needed a bank loan. I visited a local bank, who told me that the business was a daft idea and it would never work. So I spruced up and promptly drove down to London, where a large bank liked the idea and supported me; today I employ more than 40 staff.

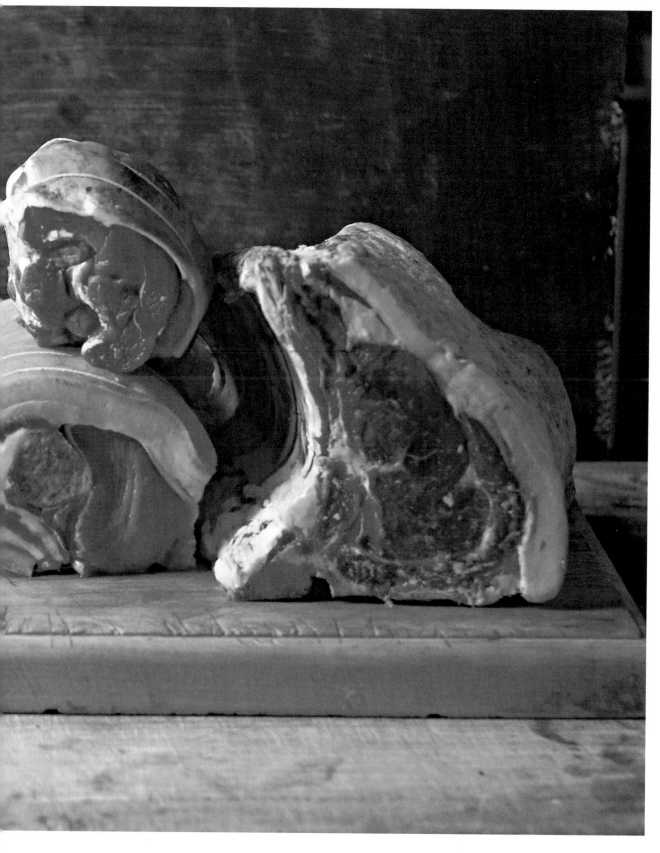

MEAT

MEAT

High-quality meat starts well before it gets to the butcher: with the farmer. In order to produce the best meat it is important to farm the right breeds, as each is suited to different parts of the country and to various methods of farming, and each has its own unique qualities for cooking.

At The Ginger Pig, we select breeds that are often rare and native to the British Isles, and allow them to mature naturally. This slow development enables us to deliver a superior quality of meat for the cook and diner. Think twice before you sling a polystyrene-encased plastic-wrapped cut of meat into your trolley; will you really enjoy it or will it just suffice?

Selecting the right meat

When buying meat, be aware of how you want to cook it. There are 3 distinct areas on animals, and the method of cooking each for the best results is different due to the way that the muscles have been worked.
1. The hardest working muscles support the head and front of the animal: neck, shoulder and fore shin. These all need long, slow, moist cooking.
2. The muscles that do no heavy work are in the middle of the animal: ribs, sirloin and fillet. These need quick cooking, and can be served rare.
3. The medium-worked muscles are at the rear of the animal: silverside, rump and shin, and these can be grilled, roasted or braised.
See pages 26-29, 48-49 and 68-69 for a more detailed guide to how to cook these different cuts from a pig, a cow and a sheep.

Supermarkets like to sell boneless meat, as sharp bones can pierce their packaging, meaning it cannot be sold. But a good butcher will encourage you to buy bone-in meat, especially for slow cooking, as it enhances and adds depth to the flavour.

Meat needs to 'breathe', so store it with cool, fresh air circulating. When you buy meat at a butcher, it should be wrapped in greaseproof paper. At home, unwrap it and put it on a plate in the refrigerator.

Talk to your butcher

Make friends with your butcher, discuss what you want to cook, listen to him and be led by his advice. If you're not satisfied with the guidance you receive, talk it through with him next time and ask where you went wrong. All good butchers enjoy customers who want to learn more.

An early-morning delivery to the Moxon Street shop from our farm in Yorkshire.

Enquire which meat offers good value, as the priciest cut is not always the best, and you need to shop according to what you can cook, the limits of your budget and the seasons. I recall a customer coming into the shop and seeing a gleaming, perfectly marbled piece of topside. They said they wanted a large slice of it. When I asked how they were going to cook it, 'fry' came the answer. I stopped them buying it and suggested a piece of tasty rump, which is far better for frying. They arrived back a week later and asked for another suggestion.

Rolled brisket hanging at the butchers.

Knives and knife skills

It is not important to have the most expensive, desirable or fashionable knives on the market; what is critical is how you look after them. You should sharpen them constantly and gently on a wet stone or steel. The vital thing is the angle at which the knives are run down the steel; it must be at 25 degrees to the steel. You only need to apply gentle pressure; with knives in good condition it should only take four or five sweeps each side to sharpen the blade. Never put your knives in the dishwasher (it blunts the blade) and store them on a wall magnet or in a knife pouch; not in a drawer being bashed and blunted. Try not to share your knives with others, they should become moulded to your hand only. This is hard in family life, but maybe you could hide away your most used and favoured knife, so you can be the master of a beautiful and well-tooled instrument.

A good butcher is gentle with his tools, whether he is sharpening knives or butchering a carcass, and so should you be when handling meat and knives at home. No blade should be forced through a cut with brute strength; it is all about making long, clean, gliding cuts through the meat, which will leave it with a lovely clean slice and sheen.

Butchers have a neat and concise collection of knives: a 12-inch blade for slicing steaks; a six-inch blade for boning out; an 8-inch cleaver for chopping; a 12-inch saw; a trussing needle; and a steel and wet stone to keep knives sharp. (A saw can't be sharpened; you have to replace the blade.) You will only need a few knives to do everything.

When seaming or cutting out bones, only use the tip of your knife and employ a gentle stroking, cutting motion. Feel for the bones with the tip of the knife and gently cut around them where possible so that you end up with a naturally formed piece of meat.

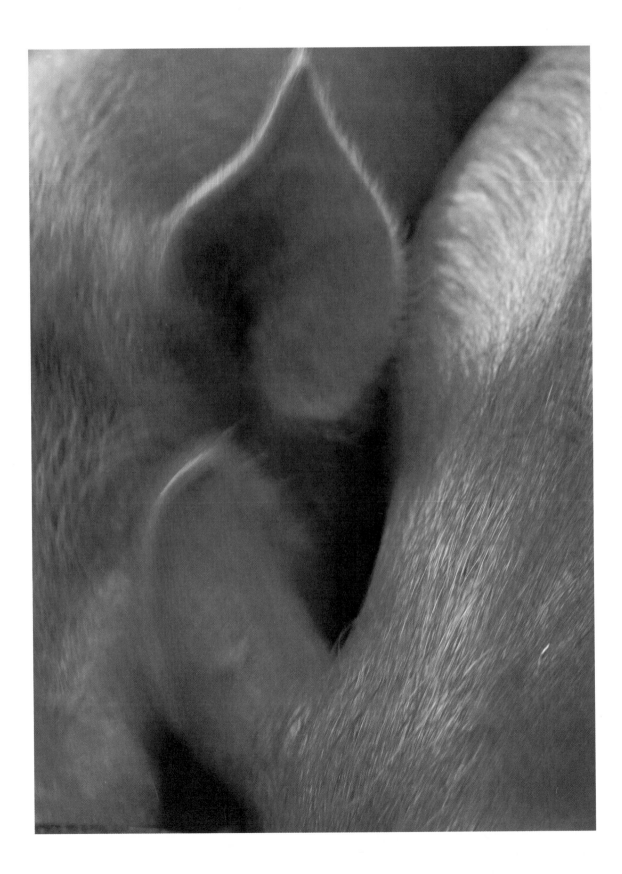

PORK

Fifteen years ago we started The Ginger Pig farm with three gilt (virgin sow) Tamworth pigs – Milli, Molly and Mandy – and a boar called Dai Bando (the name was inspired by *How Green was my Valley*). Each of the gilts delivered eight piglets, so within four months we had 24 piglets.

Pigs breed – and piglets grow – so fast that it became, for us, an addictive game. More boars were bought, to produce a good strong strain. It was going so well that we ran out of pens, so Chrysanthemum farrowed under the kitchen table, producing a litter of 8 little squeakers.

Today we have 1,000 pigs, both breeding stock and fattening pigs, and 6 breeds: Tamworth, Gloucester Old Spot, Berkshire, Saddleback, Lop and Welsh. I've just added the Plum Pudding (or Oxford) breed; it was prized by the Victorians and was a traditional smallholding pig. This cross between a Berkshire sow and Tamworth boar is a hardy, docile, pig with a coat of orange with black splodges (hence the name of the breed, Plum Pudding).

About pig breeds

Old-fashioned pure-breed pigs have some in-built problems. Pure-bred Gloucester Old Spot, for instance, can carry excessive amounts of fat. This was not a problem when most pork was eaten by manual workers who spent long hours in the cold outside, but doesn't suit today's more sedentary lifestyle. And Tamworths have a litter size problem – it can vary greatly – which makes things difficult for the farmer. So in Britain we cross-breed our pigs to create strong, healthy animals that make excellent eating, but sometimes cross-breeding is done more with profit than quality in mind. Of course, many small producers do carefully cross breed for quality in the final product.

Mass-produced breeds

The pork that mass-production farmers produce has changed, mostly due to the demands of supermarkets. These corporate monoliths and their customers don't want cuts with much fat. Also, pigs that have small litters are unprofitable for mass-producers. So farmers have selectively bred, using lean, fast-growing pigs such as the Dutch Landrace that, when crossed with the British Large White, produce big litters. This means the farmer gets lots of quick-growing piglets and a speedy profit, especially

The loving ears of Tamworth pigs.

15

Left, top:
Tamworth piglets –
the breed of ginger
pig after which
the business
was named.

Left, below:
Sarah, our
stockwoman
feeding a proud
Berkshire mum
and her one-week
old beautiful Plum
Pudding piglets.

when the pigs are kept indoors, often in a confined space. They look for an average of 12 piglets per litter and a slaughter age of 20 weeks. This farming style has rapidly led to the decline of traditional British breeds.

Rare breeds

A few passionate farmers have kept the traditional breeds going, feeling that the fabulous flavour of their meat and the truly wonderful individual characteristics of the breeds make for a far more pleasurable farming life. Although these traditional pigs are becoming more popular now, because of their rarity the gene pool is far smaller than it was 100 years ago, which makes it more of a challenge. By carefully crossing breeds, a process that is known as 'hybrid vigour' steps in, increasing both litter sizes and the strength of the piglets. And, by selecting the right boar – perhaps a leaner Lop to cover (mate) a fatter Gloucester Old Spot, for instance – we can achieve leaner pork.

Each breed has its own special quality that is important for the final meat. Some have long backs to make excellent bacon, others produce the best roasting cuts; some have wide, strong bums for fine hams, others have a meat-to-fat ratio that makes fantastic sausages, pies or charcuterie. We need this variety of qualities to be able to offer the best in the shops.

We have also chosen some pigs to help maintain rare British breeds for the future; some of our breeds' ancestries go back hundreds of years. They have earned their place in farming and at the dinner table.

The difference in taste

All stock are only as good as the food they eat and at The Ginger Pig our pigs are all fed the same unrefined diet – mostly cereals and greens grown on the farm, with added soya and peas for protein, and molasses as a treat. All our pigs grow at their natural rate to a normal weight while ranging freely over the land, laying down fat to keep warm, and producing meat that is packed with moisture, sweetness and flavour.

The modern hybrid pig, however, has been bred to convert high-protein, body-building feeds into lean meat at an unnaturally fast rate. It's what the supermarkets request, but it gives little joy at the table; frequently the meat is dry, almost ropey, when cooked.

Pork and seasonality

It is important for pigs to have a generous amount of fat, as this is vital for sausages, bacon, ham, charcuterie and roasting joints. During cooking the fat provides sweetness and moisture. Through the year, the amount of fat on a pig varies, so the meat changes seasonally. In the summer pigs don't have as much fat, but in the winter they lay down more to help them keep warm. Think of it as a winter fat 'jumper' and it makes total sense! Winter pork is also better for the cook.

The importance of fat in cooking pork

Pork is best cooked on the bone with its fat, as both bones and fat deepen the flavour and enrich the final dish. The importance of pork fat cannot be underestimated; it gives sweeter, better-flavoured meat, bastes the pork in the oven and stops it drying out.

So, never trim the fat from pork before cooking. It can be trimmed off on your plate if you prefer, after it has done its work. If cooked properly and slowly, pork fat will melt, seep through the meat and then disappear into the cooking juices from where it can be skimmed off, leaving a sweet and tender, juicy piece of pork and a greaseless sauce. This is vastly different from the lean, fast-growing varieties of pork that all too often come at a suspiciously bargain price.

With meat there is no such thing as a bargain; cheap meat will always come with a compromise, both to the animal's quality of life and to the flavour of its meat.

Right, above:
Johnny feeding a
Lop sow.

Right, bottom:
A Saddleback sow
and a baby piglet.

Following spread
Top: A Saddleback
sow feeding her
piglets.

Bottom:
A Gloucester
Old Spot gilt.

Stages of a pig's life

Piglet	New born
Store pigs	12 weeks, until slaughter weight achieved
Weaner	5–8 weeks old
Hog	Castrated male
Boar	Uncastrated male over 6 months old, ready to become a father
Gilt	Young female pig who has not yet produced a litter
Sow	Female who has produced a litter, or 'farrowed'
Porker pig	Ready to be turned into pork cuts. Lightweight porkers about 60kg (132lb).
Bacon pig	Heavyweight pig around 80–110kg (176–242 lb).

Characteristics of pig breeds

A pig's ears tell you a lot about the animal. Tamworths' pricked-up ears allow clear vision and make them adventurous. They need strong fences! Lops' ears flop over their eyes, limiting their vision and making them calm and easy to manage. Different breeds also have their own body shapes and varying amounts of fat. This affects what their meat is used for.

Tamworth: With their ginger coats, Tim affectionately calls these pigs 'chuckly chops' because they are chatty and happy. They have long bodies, great for bacon, but they slope off at the back end so their hams are smaller. If crossed with a Gloucester Old Spot we get a pig good for both bacon and ham. Meat qualities: large and long animals great for bacon.

Gloucester Old Spot: Sporting a white coat with black patches, this was the original cottagers' pig, used for grazing in orchards. It grows to a huge size, both large and long, so it's great for bacon, while the shoulders make great hams. A mature breeding pig can weigh as much as 300kg (660lb). Gloucester Old Spot makes terrific pork but can be a plain-looking pig. Meat qualities: a very large pig producing great pork and bacon.

Berkshire: A black pig with white socks and a blaze of white on the forehead, this breed is smaller and shorter. It gives good pork if slaughtered while still on the small side at 65–70kg (143–154lb), as larger Berkshires develop too much fat. When crossed with the Tamworth, these pigs produce the most striking piglets of all, with a ginger coat with lots of black splodges: the Plum Pudding pig. Meat qualities: small, chubby rears, very good for traditional roasts.

Saddleback: This breed has a black coat with a broad white band around the middle, and has great mothering and breeding abilities. A native of East Anglia, it produces good juicy pork that can be a little greasy. However, when crossed with a Tamworth, the result is a pig that is longer and slightly leaner with a fabulous ginger colour and a white saddle. Meat qualities: produces both good bacon and pork.

Lop: With their plain white coat, this is the rarest of all English pigs, as their unassuming looks led to a lack of popularity in the days when people kept rare breeds mainly because of their interesting colours. But this pig has a fantastic shape with wide rears producing good hams, length for bacon and stout legs to support their weight. (Farmers call their stock's body shape 'confirmation'.) Lops are docile, make good mothers and usually deliver good litters. Meat qualities: great bacon and good hams.

Welsh: A white coat with good confirmation and great mothering instincts, these pigs make wonderful breeders, and are often crossed with Gloucester Old Spot and Tamworth. They have meat that is good for sausages and pies. Meat qualities: good for bacon and small goods.

Large White/Yorkshire: Unsurprisingly white coated, these pigs, with their pricked-up ears, are a good size, giving a long length for bacon, but are not great for hams as they have small, skinny rears. They are easy breeders and the largest pigs in the UK. Meat qualities: sound bacon and pork.

Plum Pudding/Oxford: An orange coat with black splodges, these pigs are medium sized but have a good length for bacon. They are blessed with a sweet temperament and superb mothering skills. Meat qualities: both pork and bacon.

Slaughtering pigs The Ginger Pig way

At our farms we are fortunate enough to be within a 30-minute journey of the abattoir. The stockman, Kevin, looks after all the pigs on a daily basis and knows them individually. He calmly loads them into a small trailer, then they are taken 12 miles away, considerately slaughtered, cleaned and returned to the farm that day. The meat is hung in walk-in refrigerators ready for butchery the next day. Pork does not need to be hung; it can be eaten within 24 hours of slaughter, but will keep, in perfect butchers' conditions, for seven to 10 days.

At the abbatoir, the pigs are killed then cleaned and have all their bristles removed. This is done by dipping them in hot water, then scraping. Then they are hung by their legs while the head is removed and used to make brawn, the blood is collected for black pudding, the guts are removed and cleaned for sausage skins and the pluck (heart, liver and lungs) kept together for eating. The caul, a web-like membrane of fat enclosing the intestines, makes wonderful casings for faggots, while the trotters (now fashionable in restaurants) can also be used for making gelatine.

On average our pigs are slaughtered when they are seven months old and weigh 100kg (220lb). Some breeds, such as Tamworth, Lop and Welsh, live for as long as 10 months, as they are larger and need the extra time to grow.

Commercial slaughter

In the past the pig was the mainstay of rural cottage life. Smallholders would take a piglet in spring, feed it the household scraps, then slaughter it at the end of autumn or in early winter. The meat would be preserved, smoked or cured to provide good winter meals and nourishment for the colder months. The urgent need to keep warm could be satisfied with an insulating, rich and fatty meal, as often the only heating in a cottage was a log fire and – perhaps – a cooker.

Today, the commercially bred pig's unnaturally rapid growth and high-protein diet puts great stress on its heart and, unless the animal is slaughtered within 20 weeks, it is very likely to have a heart attack. Its forced, quick existence results in an unhappy life for the pig and lower quality meat, but fast money for the farmer. None of this encourages cooks or makes for a tasty, enjoyable meal.

Commercial pigs reach their 65–72kg (143–158lb) slaughter weight at just 16–17 weeks; at The Ginger Pig, ours will have lived a much happier life for 7–10 months.

Butchering

The pig is the most versatile of all the animals we eat, and almost all of the carcass can be used in the kitchen.

Now it is ready to be butchered, the pig is cut in half down the spine. The 'leaf fat' is removed from the stomach and rendered down into lard. The prized tenderloin running down the spine is taken out and the back legs removed for hams. The shoulder is then cut from the carcass between the fifth and sixth ribs; this is used for sausages and shoulder hams, or jointed for roasting. Both the backbone or 'chine' and the ribs are removed, leaving a whole side ready to cure for bacon.

Choosing pork

What to avoid

Inferior factory-farmed pork is white with damp flesh, which suggests that the meat could have been either injected with water or soaked after slaughter to boost its weight and therefore its profitability. The water will evaporate during cooking – and you will have been tricked both into buying water and serving a bland piece of pork.

The presence of red blotches, especially in the loin, is an indication of stress for the animal, usually incurred at slaughter. Under stress all animals produce adrenaline that adversely affects the flavour and texture of their meat. Stressed meat also has a surface sheen similar to the effect you get when a splash of petrol floats on the top of a puddle of water.

What to look for

Good pork is easy to spot; it will be firm to the touch and rosy pink in colour, with no trace of excess moisture. It will have a good layer of pure white fat between the flesh and skin. This keeps the meat moist while cooking and, vitally, increases the temperature next to the skin, giving golden crackling. The skin should be even coloured, smooth and soft to the touch, and dry without being leathery.

Choosing the right cut

There is a saying, 'You can eat all of the pig except his squeal.'

Fore end cuts

As is the case with all animals, the meat closer to the front of the pig (the fore end) is the sweetest tasting. This is because most of the pig's weight is carried by the front legs, and most of the body's movement takes place at the front of the pig, with its head, neck and front legs.

All this constant exercise bulks up the muscles and adds fat marbling throughout. The meat from this area – with all the connective tissue around its complex muscle structure – needs to be cooked long and slow to break down the muscles, while the extra fat will add flavour and melt through the meat to increase moisture and give a juicy, tender plateful. In short, the front of a pig gives great, sweet-tasting meat that is always sold at a relatively good-value price.

Middle cuts

Pigs have exceptionally long backs and occasionally one extra rib, called a floating rib. The middle of the pig offers great-quality meat in the upper part of the body and of course the wonderful belly, which is very popular roasted with its crispy crackling, or cured and turned into streaky bacon.

Hind end cuts

The rear of the pig (hind end) has less fat running through the meat and this part is used to make the classic British ham. You can also roast the back leg, but careful attention is needed so that the meat doesn't dry out while cooking due to the lack of marbled fat within the muscles.

Sides of back bacon including Berkshire, Tamworth, Gloucester Old Spot and a cross-bred pig.

British pork cuts

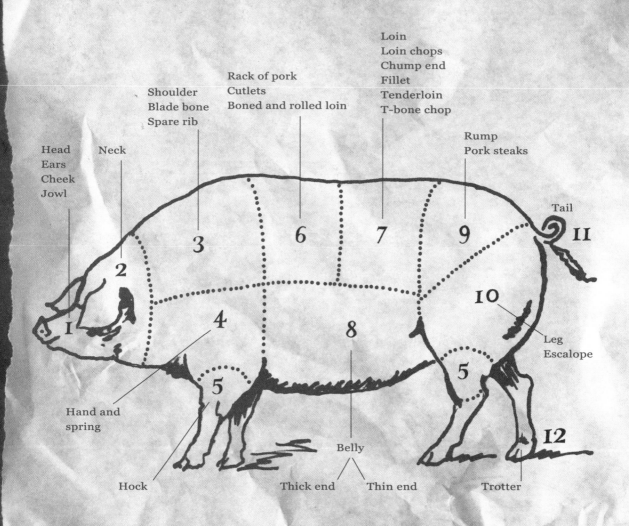

Head
Ears
Cheek
Jowl

Neck

Shoulder
Blade bone
Spare rib

Rack of pork
Cutlets
Boned and rolled loin

Loin
Loin chops
Chump end
Fillet
Tenderloin
T-bone chop

Rump
Pork steaks

Tail

Leg
Escalope

Hand and
spring

Hock

Thick end   Thin end

Belly

Trotter

Fore end

1: Head

The head is traditionally used to make brawn (also known as 'head-cheese') by pot boiling. The brains and tongue can also be extracted and cooked separately.

1: Ears

Frequently eaten in France but not so popular here – yet. Simmer to soften, then dip in butter and breadcrumbs and fry until crisp.

1: Cheek|Jowl

Exactly as it says, this sweet nugget of meat comes from the cheek and is traditionally called a Bath Chap.

2: Neck

A cut with many muscles. Good for sausages, pies and stews.

3: Shoulder

Whole (or boned) and slow-roasted, this is a very juicy cut, good for a large gathering as it's pretty big. Diced or minced, it makes excellent casseroles, sausages, terrines and pies.

3: Blade bone

The top side of the shoulder, this can be boned and stuffed, slow-roasted or braised.

3: Spare ribs

Cut from the upper part of the shoulder with 4/5 ribs. Tasty sweet and succulent due to the generous amount of marbled fat. Cook whole, boned and rolled and slow roast, diced and casseroled or cut in cutlets to barbecue or grill. Versatile and economical.

4: Hand and spring

This cut comes from the lower part of the shoulder/upper part of the front leg. It is good slow-roasted, or braised with vegetables and is often minced or diced and used in pies, terrines and sausages.

5: Hock

The lower part of the leg, which has sweet-flavoured meat. This cut is best braised or pot roasted.

Middle end

6: Rack of pork

Since this cut comes from the rib area of the loin, it contains more fat, adding flavour. Can be tied to form a crown roast, similar to that you make using rack of lamb.

6: Cutlets

Taken from the front of the loin, these should be grilled or fried.

6: Boned and rolled loin

Classic premium boned and rolled joint, with lean meat and a good coating of crackling.

7: Loin chops

Taken from the middle of the loin, these should be grilled or fried.

7: Loin

Running along the back of the pig from the shoulders to the rump, this is served on the bone (ask your butcher to remove the back-bone to make it easier to carve).

7: Chump end

The very rear of the loin. Roast it whole, or cut it into chump chops for grilling or frying.

7: Fillet|Tenderloin

This cut lies inside the ribs along the length of the loin. It is removed as one piece of meat and, as the name says, it's tender! Grill, fry or roast.

7: T-bone chop

This is a butcher's cut that is not commonly known in the UK.

8: Belly, thin end

Best left on the bone, this makes wonderful crackling when roasted. Great for sausages, pies and terrines.

8: Belly, thick end

This is the part of the belly from the shoulder end, and benefits from its thickness. Roast or braise. Good for barbecues.

Hind end

9: Rump

Large lean muscle that is tasty when roasted. Also cube and skewer for grilling or barbecue.

9: Pork steaks

Large lean muscle that can be sliced to make pork steaks.

10: Leg

The classic roast. Ask your butcher to score the skin to help create crisp crackling. It makes a great pot roast, braise, or boned, rolled and roasted. Your butcher can also slice it into steaks to grill or fry. It's sometimes considered dry, but a good-quality leg of pork should have enough fat marbling to keep its meat juicy.

10: Escalope

Cut from the leg and beaten to flatten them, these are usually bread-crumbed and fried.

11: Tail

Great when used in the stockpot, the tail is also deep-fried and eaten by enthusiasts.

12: Trotter

The foot makes great gelatine when braised. Trotters are also highly nutritious and used in cold meat pies. The whole foot can be breaded and cooked until crisp, or Michelin star chefs skilfully de-bone, stuff and braise them slowly, allowing the sinews to melt into a fabulous, gelatinous dish.or for making gelatine.

Pork offal

Liver:

Strong flavour, used in pâtés and terrines.

Kidneys:

Left in a loin chop for a real treat, or in steak and kidney pies, or grilled or fried.

Other

Back fat|hard fat

From the length of the pig, this fat is vital in sausage production. While the meat cooks, the fat keeps its form and moistens it. It is also sliced into sheets for barding lean roasting joints of pork and beef.

Soft Fat|flair fat|leaf fat

From inside the carcass, this fat is rendered down to make lard.

Bacon and ham cuts

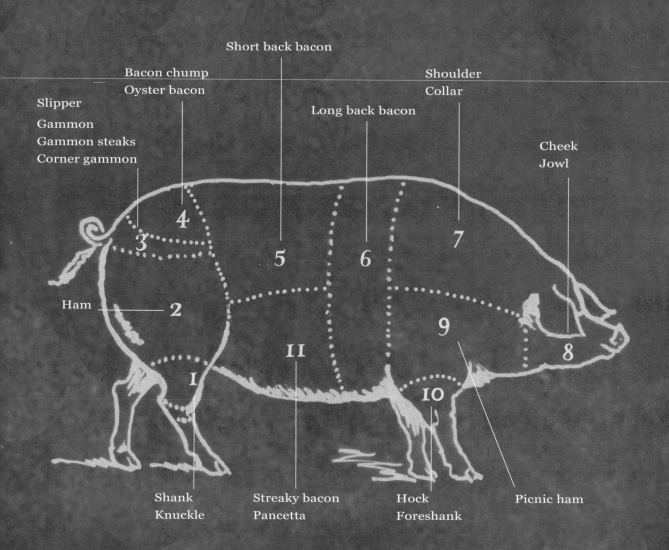

Short back bacon

Bacon chump
Oyster bacon

Shoulder
Collar

Slipper

Gammon

Gammon steaks

Corner gammon

Long back bacon

Cheek
Jowl

4

3

5

6

7

Ham — 2

9

II

8

I

10

Shank
Knuckle

Streaky bacon
Pancetta

Hock
Foreshank

Picnic ham

The traditional breeds of pigs Tamworth's, Lops and Welsh are all good for bacon. They can be taken to a heavier weight and then slaughtered at 12 months, weighing 180kg, which will deliver a carcass weight of about 120kg. As bacon pigs, they are larger than pork pigs and they naturally produce a greater amount of bacon that will have a good proportion of fat to lean meat, which is important for good tasty cooking.

We don't often keep pigs for longer than 10 months as, once their muscles have fully grown, the pigs just start to lay down fat, making the fat-to-lean ratio unbalanced. But there is always an exception. We keep a few 'oversized pigs' back to make old-fashioned bacon, which has a tiny bit of lean meat and a whopping three to four inches of back fat. We have a local customer in Yorkshire who loves to buy a 3–4lb piece of what he refers to as 'proper fat bacon'. He is well into his 90s, very well and enjoys eating natural fat, as he has done throughout his life.

These days, we break the carcass for curing down into its major joints allowing us to cure the shoulder and the heavy and dense legs for a longer period and the middle for less time. Bacon is a thinner joint and varying the curing time in this way prevents it from becoming too salty and enables the curer to deliver exactly the required cure.

Note all bacon can be cooked as pork but will just have the added salty flavour and possibly smoked aroma of bacon

1 & 10: Shank|Knuckle| Hock |Foreshank

Lower part of the leg that is just above the trotter. Economical Sweet flavoursome meat, green or smoked, needs long slow boiling or braising, never discard the stock its good for adding to soup along with the meat. classically used for jambon persille, hock pot or sauce for pasta. The hock or foreshank is taken from the upper thick part of the lower leg and is economical and often sold smoked.

2: Ham

The king of cured meats both on and off the bone, hams can be broken down to make smaller hams. Boil or roast and then decorate and glaze for the centrepiece at celebration table.

3: Slipper|Corner gammon

Between the leg and the rump, this makes a neat, boneless joint. Try it boiled or roasted whole, or sliced into rashers for grilling. Small exquisite ham that makes a great midweek supper.

3: Gammon

This cut comes from the end of the back and very top of the bottom. Gammon is a lean meat with only an outer coating of fat. Boil or roast whole for a large gathering. This cut is often incorrectly called a ham. When raw it is a gammon and only when cooked can it be called a ham.

3: Gammon steaks

These rounds are cut from the gammon, for frying or grilling.

4: Bacon chump | Oyster bacon

This a premium cut of bacon, now less-well known by this term but still requested by connoisseurs. Located between the end of the back and the top of the leg, the wedge shape of this joint makes a good, economical cut. Very lean, it is best sliced thinly and grilled or fried.

5: Short back bacon| Bacon chops

This is the premier of all bacons and is taken from the rear of the back with a large eye of meat and layer of fat just under the rind. Bacon chops are thicker slices on the bone and are suitable for grilling or frying. Try roasting a large piece of short back for a delicious and different treat.

6: Long back bacon

This comes from the middle of the back, running down the pig to belly bacon with an eye and streaky so giving both flavours in one cut.

7: Shoulder|Collar

This cut delivers a wide slice that is usually thinly cut. It is frequently used in the catering trade. Economical collar has a delicious sweet flavour and is boned, rolled and boiled to be used in pies or as a classic boiled ham, served with parsley sauce and peas.

8: Cheek|Jowl

The cheek is a nugget of meat and the jowl the whole part of the animal with fat, also known as Bath Chaps. This needs long slow cooking, boiling or braising and makes tasty pasta sauces or slow roasts.

9: Picnic ham

Often called 'poor man's ham', this cut forms part of the shoulder, which, due to its muscles, needs long boiling.

10: Hock|Foreshank

See Trotter knuckle

11: Streaky bacon| Pancetta

This meat, taken from the belly, makes delicious crunchy bacon if cooked for long enough. Try roasting a large piece.

Boning, stuffing and rolling a loin of pork

1. Before rolling, score the skin. Use a medium knife to make small incisions all over, then cut the ribs from the loin using small, sweeping movements.
2. Lift the ribs up and away from the loin, so you can reach the ends of the bones.
3. Slice the ribs free from the meat in one length.
4. Flatten the meat out, trimming if necessary to make it neat.
5. Fill with a cylindrical roll of stuffing, if you wish.
6. Roll up the boneless loin around any stuffing and tie at even intervals about three fingers' width apart with kitchen twine, using butcher's knots.

Boning and rolling a shoulder of pork

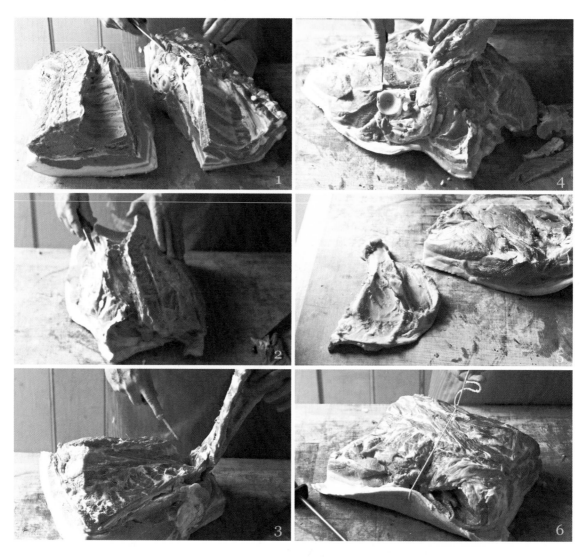

1. Use a medium knife to cut the shoulder in half lengthways, slicing next to the short ribs. You will be working on the piece shown to the right of the photograph; the piece on the left will be turned into bacon.
2. Carefully cut around the knuckle to release the blade bone. Start cutting away the spine and ribs.
3. Trim away the spine and lower ribs to remove in one length.
4. Trace the knife, using small sweeping movements, to cut around the shoulder blade.
5. Remove the whole shoulder blade.
6. Roll up the boneless shoulder and stitch and tie it with a butcher's knot.

BEEF

The legendary British beef

In the past, the UK beef farmer produced some of the best beef in the world. These days, our bloodlines have been weakened, partly due to the exporting of the best animals of many of our breeds to other countries. Canadians, especially, took our breeds and mixed them with their own domestic cattle to improve the size and quality of their own stock, and the speed at which their beef got to market. In the UK we have in turn mixed our cattle with continental breeds to try and improve their quality, so our pure bloodlines have really diminished. But there is now better news. Over the past 10 years, enthusiastic beef breeders have travelled abroad and brought back the few remaining cattle with our original bloodlines. They have been bred with British stock to try to restore the quality and purity of our breeds. Slowly, changes are being made by farmers who do not want to lose the heritage of excellent British beef. Unusually – and thankfully – the British Longhorn has never been exported and so its bloodlines remain totally British.

About cattle breeds

Longhorns

My first Longhorns were two heifers, Generous and Holly. I bought them both in calf from top breeders in Leicestershire. I wanted the Longhorn breed mostly because they are handsome and I like beautiful animals on my farms. The heifers produced two great bulls, which were not really what we wanted; in order to expand my herd, breeding heifers would have been ideal in a perfect world. Breeders say that you should not keep bulls from a first birth, so I slaughtered them. This was my first mistake. I should have followed my instincts and kept them, as they were both strong. Arthur was a beauty, with a red coat, and would have made a wonderful bull for my herd today. He was the very first Longhorn we slaughtered and was a great success at the kitchen table, so all was not lost. We had found exactly the breed of cattle that we wanted.

We added another three females, borrowed a friend's bull (we couldn't afford to buy our own) and covered (mated) my cows and heifers, increasing my herd from five to ten. It has expanded every year since.

One of Tim's prized-winning Longhorns.

Longhorns are majestic, mighty beasts weighing in at almost a ton, with
beautiful horns that turn down almost to their noses. These often look a
bit like a bonnet. Their coat is a red-brown dappled with white; think of
a brown canvas that has had a bag of flour thrown at it. No two cows are
ever the same, but they all have a white stripe running down their backs.

Their meat is exceptional and very much in demand both by chefs and
knowledgeable cooks. Longhorns are a slow-growing breed – as are all
native English cattle – but this gradual development enables the beasts
to lay down fat and deliver a splendid flavour, both things the beef-eater
desires at the table.

That the Longhorn breed exists at all is thanks to Robert Bakewell, one of
the most important figures in British cattle breeding and the agricultural
revolution. Bakewell was a gentleman farmer, who developed the breed in
1760 when he crossed a horned heifer with a Westmorland bull, creating
the Dishley Longhorn, today known as the English Longhorn. The breed
was widely farmed until the 19th century, when the Shorthorn took over.
Sadly, Longhorns declined and became rare in the 1960s, but in 1980 they
were rescued by the Rare Breeds Survival Trust and have made a good
comeback. There are now more than 4,000 Longhorn cattle in the UK.

Longhorns are good milk producers as well as good beef animals and
their milk has a high fat content. In fact, it was used to make the first
Stilton cheese. One day I would like to start a dairy herd of Longhorns,
though this has not been done since 1973. We may have the largest herd
of Longhorn cattle in the UK, with around 360 cows and calves, although
the numbers vary according to the time of the year.

Shorthorns

In 2006 we purchased some Shorthorn cattle, another native breed and
a great cow for beef, to enable us to offer a wider variety in the shops. Like
Longhorns, these beasts are easy to manage and produce brilliant meat
when allowed to mature naturally for at least 30 months before slaughter.
They are average sized, with mahogany-coloured coats, sometimes flecked
with white. The breed used to have short horns, as you'd expect, but they
are now 'naturally polled', which means the horns have been bred out.

Herefords

We also added Herefords in 2006. This breed has been extensively exported to the Americas and Australia and bred with other cattle to improve the quality of meat and speed of growth. Herefords today are often
bred for the mass market and slaughtered at an early age of 20 months,
but I don't consider the beef to be at its best until they are 30 months old,
as they need time to mature and lay down the all-important layer of fat.

Belted Galloways and Riggits

We have a small herd of Belted Galloways, and have just started to breed the red-coated Riggits, which were very popular in the 18th and early 19th centuries. Red Riggits are now seldom seen, and I really want to build up a new herd by crossing my Belted Galloways with my new red Riggit bull to try and get a pure red calf. I seem to have a liking for ginger or red hides. It all started with my Tamworth pigs, followed by reddish-brown marbled Longhorns, and that's not to mention the Plum Pudding pigs!

A White Galloway called Beauty, who carries the Riggit gene.

Riggits are the original Galloway cow from south-west Scotland but are now a very rare breed and virtually unknown flavour. We are breeding them to develop a herd; it will take a while, however, as we are keeping all the females for breeding on and will only kill mis-marked bulls (those with white patches in the wrong place). That's because we only want the bulls with perfect markings to sire our new herd. It's a long, slow process to get a herd right, with just one calf being born from one female every year – and that's only if you have 100 per cent success.

Other breeds

I am planning to add Murray Greys (a cross of a female Shorthorn with a Galloway bull, which is very hardy) and Red Devons. The desire for Red Devons comes from my admiration of Anton Coaker, from whom I bought my red Riggit bull last summer. He farms Red Devons on 15,000 acres on Dartmoor and they roam happily, producing excellent meat. I'd like to do the same in the north of the country.

Good and bad husbandry

Originally there was very little difference between dairy and beef cattle in terms of their rearing methods, but today cows are commercially reared as either dairy or beef. Dairy calves are often removed from their mother after just one day, then fed on a powdered milk mix while the mother returns to the milking herd. Once the older cows are not producing enough milk, they go to the meat processing market. The male calves become veal or mature into beef or a bull, and the female calves go back into the milking herd as soon as they're old enough. Each female produces a calf every year, repeating this ugly cycle.

But not all farmers follow this practice. Our cattle are naturally reared, born in the fields in April with little intervention. They spend spring and summer roaming the pastures with their mum, suckling until they are 10 months old (before her next calf is born). They come into spacious barns in winter if needed and are fed home-grown barley, wheat, soya or peas, topped up with molasses. Cattle reared this way are called 'suckler herds'.

Sadly, most of the beef consumed in this country today comes from dairy breeds. In the UK we have many Holstein Friesian cows, which are much desired for their ability to produce a lot of milk daily. To keep these cows producing such vast quantities of milk, they need to deliver a calf annually.

All the male calves are of little worth to a dairy farmer. Animals from this breed do not have large muscles and have a very lean – almost bony – rump, making their beef of little value. A common way round this problem is to cover (mate) the mothers with a good beef-breed bull, which will produce a dairy-cross.

The male dairy-cross calves can then be fattened up intensively and quickly, and sold into the beef market as 'bull beef'. This is a very large percentage of the beef that is eaten today. But 'bull beef' is the worst type; it comes from an uncastrated male beef cow that has been fed a high-protein feed to maximize muscle growth and development, so it puts on weight rapidly, reaching 300kg (660lb) in 10–12 months. Used by the manufacturing and catering industry, this meat has very little waste, but it bruises easily and offers a poor flavour in comparison to the real thing.

These commercially reared cattle sometimes have 'double muscle', which gives them a body builder's image. All this is good for the producer but poor for the consumer, as the animal will deliver flesh that is floppy and without density. This unnatural feeding and early end to life results in a faster profit for the farmer and very lean meat for the supermarkets, but the meat is of poor quality and the animal has not had a happy life.

Slaughtering cattle at The Ginger Pig

Cattle at The Ginger Pig are never slaughtered before 30 months, unless it is for health reasons. Generally, most farmers consider 30 months the maximum age for beef cattle these days, as they can then go on to butcher the whole beast without the bureaucratic trouble involved in the slaughter of older animals.

This state of affairs is due to legislation brought in following the bovine spongiform encephalopathy ('mad cow') epidemic of the 1980s. Although animals older than 30 months can legally be killed in Britain, they must be sent to a special abattoir that will only be killing older animals on that day so no cross-contamination can occur. Their backbone and spinal cord are removed and a sample of the cord and brain cells sent to be tested by DEFRA. Only once the results come back clear is the beef allowed to leave the abbatoir and enter the food chain.

When our cattle are in their prime they are selected and fed for six weeks on a supplemented diet of home-milled barley and molasses to lay down fat. This is important both for cooking and for hanging, as the fat protects the meat from deteriorating. This layer of fat is a very important factor in the quality of air-hung beef.

Slaughter must be done in a calm and considerate manner, as a perfect animal will be wasted if this process is badly managed. If the cow is in fear at the time of death, adrenaline will pump round its body, causing muscles to tighten and giving tough meat with a reflective sheen and a purple colour.

Stages of a cow's life

Calf	An animal less than one year old
Baby beef	Slaughter cattle weighing 315–450kg (693–990lb) at 9–15 months, these need to have been graded 'good' or better for good-quality meat
Beefling	A fat young cattle beast weighing 500kg (1,100lb) at 18 months to two years old
Store cattle	Cow not ready for killing ie. it needs finishing (feeding) to achieve optimum weight to size to age
Yearling	An animal in its second year
Stirk	A half-grown heifer or bullock, 6–12 months old
Beast	General descriptive term for an adult cow
Bull	Uncastrated male used for breeding, usually more than one year old
Bullock/Steer	A castrated male destined for beef
Bull beef	From uncastrated animals, usually leaner than the bullock or steer, these tend to be from dairy herds
Maiden heifer Bulling heifer	A young virgin female cow
Heifer	A young female who has one calf or is in lactation following her first calving
Cow	A female that has given birth
Fat stock/Finished stock	Animals that are ready for slaughter

Characteristics of cattle breeds

One of the first things to find out about your beef is its provenance and breed. If your butcher doesn't know, it implies they don't care or don't consider this important. But it is vital. Every breed of cow has its own unique qualities, which make its meat suited to cooking in a particular way. Here is a guide to the breeds we farm, and their special advantages.

Longhorn: This very handsome beast has a reddish-brown coat with a splattering of white and a white stripe running the length of the back. They are large animals, with their distinctive down-turned horns, and were originally bred in Dishley in the Midlands. They were the first cows we farmed, and their meat is fabulous. Meat qualities: large bone structure that lays down big muscles, delivering great substantial joints. Very well-marbled, great-tasting beef.

Shorthorn: With a variable red and white coat, these cattle grow to a good size, but they do their growing very slowly. The breed is originally from Durham. When Shorthorns are cross-bred with Longhorns, the resulting cattle always produce a generous and fine rump, arguably one of the best-tasting cuts of beef. Meat qualities: good flavour and marbling, tremendous, large fillets.

Hereford: A solid red coat with a white face, chest and socks. This is a large, strong animal, often crossed with other breeds, so our pure-bred variety is a rare thing. Meat qualities: gives good marbling and a medium carcass, producing slightly smaller joints and good steaks.

Galloways: (including the Belted Galloway, Galloway and Riggit breeds). These are all originally from Scotland. They are medium sized, very hardy, easy to manage and slow to mature. The cattle graze freely, picking what they can find from the hedgerows and land, and this scavenging adds flavour to their meat. Belted Galloways have a black coat with a ring of white around their middle, so they are often called 'Oreo' cows, after the American biscuit. The Galloway has either a black, white or red coat, sometimes a mixture. Riggits have a white line down the length of the back and a black and white, or red and white, splattered coat. Meat qualities: marbled meat that hangs and matures really well, delivers a great sweet taste and good texture. This is the smallest of all the breeds on the farm but they are very compact animals, giving chunky, chubby joints.

Ageing beef

Beef cannot be eaten straight from slaughter; it needs to hang, allowing it to mature and develop flavour and for the meat to become more tender.

There are two methods of ageing: dry-ageing and vat-ageing. Dry-aged beef is far superior but in the UK only 10 per cent of shoppers buy it. It is of a higher quality, texture and taste because it is allowed to age naturally by hanging.

Once the animal has been slaughtered, the carcass is cut in half and then hung in a walk-in cold room, allowing cool air to circulate freely. Beef can be hung for 14–50 days, or even longer for rumps, but very long-hung meat has an acquired taste that may only suit a connoisseur. Usually, we hang our beef for 35–40 days. Dry-ageing is a natural process that takes place when the enzymes in the meat react with the fibres in the muscles, making them tender and elastic. While air-hanging, meat will lose a lot of moisture, which means the flavour will intensify and the meat will not dry out while cooking.

This is the best place to share with you an old English rhyme; it shows perfectly the versatility of a generous Sunday roast.

Hot on Sunday
Cold on Monday
Hashed on Tuesday
Minced on Wednesday
Curried on Thursday
Broth on Friday

Dry-aged meat is expensive, due to the time taken to hang it and the loss of moisture from the carcass (which results in a lower weight, making it less profitable as meat is sold by weight). It also needs to be trimmed after hanging, to remove and discard connective tissue and an outer layer that has a light build-up of bloom (safe bacteria, but not to be consumed). Though this is a further weight loss, it's worthwhile for the superior taste and texture.

Dry-aged beef

When shopping, you can easily spot well-hung beef. It will be dry on the outside, cushion-soft and will hold a thumb print when pushed in for a few seconds. It is a beautiful dark red, almost mahogany colour, and when it is cut, it will be a brighter cherry red inside, with a lovely gamey smell and slightly wet surface.

The meat should be evenly coloured. Beef that is tinged with purple shows there has been stress at slaughter; it means that adrenaline has pumped around a frightened animal at the time of death, bursting the capillaries and leaving red spots in the meat.

Only good-quality beef can be dry-aged. This is due to the all-important marbling of fat through the muscles. The most vital thing to look for in beef is this marbling, which runs around and through the muscle in varying amounts. You will see fine threads of creamy white fat travelling through the meat and generous layers of fat around the muscles. This fat melts and bastes the meat during cooking, helping to make the beef juicy and pleasing at the table. The thicker layer of fat around the outside of the carcass helps to protect the beef from contamination while it is air hung.

If you are worried about your fat intake, leave the fat on your meat during the cooking process, then trim it off at the table and do not eat it. Never trim the fat off your meat before cooking as this will adversely affect the texture and flavour of your finished meal. And remember, if you choose to eat the fat, that you are eating something totally natural, unlike many other synthetic and unhealthy fats found in most processed foods today.

Vat-aged beef

Vat-aged beef is what 90 per cent of the UK population eat. Vat-aged beef is slaughtered, butchered and vacuum-packed, all within 24 hours. As the meat sits in a bag of its own blood, it locks in all the moisture, which expands while cooking, splitting the fibres and allowing the juices to run free, leaving the cook with drier beef.

The beef sits in these bags in a cold room, but can still be labelled 'aged for 28 days', so the customer might think they are buying quality beef. This is not the case, as the meat is not allowed to intensify its flavours and, when you cut open a bag of vacuum-packed meat, there is always a pool of blood that needs to be poured off, plus a rather unpleasant smell. Vat-aged beef is not good for the customer, but the producer loves it as there is no loss of weight, so there is more profit.

Choosing beef

Beef is the meat that offers the greatest variety but often the toughest challenge to the cook. There are cuts of meat to suit all cooking methods, as well as those suited to preserving, either by pickling or salting.

Non-aged (to the left of the picture) versus aged (to the right) ribs of beef. Note the dark colour and fairly dry appearance of the air-dried meat (on the right).

Choosing the right cut

Before you go shopping for your beef, you must understand what cuts from different parts of the animal can give you in your kitchen. There's no point in trying to flash-fry a tougher cut with more cartilage that is best for braising – you will end up with rubber – or in wasting a prime, tender cut in a slow-cooked casserole. So here's the essential knowledge: first you must consider how you wish to cook the meat, as different parts of the animal need very particular methods of cooking. The hard-worked muscles – such as those from the leg, neck and shoulder regions – are tasty and with good fat content. They need longer, slower, moist cooking and take well to casseroles and pot roasts. The less-worked muscles – such as the rump and fore rib – are packed with flavour and are best for grilling, pot-roasting and roasting. The muscles that do no heavy work – such as the sirloin and fillet – are very tender and need very little cooking. Just a quick flash-searing or grilling are fine.

Fore end cuts

The meat closer to the front of the cow (the fore end) is sweeter and tastier. This is because 70 per cent of the animal's weight is held up on the front legs and most of the movement takes place at the front of the cow, with its head, neck and front legs. All this movement increases muscles' bulk and adds fat and marbling through the huge joints. The meat from this area needs to be cooked long and slow to break down the muscles and the extra fat in the joints adds flavour and bastes the meat, keeping it moist. These cuts are usually the cheapest but, if cooked with skill and not rushed, they deliver deep and rich flavours with robust textures, making wonderful casseroles.

Middle cuts

The middle of the cow offers great-quality meat in the upper part of the body and great-value flank, which can be barbecued or used in pies. These lesser-worked muscles deliver a finer, more delicate flavour and texture that needs far lighter cooking.

Hind end cuts

The rear of the cow has less fat running through the meat. This part produces what I consider the tastiest steak – rump – and good joints for pot-roasting or roasting. But, due to their lack of fat, these cuts need moisture or 'barding' with thinly sliced pork fat or streaky bacon, whilst cooking.

Our Black Galloway, Ginger Beauty (left), with a White Galloway, Toffee Apple. Both are heifers on the way to being cows.

British beef cuts

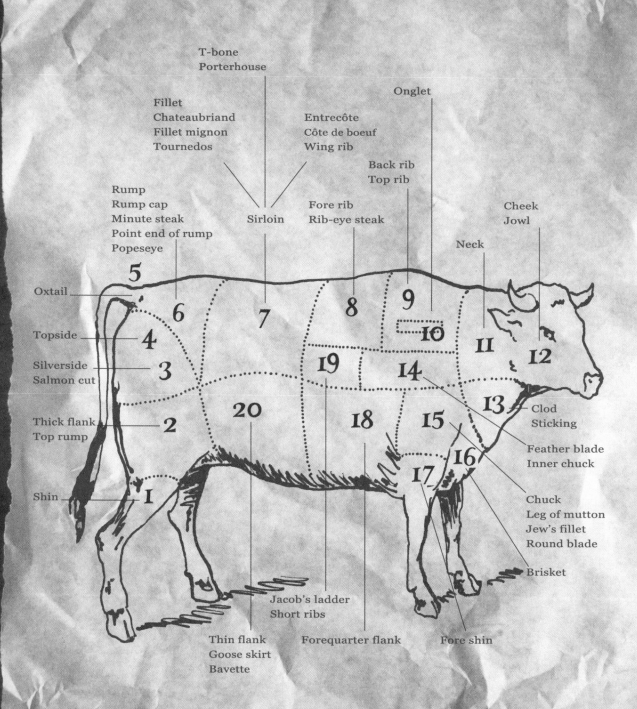

T-bone
Porterhouse

Fillet
Chateaubriand
Fillet mignon
Tournedos

Onglet

Entrecôte
Côte de boeuf
Wing rib

Back rib
Top rib

Rump
Rump cap
Minute steak
Point end of rump
Popeseye

Fore rib
Rib-eye steak

Sirloin

Cheek
Jowl

Neck

Oxtail

5

6

7

8

9

Topside

4

10

11

12

Silverside
Salmon cut

3

19

14

13

Clod
Sticking

Thick flank
Top rump

2

20

18

15

16

Feather blade
Inner chuck

17

Shin

I

Chuck
Leg of mutton
Jew's fillet
Round blade

Brisket

Jacob's ladder
Short ribs

Thin flank
Goose skirt
Bavette

Forequarter flank

Fore shin

Hind end

1: Shin
From the top of the back legs, with lean muscles and much connective tissue, for casseroles.

2: Thick flank|Top rump
From the upper back legs, good for braises, casseroles or pie, or can be flash-fried in thin strips.

3: Silverside
The lower part of the rump. For pot-roasts, braises or casseroles, a favourite for salt beef.

3: Salmon cut
A 1½ kilo joint to roast quickly at a high heat, rest, serve pink.

4: Topside
For pot roast, casserole or braising. Well hung and barded, a good roast to be served pink.

5: Oxtail
Buy this sliced into 7cm-thick rounds. An excellent braise or casserole, as it needs long, slow moist cooking. A tender meat packed with flavour, and has gelatine to enrich and flavour cooking juices.

6: Rump|Rump cap
The upper part of the rear, this cut sits next to the sirloin. Ask for a slice from the upper end. It must be well hung and will deliver a great-tasting steak, or roast it fast at a high heat and serve pink.

6: Minute steak
Finely sliced, this should be fried.

6: Point end of rump
Has great flavour, though some say it's a little tough. Needs to be cooked medium-well and rested.

6 Popeseye
A large muscle from the rump, this joint represents great value. Roast quickly on a high heat, leave to rest, carve and serve rare.

Middle

7: Sirloin
Top-quality roast on or off the bone, or steaks to grill or fry.

7: Entrecôte
Steaks cut from the sirloin.

7: Wing rib
An excellent cut roasted on the bone, or boned and rolled.

7: T-bone|Porterhouse
Cut with the sirloin steak on one side and the smaller fillet on the other. Grill or fry. You'll never get a perfect result as the fillet needs shorter cooking than the sirloin.

7: Fillet
From the sirloin, roast, fry or grill.

7: Chateaubriand
For Beef Wellington, roasts or steaks.

7: Fillet mignon
The lower, narrower end of the fillet, slice into small steaks.

7: Tournedos
Small rounds of fillet. The tail end of fillet should be half the price of the rest and is good for stir-fries.

7: Côte de boeuf
French name for trimmed fore rib of beef.

8: Fore rib
Upper part of the back. Makes a great roasting joint, due to the layer of fat that bastes the meat in the oven. Best cooked on the bone, but can be boned and rolled.

8: Rib-eye steak
Comes from the fore rib. Juicy, due to its marbling of fat.

Fore end

9: Back rib|Top rib
Good-value, tasty cut best for slow pot-roasting, and great boned and rolled and slow or pot roasted.

10: Onglet
A barrel shaped muscle running along the spine, tasty for flash cooking or long braising.

12 Cheek|Jowl
A large nugget of muscle that needs slow cooking. It has a similar flavour to oxtail.

11: Neck
Economical cut of meat used for stewing, braising and casseroling.

13: Clod|Sticking
Very rich. For casseroles or mince.

14: Feather blade|Inner chuck
Very tender, richly flavoured and well marbled. Must be quickly seared or used for slow, moist cooking – anything in between just does not work well.

15: Chuck
Braise, casserole, pot-roast or mince.

15: Leg of mutton
Often diced and called chuck or braising steak and used as such, this cut can also be cooked whole, which needs long slow-roasting.

15: Jew's fillet|Round blade
A small, tasty fillet-shaped cut from the top rib, with gristle that melts with slow cooking running through its centre. Great value.

16: Brisket
From the lower shoulder, this cut is good for pot roasting, braising and pies. Well wrapped in fat, adding flavour, and the classic cut for salting.

17: Fore shin
A cut with connective tissue that, when cooked slowly, makes a sticky, rich and unctuous casserole sauce.

18: Forequarter flank
Cut taken from the lower chest running into the upper belly.

19: Jacob's ladder|Short ribs
These cuts are very popular in the USA and becoming better known in the UK. Braise for tasty, big ribs.

20: Thin flank|Goose skirt|Bavette
A flat sheet of meat with a coarse texture. It either needs long, slow cooking (good for casseroles or mince) or marinating and flash cooking and slicing into thin, tasty ribbons with a good texture.

Beef offal

Liver
Very strongly flavoured, slice and braise with vegetables.

Kidneys
A speciality cooked whole with sauce or used for steak and kidney pie.

Heart
Slice and casserole slowly.

Preparing a côte de boeuf

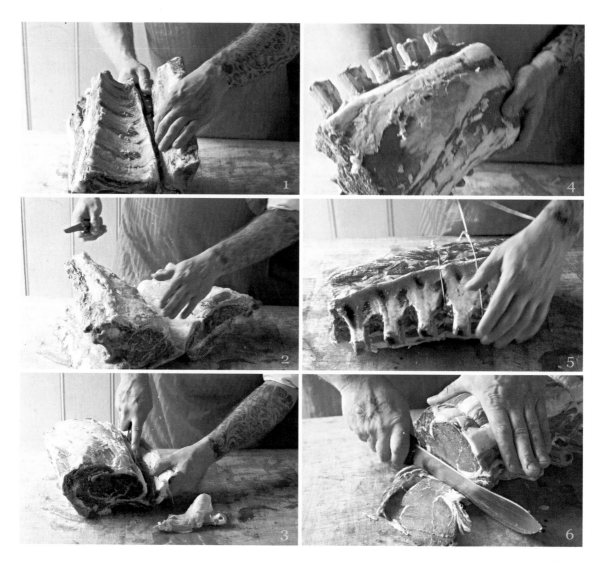

1. When buying your meat, ask the butcher to 'chine' it for you, sawing through the spine. At home, using a medium knife, remove the spine from the joint.
2. Cut away the outer flap of skin, slicing through to reveal a neater piece of meat beneath.
3. Trim excess fat, revealing the fillet of meat. Trim away 5cm (2in) of meat from the ends of the ribs, and carefully scrape the meat and sinew from each bone.
4. You will now have the classic côte de boeuf presentation.
5. Tie the joint at evenly spaced intervals, knotting with kitchen twine, giving a good shape (butcher's knots are optional).
6. Trim a thin slice from each end for perfect presentation. All the trimmings can be minced or casseroled.

Onglet

Point steak

Bavette
Goose skirt

T-bone
Porterhouse

Feather steak

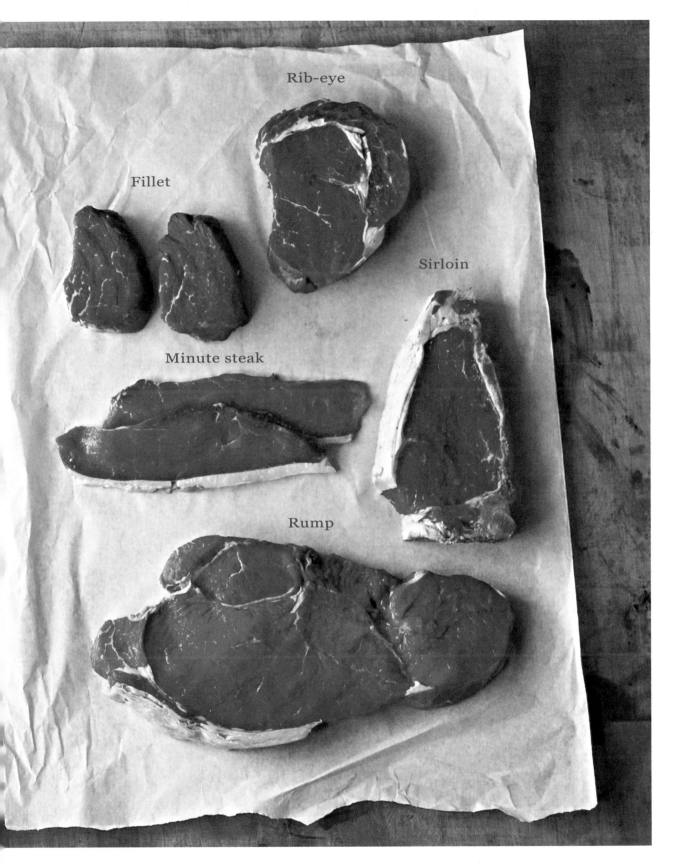

Rib-eye

Fillet

Sirloin

Minute steak

Rump

Steaks

Steaks: the knowledge according to Tim

Always remember that steaks fall into two categories. They either have great flavour or they have tenderness; it is rare for both qualities to go together. Read on to find out what steak suits you best.

Feather blade

The inquisitive foodies' steak. This is not a very well-known cut. It comes from the shoulder blade and isn't very big, but packs lots of flavour and should only ever be cooked rare or else it will toughen. It is not at all expensive.

Sirloin

The City boy or snob's steak. From the middle back of cattle, this has a good size and is well marbled, but lacks true depth of flavour. It is eaten a lot more now than it used to be because modern butchers hang it to add beefy flavour. Expensive, tender and juicy, it is beginning to be sold on the bone a little more, which also adds flavour.

Rib-eye

The youthful trendy eaters' steak. This comes from the fore rib. It is marbled with a central piece of fat and, because of this fat, is very tasty.

Fillet

The ladies' steak. The fillet comes from inside the sirloin. This muscle does no work at all, so it's very tender and has no fat, but on the downside it doesn't have a tremendous amount of flavour. It can't be hung for very long, but is good flash-fried with a sauce to add flavour.

Rump

The steak-eaters' steak. This is full of flavour. It comes from the backside and must be well hung. It's best to buy rump 5cm (2ins) thick, flash-fry on a good high heat, then slice into ribbons. This is my favourite steak, so what are you waiting for? Get shopping!

T-bone/Porterhouse

The 1970s Saturday-night-out steaks. From the lower middle of the animal, these cuts are part sirloin and part fillet. Both cook at different rates, so you will have a problem cooking the perfect T-bone. The Americans adore it, but it may have seen its best times in the UK.

Onglet

The European travellers' steak. This is a large, sausage-shaped, textured strip from the centre of the animal, running next to the diaphragm. Smaller but almost fillet-like in shape, it has dark red meat, a dense texture and great depth of flavour. It is often carefully cut into, to open up and flatten out. It's tasty, not melt-in-the-mouth, but very good if thinly sliced.

Goose skirt/Bavette

The thrifty but knowledgeable cook's steak. From the other end of the inner flank at the bottom of the diaphragm, just above the liver and kidney. A flat sheet of meat, well marbled, with a soft texture and a delicate flavour.

Point steak

The knowledgeable, mature, clever shopper's steak. Older customers tend to stick with this quirky steak. It is from the pointed, thin end of the rump where it joins the sirloin. With a funny triangular shape, it has all the flavour of rump with the tenderness of sirloin.

Minute steak

The hungry, economical cook's favourite. From the rump cap, when thinly sliced and quickly fried, this is the ideal cut for a steak sandwich.

VEAL

Rose veal

We are not a nation that consumes great amounts of veal. I do not produce it, but I do buy it from a reliable source for our customers. The veal we sell in the shops is from the Limousin breed, and also from the Limousin region of France. It has only been fed its mother's milk and allowed to roam free in the fields. This veal is called *sous la mère*, meaning 'under the mother'. Slaughtered at five and a half months, it produces the best calf meat one can eat. It has had a natural life and the calves are well cared for and happy. The meat is a light rosy pink, with a firm texture, very little fat and a delicate flavour.

Choosing veal for your dinner plate is no different from eating lamb or pigs that have been commercially killed at five months. And remember that standard chickens are relative babies, having lived only 41 days.

In the UK we produce rose veal, which has been reared humanely. It gets its name from its pink colour. When shopping, it is always important to know where and how your produce has been reared. If your butcher fumbles when you ask him these questions, don't believe him. It's a good butcher's duty to know where his produce has been reared and how.

Mass-produced veal

This meat is a very different thing. It is solely a by-product of the dairy industry as, in order for a cow to produce milk, she must deliver a calf every year. But it is only the females that are of any use to the dairy farmer. The males are not considered favourable, as a dairy-cross male won't produce great beef for the connoisseur cook. So these young calves are separated from their mothers at a few days old and only go on to live for eight to 16 weeks, when they are then slaughtered for the 'white meat' veal market. Fortunately, this cruel practice is not allowed in the UK. White veal is from a calf that has never seen daylight, hasn't been allowed to roam freely – or may even have been confined to a small cell – and has lived solely on a diet of milk that it has not suckled from its mother.

LAMB

Traditional sheep farming

I never planned to farm sheep, but when I purchased Grange Farm ten years ago it came with a flock of sheep for grazing on the moor. This was a 'hefted' flock, which means ewes and lambs that for generations have been bred on the same piece of fenceless moorland and naturally stay together as a group, only ever grazing in the same area. In reality, the whole moorland can be seen as a mosaic of different hefted flocks.

A hefted ewe possesses knowledge that she passes on to her lambs, teaching them where to graze to find protein-rich new shoots of cotton grass, where streams or bogs are shallow enough to be safely crossed and where is best to take shelter in bad weather. Most of our ewes are brought into the farm for lambing and then all returned to the moor, where the lambs quickly learn a natural homing instinct for their patch.

Hundreds, possibly thousands, of years ago, a patient and hardy shepherd tended his sheep on the moor, protecting them from predators and preventing them from straying; his legacy lives on in the hefted flocks of today. I couldn't break with this traditional method of farming and so kept the sheep that came with the farm. Today we have 1,500 breeding sheep, which increases to 4,000 animals after lambing at the end of April. Every year we keep back 20 per cent of all our lambs to add to the next year's breeding stock.

A farmer could receive anything between £28 and £100 for a lamb carcass. At the moment lamb is in short supply in the UK, because exchange rates mean it is cheaper for continental butchers to import much of our meat than to buy locally. Farmers have been cashing in on the resulting high price, so the national flock has dropped dramatically, which is not good for long-term production.

Lamb can vary enormously in taste according to where it has been living and what it has been eating. Our Blackface sheep live on the moor, eating a modest heather and scrub diet, which both suits them and produces some of the finest-tasting lamb with a unique flavour. The other breeds live on the fields around the farms.

Dorset ewe tending her newborn lamb. Dorsets are the first breed to lamb in the winter.

There are regional variations in taste and texture in lamb, and all are worth exploring. There is salt marsh lamb from East Kent, lambs that feed on the clover meadows of the West Country or others that eat wild herbs and heathers from the hills in the Lake District. All have subtly different flavours and eating qualities.

Commercial sheep farming

Britain is famous for lamb and we produce enough to be self-sufficient. Yet we import lamb from New Zealand and Australia, to cover our lack of the meat in the late winter and early spring months, and most of this is sold in supermarkets. The meat is usually from Dorset sheep, because this is the only kind you can breed all year round. In New Zealand, many farmers produce three sets of lambs every two years, pushing their stock to breed at the maximum rate, which is not natural. These sheep are also farmed in huge numbers, which helps keep costs down. The meat is usually vacuum-packed within hours of slaughter and can be kept in this form for up to a year if packed in sterile conditions.

Lamb and seasonality

Our lambing season starts in early December, with the Dorsets that were tupped with Dorsets, Charollais or Suffolks. These lambs will be weaned in mid-April at about 18 weeks old and are usually ready for the Easter market. They should weigh 40kg (88lb) for slaughter, which is heavier than a commercially grown lamb, but, unless it is for health reasons, I will never slaughter an underweight animal.

In March we lamb the Mules, who were tupped with Texels and Charollais and will be weaned in early July for the summer market.

Finally, in April we lamb the Blackface from the moor. These sheep were tupped with other Blackface or Bluefaced Leicesters. In this month we also lamb the remaining Mules. These lambs will be weaned in late August and will provide lamb for autumn and early winter.

Mule sheep with no horns that live in the fields by the farm and Blackface sheep with horns – these are the strongest breed and this breed live on the moors.

Slaughter

The earliest lambs are killed at 16–18 weeks, which is the norm, though I ensure that ours weigh at least 40kg (88lb) before slaughter. Each week we slaughter around 35 animals. Our lambs are weighed, hand-selected and brought into a field by the farm. The following day they are driven 12 miles to the abattoir, where they are calmly slaughtered, cleaned and returned that same afternoon to hang in the cold room for a few days before being sent to the shops in London.

A lamb born in December and slaughtered for the Easter market is four to five months old. It will have a delicate flavour and lightly-coloured meat perfect for the Easter table, but it would be much better to leave this youngster to grow for a few more months so that it can develop in flavour, texture and size. All meat that is sold as lamb is from animals aged between four and 10 months.

Hogget and mutton

Any lamb that enters its second spring becomes a hogget, then from two years old it will be called mutton. We should enjoy hogget and mutton in the winter, giving us a greater variety of flavour from sheep meat through the year. Hogget and mutton meats have a deeper colour and a more developed flavour than lamb.

Hogget and mutton animals should be physically mature and in their prime. Their meat has a tougher texture than lamb, but they are a pleasure to eat if slowly cooked, or they can even be enjoyed pink and very finely sliced. Mutton should be hung for at least two weeks, allowing it to mature and improve.

Until the 1950s the value of a sheep was all in its wool. The value of wool was high – meat was merely a by-product – so people happily ate a lot of hogget and mutton from animals that were farmed primarily for their coats rather than their meat. But, with the introduction of man-made fibres, the demand for wool declined and the sheep farmer fostered the market for lamb through necessity (in 1960 each fleece was worth £12; today it is only worth around £1). Happily, there is now a resurgence in the eating of mutton, with top restaurants starting to offer it on their menus, and mutton is also being seen once more in the domestic kitchen.

Choosing lamb, hogget and mutton

Texel-cross sheep
surrounded by
Blackface sheep
and a lone Dorset.

First you should select what you want to cook: lamb, hogget or mutton. It's important to know how you want to cook lamb: as with all animals, the fore end is really tasty but needs longer cooking; the middle is sweet and tender, needing less cooking; and the hind end offers large, lean muscles that require medium cooking.

The meat you choose should be fresh and have a bright colour. Whatever its colour, the fat should be hard and certainly not oily, the meat moist and evenly coloured throughout, and the skin dry but not leathery. Never buy grey or wet-looking lamb, hogget or mutton. The legs should be compact and plump with meat, the result of a good and well-fed life.

What the meat looks like

Sheep meat is eaten at many different stages of the animal's life and it is important to be able to recognize the differences.

Baby or milk lamb

Very small bones with no fat and moist, light pink meat that almost looks like veal due to the fact that it has only fed on its mother's milk. A baby or milk lamb will be fewer than three months old.

Spring lamb

With white fat and a good amount of marbling through the meat, the meat of a spring lamb is a deeper, rosy pink – but not red – and is moist when cut. A spring lamb will be four to nine months old.

Winter lamb

These are similar to spring lamb, but a bit larger and with meat that is darker coloured and has a little more fat. Winter lambs will be 10–11 months old.

Hogget

Hogget has creamy coloured fat and good marbling through its dark red meat. This meat will have a good grainy texture and will be moist when cut. Hogget will be 12–23 months old.

Mutton

Mutton has dark, creamy fat with generous marbling through the dark red/mahogany-coloured meat. This meat has a grainy texture and will be moist when cut. It comes from an animal that is at least two years old.

Breeding combinations

Females		Males	Result
Dorset	+	Dorset	Pure Dorset. Best females to the flock, males sent for meat.
Dorset	+	Charollais	Dorset cross. Good meat.
Blackface	+	Blackface	Pure Blackface. Best females to the flock, males sent for meat.
Blackface	+	Bluefaced Leicester	Mule. Best females to the flock, males sent for meat.
Mule	+	Texel	Mule cross. Good meat.
Mule	+	Suffolk	Mule cross. Good meat.
Mule	+	Dorset	Mule cross. Good meat.

Stages of a sheep's life

Lamb	Young sheep before its first main teeth are cut.
Cade lamb	Regional term for an orphan lamb.
Fat lamb	Lamb ready for slaughter, about 4 months old.
Wether	Castrated male.
Store lamb	Lambs that didn't reach slaughter weight in time for summer sale. 'Fed on' until heavier.
Shearling	Regional term. Sheep up to first shearing at one year. Kept for breeding. '1st shearling', '2nd' etc, according to the number of times sheared.
Ram	Uncastrated male, more than six months old.
Tup	Uncastrated male sheep.
Hogget	Castrated male sheep, 10–14 months old.
Tegs	Regional term. Fat lamb in its second season.
Gimmer, Theaves	Regional terms, ewe not yet a mother.
Ewe	Female sheep of breeding age.
Cull ewe	Ewe at end of useful breeding life.

Characteristics of sheep breeds

Sheep may at first glance all look alike, but the breeds are very different. Each breed has its own qualities and can deliver certain characteristics for the butchers, for breeding stock, or for tups. Not all pure breeds have good meat; many need to be cross-bred.

Blackface: These hardy, horned moor sheep are good looking and make great mothers. Purebred Blackface make the best hogget, straight off the heather at one year old, while they're even better as mutton at two or three years old.

Bluefaced Leicester: The most unusual sheep in the world, with Roman noses. These sheep do not like hard weather, but when crossed make good Mules with strong, broad shoulders and a fine length in the neck and back. The breed also provides great randy tups.

Charollais: When crossed with the Dorset, this breed gives a well-muscled sheep with good legs, making good meat. Pure-bred Charollais tups are great to cross with other sheep, though as a pure breed the meat is not good.

Dorset: This breed has a natural ability to breed throughout the year. Dorsets have good chubby rear legs, a great shape and a heavy weight with a good amount of natural fat. Dorsets are a great choice for Easter lamb.

Mule: The most prevalent breed of sheep across the UK, a Mule is the product of any horned and Borders sheep mix. So a Blackface crossed with a Bluefaced Leicester will produce a Mule. Mules are hardy with big hindquarters. They make good mothers and produce a generous amount of milk.

Suffolk: This breed produces great tups for cross-breeding and puts on weight quickly. Suffolks have good meat, though as a pure breed there is more bone than meat. When crossed with other breeds, Suffolks produce the same excellent, tasty meat but in a larger quantity.

Texel: This breed makes a good sire, with wonderful proportions and very big, strong back legs.

Lamb loins ready for roasting: the one on the right, when cut, makes lamb cutlets, and on the left, lamb loin chops.

British lamb cuts

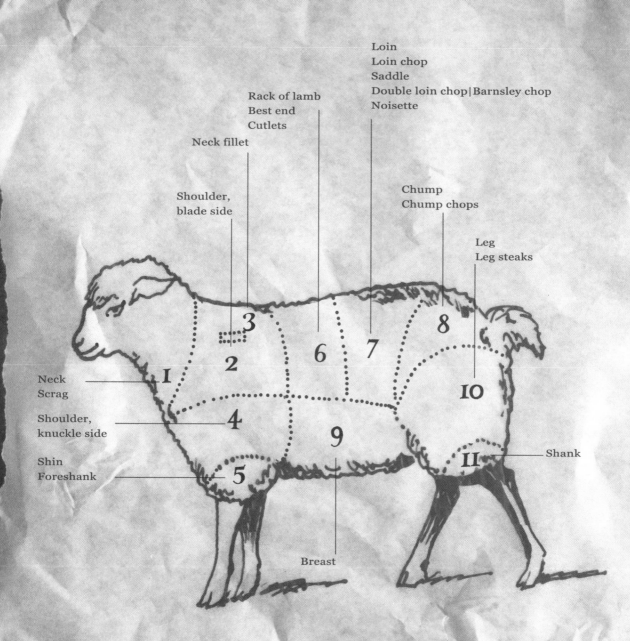

Loin
Loin chop
Saddle
Double loin chop|Barnsley chop
Noisette

Rack of lamb
Best end
Cutlets

Neck fillet

Shoulder,
blade side

Chump
Chump chops

Leg
Leg steaks

3

2

6

7

8

Neck
Scrag

I

IO

Shoulder,
knuckle side

4

9

Shin
Foreshank

5

II

Shank

Breast

Fore end

1: Neck|Scrag

From the top of the neck, this cut is ideal for braising (long, slow cooking in liquid). If you cook it on the bone, it will add extra flavour to your pot.

2: Shoulder, blade side

This has the most flavour and is very succulent, perfect for slow-roasting on the bone for added flavour. Boned and rolled, the joint lends itself to stuffing before being slow-roasted or pot-roasted; the natural fat bastes the meat while cooking. It can be minced or diced.

3: Neck fillet

This cut runs along the top of the shoulders. The small, marbled fillet used to be great value but is now pricier due to demand. It is versatile and can be roasted, fried or casseroled.

4: Shoulder, knuckle side

Again flavoursome, great for slow roasting or ask you butcher to cut into 4/5 chunks, we call them 'henrys' or 'trunks'.

5: Shin|Foreshank

From the front leg, this cut can be sold as part of the shoulder or on its own for braising or pot-roasting.

Middle

6: Rack of lamb|Best end

The first seven ribs of the back. When trimmed this cut becomes a French dressed rack. Two racks shaped into a circle and stuffed, become a Crown Roast, which delivers wow factor at the table. Serve pink.

6: Cutlets

There are seven cutlets on each side of the animal. They are individual ribs cut from best end of neck. Grill or fry and serve pink.

7: Loin

From the middle of the back, this is a good roasting joint. Very tender, sweet meat and one of the tenderest cuts of lamb – so serve it pink. Boned and rolled, it is great for those who do not like coping with bones!

7: Loin chop

From the rib end of the loin, perfect for grilling and frying. Serve pink.

7: Saddle

This cut is made from both sides of the loin still joined by the backbone. A great celebration joint to roast and serve pink.

7: Double loin chop|Barnsley chop

This comes from the loin, with chops from both sides. For the hungry eater. Grill or fry.

7: Noisette

This is boned, rolled loin that can be sliced into perfect rounds. Noisettes are often served at dinner parties as they are easy to cook, tender portions. Grill or fry and serve pink.

8: Chump

The end of the back where it joins the leg, this cut can come on the bone or boned. It is a perfect small roasting joint, or can be sold as part of the leg.

8: Chump chops

Sliced on the bone at the top of the leg, these chops are generous in size. Grill or fry.

9: Breast

This can be cooked whole, or boned stuffed and rolled. As a roast or braise it is fatty, but gives great value with sweet, tasty meat.

Hind end

10: Leg

The most popular cut of lamb, the leg can be boned, stuffed or rolled. Roast, cook pink, or slow-cook until the meat is falling off the bone. Butterflied and boned, the leg is wonderful for the barbecue.

10: Leg steaks

Sliced from the leg these steaks are great to fry or grill.

11: Shank

From the end of the leg, this is a larger joint than the front leg. It is normally left on the leg to sell as whole roast but if removed it will need braising.

Offal

Lamb's liver

Really fresh, this is almost as good as calves' liver but at a fraction of the price. Do check with your butcher that the meat is really fresh. Lightly pan-fry or grill.

Kidneys

Often overlooked, these are sweet and tasty nuggets. Grill them, fry, or cook in a creamy spiced sauce.

Cutting two joints from a shoulder of lamb

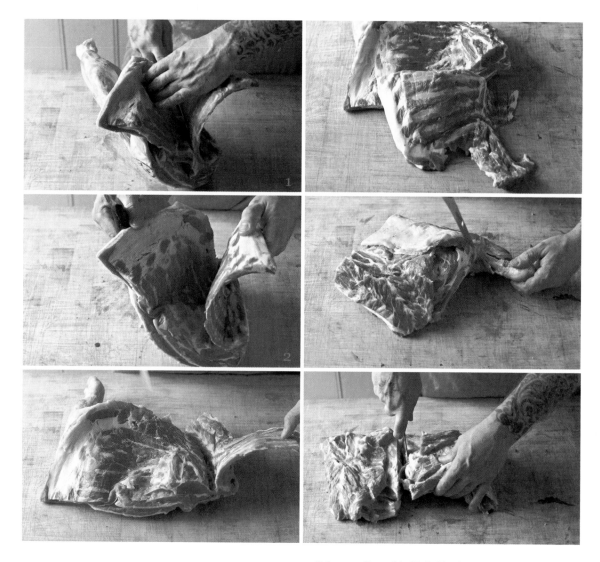

1. Using a medium, thin-bladed knife, begin to cut the ribs away from the shoulder, making sure your knife stays close to the bones and using gentle, sweeping cuts.

2. Pull the near-severed sheet of rib bones towards you, so you can reach the ends of the bones.

3. Slice the ribs free from the meat in one length.

4. The ribs are now completely separated from the shoulder.

5. Trim off excess fat and trim the shank off, producing one large meat joint.

6. Cut the shoulder into two, slicing through the knuckle bone, still using the same knife.

POULTRY

Chicken

A year ago at Grange Farm we started our own flock of chickens, with the Welsummer breed. We have now added Rhode Island Red, Light Sussex, Araucana, Leghorn and Maran, and have 120 birds. Most farmers raise chickens either for eggs or meat, but we are fortunate to be able to do both. The eggs are collected daily and only when a bird has reached its full natural size will I consider killing a bird for the table.

Good and bad poultry husbandry

These days we are increasingly aware of the terrible lives inflicted upon battery chickens and broiler flocks, but not all poultry farmers stoop to such low standards. An example of a good supplier is W.E. Botterille in Leicestershire (www.freerangebirds.co.uk), who supply us with geese and turkeys. This family business produces traditional breeds of poultry that freely wander the fields by day, are housed at night, both scavenge for food and are fed on a cereal diet, and are farmed in batches of 400 (which is small by today's standards). When ready, they are prepared on the farm, dry-plucked and hung, allowing a good flavour to develop. All these factors help produce top-quality birds that are rich in flavour and reach a good size for the table.

The best method of poultry farming is traditional free range, which should not be confused with simple 'free range' farming (which does not demand such high animal welfare conditions – see page 78 for more details). Birds reared to traditional free-range standards are a rarity.

Factory-farmed birds that have never seen daylight are farmed in batches of more than 4,000, have their beaks and wings clipped to stop them from harming each other, and are fed both on antibiotics and on foods that encourage them to rapidly and unnaturally put on weight, enabling them to reach their weight for slaughter at just 40 days.

A slowly matured, naturally fed chicken takes about 11 weeks to rear and will have a golden-yellow skin from the pigments found in grass. It will have a generous layer of fat under the skin, with firm pink meat and well-worked feet that have walked freely over the field and farmyard. These chickens will have dense bones due to their maturity; you will not

A Light Sussex in the arms of its proud owner.

73

be able to cut through the bone with anything but a sharp, heavy knife. The time and care taken to rear these chickens, and the quality of their food and housing, will be reflected in a high purchase price. However, after tasting one of these chickens, I promise you will never again feel happy, comfortable or satisfied eating a 'bargain' chicken.

Choosing a chicken

A chicken is only as good as the farmer who raised it and your butcher should know exactly where the chicken he sells comes from.

In the UK, buying poultry can be very confusing. There are many labels, and some are misleading, adding confusion to how the chickens have been farmed, the amount of time they have spent outside and the density at which they have been reared. All this is not only a question of animal welfare, it also affects the quality and flavour of the meat.

Sadly, most broilers (the name given to chickens reared for cooking) are farmed for the supermarkets and have been bred, fed and squashed into sheds to be killed at six weeks old, never seeing daylight or having their litter changed. I would far rather buy and eat poultry from reputable suppliers who consider the birds' welfare to be of the utmost importance.

When buying poultry, always look for the following farming standards:

❋ The bird was free from a young age to range outside during daylight hours

❋ It was fed on a diet that is high in natural cereals

❋ No antibiotics or additives were added to its feed

❋ It is a traditional slow-growing breed

❋ The bird was grown to full maturity (i.e. it is at least 80 days old)

❋ High standards were applied in slaughtering

❋ The meat has no discoloured patches to have suggested maltreatment.

Chickens are sold drawn (already gutted), and a good butcher will always sell chicken with its giblets, which are great for making gravy and stock. As with all kinds of meat, chicken should be stored uncovered in the refrigerator, but take extra care, as chicken is particularly susceptible to contamination by salmonella bacteria, which causes food poisoning. Always store cooked and raw meat apart, and make sure raw chicken is stored on a shelf beneath cooked meat to prevent raw juices from dripping on to cooked food below it.

Pevious pages:
Left-hand page,
top left:
A White Leghorn
Left-hand page,
top right:
A Welsummer

Left-hand page,
bottom:
A Maran
Right-hand page:
A Light Sussex
and a Welsummer
freely running out
of their chicken
house.

Opposite:
A variety of
chickens of
different breeds,
strutting around
in the fields
at Grange Farm,
with our lambing
barns visible in
the background.

British chicken labelling

Traditional free range and Free range total freedom
This offers the best standards of animal welfare and meat quality. Breeds are selected for their slow growth, the birds are fully free range (being put away only at night to protect them from predators), they live to at least 80 days old, are fed a high-cereal diet with no antibiotics or additives, in limited flock sizes. They are dry-plucked and hung to improve flavour.

Free range
This is a confusing term, the label is earned by adherance to many rules that can be changed according to the producer's needs. However, all free-range poultry must have free access to roam outside for at least half of their lives, be fed on grain, live to at least 58 days old and be kept in limited flock sizes.

Organic
In the UK, organic certification for poultry can be granted by a number of agencies, including Organic Farmers & Growers Ltd, which specifies that organic eggs and meat should be from birds that originate from an organic certified farm and that that they abide by organic feed and veterinary standards. It is, however, always advisable to check carefully the wording of the labelling on any bird you buy to find out more about its background, feed and living conditions.

Freedom Foods
Specified and set up by the RSPCA, Freedom Foods offer three standards for poultry: free range; organic; and indoor. Whichever of these three methods of farming were used, all such poultry are protected by rules that insist on a good diet, comfortable housing, freedom from pain, discomfort or mental suffering and the ability to express natural behaviour.

Red Tractor
A standard set by the Assured Food Association, which produces around 90 per cent of chickens that are eaten in the UK. This label identifies birds that have been farmed inside and have been reared quickly for retail. However, Red Tractor poultry is independently inspected during its life and slaughter and each Red-Tractor bird can be traced back to the farm from whence it came.

Corn-fed and farm-fed
There are no legal definitions at all surrounding the quality of life for poultry labeled as Corn- or Farm-fed. This label only indicates what and how the birds have been fed.

French chicken labelling

France has clearly defined labelling. The Label Rouge indicates high animal welfare and such birds are favoured by many top chefs. This label's requirements are clear and concise: farmers must only use slow-growing breeds, have a minimum barn size and a maximum stocking density. Any one farm can only have four barns, all birds must be free to roam outside from 9am until dusk in at least two acres of land and their diet must be 75 per cent cereal-based. Label Rouge birds cannot be killed before they are 81 days old and must weigh a minimum of 2.2kg (5lb) without giblets when they are prepared. Finally the birds are permitted a journey of fewer than two hours to be processed. Label Rouge poultry provide 30 per cent of the French consumers' market. They have a higher purchase price than much of the other chicken sold in France, but it seems that many French shoppers are happy to pay for a product reared with care that will deliver great taste to their tables. Due to the success of this label, it is also being copied in the USA and by some producers in the UK.

Slaughter

The Ginger Pig kills its chickens at between 80 and 155 days, depending on weight. A 2.5kg (5½lb) bird will be killed at between 80 and 100 days and a 4.5kg (10lb) bird between 100 and 155 days, but the exact age chosen also varies according to the variety and individuality of the bird. Intensive farming methods mean that intensively reared chickens are killed at 41 days for a 2.1–2.2kg bird (4½–5lbs), dressed for weight.

Dry-plucking and wet-plucking

For dry-plucking the bird is hand held and rotated near two spinning plates that extract the feathers. Sometimes they are then waxed to remove any feathers that are left and the bird is then hung to tenderize its meat and intensify its flavour. Though these birds may look dry, they will produce a beautiful crisp skin that will help to seal in all the flavours.

Wet-plucking accounts for more than 95 per cent of the poultry we eat in the UK and produces pink, wet and shiny birds. The bird is plunged in hot water, then placed in the rapidly-rotating bowl of a machine for about 40 seconds, while the feathers are extracted and the bird is sprayed with water. It is a far faster plucking method and does not require each bird to be hand held. The biggest difference between the two is the addition of water. In wet-plucking, a hole is left where each feather has been extracted through which water can enter, creating a breeding place for bacteria. This makes hanging wet-plucked birds impossible for fear of contamination.

Characteristics of chicken breeds

In the past British chickens were leggy, a body shape that delivers the most flavoursome meat, but with smaller breasts. The modern-day consumer desires larger breasted poultry and we have bred our chickens to accommodate this market demand. The French still produce a leggy, smaller breasted bird as they still demand flavour over lean white meat.

Welsumer: With flecked, rich, dark-brown feathers, originally from Holland, this breed was imported to the UK in 1928. It is an ideal bird for free ranging and produces large brown eggs.

Rhode Islands Reds: Boasting a dark, rich, glossy red coat, this breed was originally from the USA and imported to the UK in 1903. It is a very popular, heavy breed and a good layer. When crossed with the light Sussex cockerel, the males make a wonderful roast table bird. The most known breed around the world.

Light Sussex: Mostly white with speckled grey and silver head and tail feathers, this is Britain's oldest breed and is good for both meat and eggs.

Araucana: Its black feathers have a green sheen and white spots that develop with age. This breed was imported from Italy in 1888. These are good layers, producing a beautiful blue/green egg that results in a reasonable sized bird.

Leghorn: This elegant black or white bird was imported from Italy in the late 1800s. A typical and prolific laying bird it is also slender and not ideal for the table.

Marrans: With 'cuckoo patterned' dark grey to silver coloured feathers, this breed was originally from Marons in France and arrived in UK in 1800. It is a good breed for both meat and speckled chocolate coloured eggs, although the birds need space as they are prone to laziness and easily become fat. When crossed with an Old English game bird, Marrans make wonderful table pot-roast birds.

Master Gris: This brown feathered bird was originally from France and has all the French characteristics of being leggy and smaller breasted. But they are packed with flavour and therefore make great table birds.

Dorking: A silver-grey feathered bird from Sussex, it was bred in the 19th century for the London market. The ultimate broad-breasted English table bird.

British chicken cuts

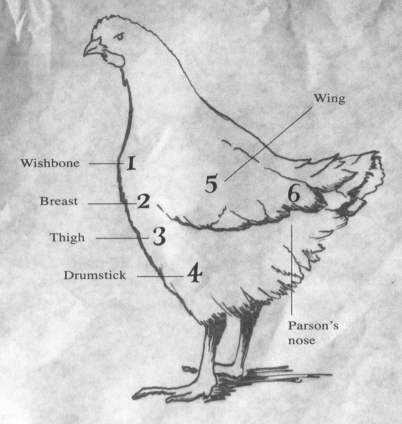

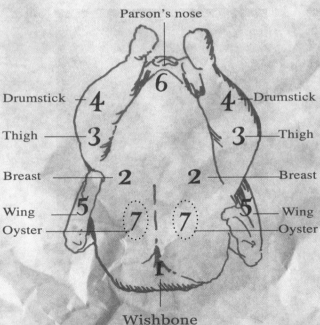

1: Wishbone

This bone is traditionally snapped at the table. Before it is snapped, two people make a wish and the receiver of the larger part will have their wish come true!

2:Breast

This cut provides lean, white meat and is very popular. With its mild taste, it can be grilled, fried, roasted, braised in liquid or barbecued.

3: Thigh

A cut that has dark, tasty meat that can be grilled, fried, roasted, braised in liquid or barbecued.

4: Drumstick

The meat from this cut is similar to that of the thigh (see above) and, when joined to the thigh, forms the chicken leg.

5: Wing

With brown meat, this cut is usually marinated for extra flavour and succulence, roasted and then eaten with one's fingers.

6: Parson's nose

By some this is considered a sweet and tender delicacy; by others, this part of a chicken is totally disliked.

7: Oysters

These are two oval discs of sweet brown meat that lie on either side of the spine just under the wings.

Offal

Chicken livers are small, soft and inexpensive. They are principally used for pâtés or quickly fried for inclusion in salads.

Turkey

Somehow, despite the acres of column inches, television air time and even whole books about the shortcomings of intensive chicken farming, turkeys have been overlooked. Yet these birds are also too often packed into sheds, deprived of daylight and frequently fall victim to ill health, such as during the bird flu outbreak at a Suffolk farm in 2007. We do not farm turkeys, but we have a good supplier of the birds for our customers.

About turkey breeds

Traditional free-range Bronze turkeys are the best turkeys available, and are farmed in the same way as other traditional free-range poultry (see page 78), roaming the fields, only put away at night and foraging as well as eating a natural grain diet. The one difference between turkey and other poultry is their size. They are larger than most other poultry so they take longer to grow. Slow-growing Bronze turkeys will take six months to reach maturity. They are dry-plucked (see page 79) and hung for 10–14 days to relax their muscles and develop a good flavour.

Bronze turkeys were originally the product of crossing domestic turkeys brought from Europe with the wild American turkey. The two produced a larger but tamer bird, which has become very popular. In 1981 a farmer in Essex, Derek Kelly, bred the Kelly Bronze turkey, which is considered a tremendous bird for the cook.

Free-range turkeys

In Europe a hen bird with a broad breast is favoured because, when cooked, the breast is the most popular cut (although I prefer the dark meat). In the USA, size is everything, so the larger bird – the male – is the king of the Thanksgiving feast. Although turkeys are most popular in the USA in November for Thanksgiving and in the UK at Christmas, the meat is now available all year round, is economical and very low in fat.

Ask your butcher to secure you a tasty, traditional free-range bird that has lived a humane life. You will probably need to place an order, as free-range turkeys are raised in small batches and are in huge demand at Christmas and Thanksgiving.

Always choose a bird with a dry, blemish-free skin with a plump breast and no rips or breaks. Make sure the giblets come with the bird, as they make the best stock for gravy.

Goose

Free range geese such as these are put away at night and roam the fields during the day.

Goose meat has a darker colour and a much richer flavour than that of other farmed birds. These birds are bathed in goose fat, a fabulous and renowned substance, one that makes it virtually impossible for the bird's meat to dry out beneath the goose's signature crispy skin. Goose fat is a valuable product in its own right, producing the crispiest and most golden roast potatoes, and it's a must when you are making a traditional cassoulet. Always keep the fat that you have rendered from cooking a goose – it will last in the refrigerator for a couple of months.

Goose is always expensive and provides less meat than other birds, but it makes a wonderful, rich and complex-tasting meal. A Michaelmas goose should be eaten on September 12th, after a summer of its grazing the fields, then dining on early autumn grain. A goose is expensive because it is an extravagant addition to a farmyard and takes a lot more feeding than any other bird, while providing less meat.

You will need to order a goose from your butcher or speciality supplier. Always select a bird with a dry, pale skin and a plump breast. Most of the meat on a goose comes from its breast (and this is also the best meat), so carve it thinly. The leg meat can be a little tough. Use the carcass to make stock for soup.

The Ginger Pig's supplier has been rearing poultry for more than 70 years. They rear geese that, by day, naturally forage in the fields and feed on home-grown wheat and vegetables. They are allowed to reach maturity for the Christmas table naturally before slaughter.

Duck

One common problem in the mass farming of ducks is lack of water. Ducks need water, not only for drinking, but also for swimming in. Many intensively reared ducks only ever see water in a small drinking trough.

You need to find a good butcher or supplier who can sell you humanely reared poultry. Select a duck with dry, pale, blemish-free skin and a long plump breast. As with all poultry, look at the label and aim for traditional free range or free range (see page 78). Duck breast can be eaten pink and well done, but legs need to be cooked for longer to make the meat tender.

If you choose wild duck, it will probably be mallard or teal. Ideally, only buy them if you or someone you know has shot them as it is often hard to know how wild ducks really are. They may have a fishy flavour, due to their diet, and can be very tough. Plump wild ducks tend to be young and can be roasted, whereas a thinner bird is best braised long and slow.

Duck breeds

Aylesbury: these birds have white feathers, are naturally quick growers and deliver a high quality of meat.

Barbary: also known as Muscovy, these have a mixed plumage of black and white feathers and produce delicious meat.

Gressingham: this is a cross of the wild mallard and Pekin duck, and is a bird with larger quantities of greatly favoured breast meat.

Guinea fowl

The guinea fowl is native to Africa, but is now widely farmed in France, Italy and Belgium. These birds make good guards and will alert you to intruders with a loud, crowing cackle. They have a beautiful coat, in shades of grey with white dots. The meat is pink and they have a purple-tinged skin, which makes you expect a strong gamey taste, but in fact their flavour is mild and somewhere between pheasant and chicken.

Guinea fowl are available to buy fresh from October to February and lay their eggs in the spring and summer. Because of this seasonal availability, people often assume guinea fowl are game birds.

Guinea fowl are not as plump as chickens and tend to have leaner legs and are somewhat flat-chested. Don't let this put you off, as they taste great. When it comes to cooking, they can be treated in the same way as chicken, so roast, pot-roast, joint and casserole, or pan-fry them.

Geese are hung for five to seven days prior to their being sold.

Butchery of poultry

Jointing a bird

Poultry can be jointed into four large pieces or eight smaller pieces. Cut off the legs between thigh and breast and set them aside if you want only four joints. If you require eight, cut each leg into two at the joint between thigh and drumstick. Cut down the length of the breastbone, then, with poultry shears, cut out the breastbone and remove it. Turn the bird over and cut beneath the wings on both sides, making your cut down the length of the carcass where the flesh of the breast tapers off. All resulting trimmings can be used for stock. For eight joints, cut each breast in half, to produce two joints that are still attached to the wing.

Boning a bird

Select a bird with skin that has no cuts or tears. Cut the tip and middle section from the wings. Cut the skin down the length of the spine with a boning knife and, with short sharp strokes of the blade, cut the flesh away from the carcass on one side, releasing all the way to the leg and wing. Repeat on the other side. At the wing and leg, release the ball and socket joints and cut the meat away from around the lower part of these bones. Continue cutting the breast meat away from the carcass on both sides, using your fingers to help you to free the meat. Eventually you will be able to lift the carcass away. Use the bones and trimmings for the stock pot. Once boned, the bird is excellent for stuffing and by getting rid of the bones you make carving very easy.

Spatchcocking a bird

This technique is usually only done to smaller birds and, to speak bluntly, spatchcocking means to split and flatten. Cut the bird down the length of each side of its spine (use the spine for the stock pot). Trim out the wishbone. Lie the bird out flat, skin side up and, with its legs turned in, firmly press down using the heel of your hand, breaking the breastbone. Snip a little hole between the leg and the breastbone and tuck in the end of the drumstick. Thread two skewers across the bird to hold it flat. It is now ready for grilling, baking or the barbecue.

GAME

Due to the high demand for game shooting, game birds are commercially bred and hatched, placed in pens in woodlands and fed on grains packed with antibiotics (due to the large numbers in which they are bred). Just before the shooting season starts, birds are set free so that shooting parties can be guaranteed birds to shoot and an expensive day out can be enjoyed, killing supposedly 'wild' birds.

Game shooting is big business and, often, shot birds are simply disposed of, as more are killed than the market requires. So when you buy game, remember that the best sources are small farms where truly wild animals are shot. However, do bear in mind that there is no guarantee of what the butcher will have for sale at any specific time – hunting is real and who knows what will flutter by on that particular day.

When you have found a good supplier, you can request how long you would like your animal to have been hung for to enrich its flavour. This timing is a personal thing, but all too often meat is not hung for long enough. By working with your supplier, you will also be able to select the age of a game bird – a younger animal is good for roasting and an older better for casseroling.

It is hard to be exact about the age of game, but obvious clues are found by looking at its size and condition. Rough skin on the feet show age and an older cock will have a long claw on the back of its leg. Also, the larger a bird is, the older it is. Soft beaks and breastbones are also age indicators as they are found on younger birds.

With rabbits and deer, again size and general health give away their age. Good teeth are found on a younger animal, as are tidy feet. Look at the antlers of deer; a huge antler can only come from an older beast.

Game is a wonderful thing. Think of game as an adventure and a fabulous alternative to farmed meats.

Quail

The quail is a small, one-portion-sized bird, very popular but too often farmed in similarly poor conditions to chicken. Free-range quail is a rarity and, unless you know the supplier or it is clearly labelled, I would shy away from buying it. Quail is a game bird that is shot year round but, if wild, is often eaten by the hunter, as they know the quality will be good.

Labradors return home with the day's shoot.

91

Partridge

A partridge is a wonderfully-flavoured, single-portion-sized bird that is available only from September 1st–February 1st. Partridge needs to be hung for a week, depending on age. You can spot a young bird as it will be plump and in good condition – young partridge is great for roasting. An older bird will have a thin, protruding breast-bone and will be best casseroled in order to tenderize its meat.

Pheasant

The most popular game bird in the UK, pheasant, due to the large numbers in this country, can often be a bargain a few weeks into the October 1st–February 1st game season. The hens need to be hung for at least 10 days and the cocks a couple of days longer. Young birds are perfect roasted, whereas an older bird should be casseroled. The age of a pheasant can be calculated in the same way as a partridge (see above).

Grouse

Believed by some to be the king of game birds, grouse is only available during its short August 12th–December 10th season. Due to their living on heather-covered moors, grouse have a lovely flavour that is slightly bitter. At the beginning of the season grouse are very expensive but, if you can wait a month into the season, the price may drop. It is important to be able to age your bird because, as with all other game birds, young grouse are perfect roasted, whereas an older bird must be casseroled. A neat and fresh beak and feet shows a young bird, while if these are old and dry, the bird is best for the pot. If you can buy grouse 'in the feather', look at its wing feathers: a young bird's feathers have pointed tips while, on an older bird, they are square.

Rabbit

Rabbits are readily available, great value, and tasty, but they are a much underused source of meat. This could be because we associate rabbits with their being our pets. They are a little fiddly to eat, due to the small pockets of meat on the bone, and they are often badly cooked and dry out. If you currently avoid rabbit, I am going to try to change your mind. First, steer clear of farmed rabbits as farming is totally unnecessary with the vast numbers of wild rabbits currently roaming the countryside. Rabbit farming conditions are not kind and deliver bland-tasting meat. Find out your butcher's source of rabbit. Wild rabbits have meat that is pinky brown, whereas farmed rabbit meat is white (I think this is where the odd, but often cited, comparison to chicken meat originates).

Braces of pheasant, freshly shot, from Blansby farm.

An older, larger rabbit needs long, slow casseroling, with some kind of liquid and a strip of pork belly or bacon to help enrich and keep the meat moist, whereas a young rabbit can be roasted wrapped in bacon, or pan-fried with chopped bacon – but, even then, you will need to test the meat with a knife for tenderness and keep cooking it if it is tough.

Classically, rabbit is jointed, then casseroled with a mustard sauce, or you can pot-roast it, pick off the meat and use it for a pasta sauce or pie filling. Rabbit makes good eating and a welcome change from other meat; especially if you have shot it, as it will be food for free.

Venison

Wild venison is available from August to the end of February, depending on its breed (see chart opposite). Much of the venison we buy originates from a red-deer herd in Scotland or the South of England, where they are culled as a result of the damage they cause to farm land or havoc on the roads. Culling is a tightly managed process, with the ratio of females to males culled being carefully considered.

Scottish red deer is said to have the edge on other breeds for flavour, but farmed deer is often more tender than wild deer as it is younger and has had a calmer, less active life.

Venison is becoming increasingly popular because it is lean and low in fat, but it needs to be hung for three to four weeks. When roasting venison, bard with pork back fat or wrap it with bacon. Roast venison is best cooked in a high oven for a short time and served pink and juicy. The best roasting cuts are the leg, or 'haunch', and the saddle. Larger red deer can be butchered in a similar way to lamb, producing rack, loin, chops, fillets and steaks.

The best venison cuts to use for casseroles and pot roasts come from the shoulder, breast and neck. As venison is lean, it's a good idea to marinate the meat before casseroling or braising, and to add a strip of pork belly to the pot to provide extra succulence.

Farmed deer is available all year round and is the most readily available venison on the shelves. The box opposite shows all British deer, but true wild game is not shot to order, by breed, and is therefore sold under the general term of venison, irrespective of the breed.

Seasonal availability of game

This chart shows the dates between which it is permissible to shoot game in England (E), Scotland (S), Wales (W) and Northern Ireland (NI). The shooting seasons listed here determine the availability of fresh game. At all other times, any game sold has been farmed, frozen or imported.

Feathered game

Goose and Duck (inland): Sept 1 - Jan 31 (E, S, W); Sept 1 - Jan 31 (NI)

Goose and Duck (below high-water mark): Sept 1 - Feb 20 (E, S, W); Sept 1 - Jan 31 (NI)

Partridge: Sept 1 - Feb 1 (E, S, W); Sept 1 - Jan 31 (NI)

Pheasant: Oct 1 - Feb 1 (E, S, W); Oct 1 - Jan 31 (NI)

Grouse: Aug 12 - Dec 10 (E, S, W); Aug 12 - Nov 30 (NI)

Blackgrouse: Aug 20 - Dec 10 (E, S, W); not available in NI

Furred game

Rabbit: should not be shot in summer breeding season

Deer: venison is a seasonal meat and meat from different breeds will be available at different times of the year, as determined by the shooting calendar.

Red stags: Aug 1 - April 30 (E, W, NI); July 1 - Oct 20 (S)

Red hinds: Nov 1 - Feb 28/29 (E, W, NI); Oct 21 - Feb 15 (S)

Red deer are native to the UK. This is the most prolific breed and is believed to be the best due to its wild lifestyle and its tendency to live and feed on the herbs and heathers of moorland.

Roe bucks: April 1 - Oct 31 (E, W, NI); April 1 - Oct 20 (S)

Roe does: Nov 1 - Feb 28/29 (E, W, NI); Oct 21 - Mar 31 (S)

Reintroduced after being hunted to extinction in the 17th century, roe deer are now prolific and often cause damage to crops and trees.

Fallow bucks: Aug 1 - April 30 (E, W, NI); Aug 1 - April 30 (S)

Fallow does: Nov 1 - Feb 28/29 (E, W, NI); Oct 21 - Feb 15 (S)

Another reintroduction, this time from the Far East in the 18th century, fallow deer have now cross-bred with red deer.

Muntjac: no statutory close season (E, W, NI); Oct 21 - Feb 15 (S)

A small animal, the muntjac was recently introduced and has caused a lot of woodland destruction.

RECIPES

SEPTEMBER

September on the farm

September is the busiest time of year on the farm, working against the clock to finish the wheat, oat and barley harvests, then preparing the land for the next crop. Everything must be ready for a hard winter. There are water pipes to check, fences to look at, equipment to service – you can guarantee that anything that can go wrong will do so in midwinter.

We're up at dawn to feed the livestock and lock-up is just before dusk (the fox comes out just after to make sure we've done our job), so I relish the clocks going back and my day finishing by five o'clock. Knowing that a delicious casserole with soft herby dumplings is in the Aga helps to allay the nagging feeling that I should be outside working later.

This is the month when I judge how good a harvest we've had. If the land has achieved three tons of grain or more to the acre, I'm happy, as grain prices hover at around £80 for a ton and it costs £190 an acre to grow. Any fewer than three tons and I wonder what I've done wrong. The grass stops growing now, so another concern is having enough grain to feed the 2,000 sheep, 500 cattle, 1,000 pigs and 140 chickens on our three farms: Grange Farm, Blansby Park and East Moor in North Yorkshire.

One of my greatest helpers is Kevin Hodgson, who's in charge of the pigs, drives the combine harvester and assists in running the arable side. He's not very optimistic – but his outlook tends to improve as the day progresses so I try to avoid him until after lunch. With the harvest coming in, I feel as if I am filling my kitchen for Christmas: I think of my barns as cupboards full of grain, hay and straw, stored for the winter.

When I was a child, we had Rhode Island Red chickens running around our smallholding. Chickens really were a lot larger then. Modern breeding has created a bird that is oven-ready in 40 days and, due to this incredible speed of production, we are now used to unnaturally small chickens. For our shops, I've always sourced slow-growing breeds with a long natural life – and now I hope to be able to produce some myself.

Before I started The Ginger Pig in 1996, I read a recipe in *The Art of Cookery* by Hannah Glasse (1708–1770), which calls for a 15lb chicken. My butcher laughed when I asked him for one, suggesting I use five 3lb chickens instead. I've carried the image of those big chickens for years, laying eggs on fresh straw to be boiled for breakfast, so I've started a new project. I want two things: a large, tasty chicken for our shops;

and differently-coloured eggs. So, because of this dream, in the corner of a friend's farmyard is a ramshackle 1950s chicken house with a tin roof and cast-iron wheels, and, with the help of my joiner Tom, a tape measure and a notepad, we've sketched the chicken house and started building our own very smart accommodation. If I'm going to breed traditional chickens, they need to have the right kind of classic-looking houses in which to live.

Making the chicken houses is proving a lot easier than finding the right birds to go in them. I want a variety of egg colours to remind me of a Farrow & Ball colour chart. Cuckoo Marans and their cousins, French Marans, lay rich chocolate-brown eggs, while a Leghorn shell is pure white. Rhode Island Reds have a paler brown shell and the Light Sussex a lovely soft cream. Unusually, the Aracauna breed produces a dull green egg, but the hen I want is the Welsummer, a bird with dark terracotta eggs.

Typically, the Welsummer is the hardest to find, but I have found a highly respected breeder. Reverend Lobb, in Ayrshire, has a strain of birds that date back to the beginning of the last century. I telephone to ask if I can buy some chicks or hens from him. The answer is no. In desperation I ask, 'What can I buy?' 'Well, I do sell fertile eggs, but I don't deliver and I don't post.' So I set off for Scotland and purchased 150 terracotta eggs, then delivered them to Mr Todd of Ampleforth, who has the incubators. Three weeks later, Mr Todd rings to say only 85 chicks have hatched (and that half of these will be cockerels).

I buy heat lamps, chick feeders, brooders (boxes that simulate a mother-hen environment), thermometers, water containers, wood shaving. Just how much equipment do 85 tiny chicks need? For two weeks I watch my flock develop, growing feathers and becoming more adventurous in their warm shed. I am inwardly congratulating myself when my friend and great helper on the farm, Sarah, rushes into the kitchen to say there are dead chicks in the brooder. I run to the shed to discover that my chicks have become cannibals. After a few frantic phone calls I learn that cannibalism and bullying are traits of the Welsummer. I hope we can salvage a few to place in the smart new chicken house.

But September is not all about chickens. Three years ago I needed more land for my pigs and rented West Farm, Blansby Park, from the Duchy of Lancaster. I moved the pigs across from Grange Farm, but I've really missed their funny ways, so I'm buying more. I've sourced the best gilts (virgin sows) and chosen a boar –who is now called Turpin – from the

Golden Ranger line (a desirable, well-known family in the pig world).
It's a joy to have contented, grunting pigs back at Grange Farm and
to be able to get to know them all as individuals.

With the new chickens and pigs I'm so busy that Sarah takes my place
on a trip to Duchy Home Farm, Tetbury, to attend the Riggit Galloway
annual meeting. The Prince of Wales is our patron – he is a great
supporter both of British farming and of minority breeds and I am sad
to miss out. But the barns are full to bursting with the harvest, the yard
looks organized, the chickens are settled and the pigs growing by the day,
while the dimming light reminds us that winter is almost here.

My fabulous
chicken houses
at dawn.

Meatballs in tomato sauce

When tomatoes are abundant, make your own sauce (see page 325) to go with these delicious little meaty nuggets. To add your a personal twist to the sauce, try adding a few chopped olives, a well-judged sprinkling of dried chilli flakes or some torn basil leaves.

Serves 6, makes 24 meatballs
Takes 1½ hours

1kg (2lb 4oz) tomatoes or 600ml (1 pint) passata

1kg (2lb 4oz) lean minced beef

1 onion, peeled and finely diced

1 garlic clove, crushed, peeled and finely diced

sea salt

freshly ground black pepper

leaves from 1 bunch of parsley, finely chopped

1 egg

2 tbsp olive oil

200ml (7fl oz) white wine

1. Skin and deseed the fresh tomatoes, if using: bring a saucepan of water to the boil, make a small cross in the skin of each tomato, plunge them into the boiling water for 20 seconds and remove. When cool enough to handle, the skins should slip off easily. Cut the tomatoes into quarters, scoop out and discard the seeds with your fingers and roughly chop the tomato flesh.

2. Preheat the oven to 180°C/350°F/gas mark 4. Place the minced beef, onion, garlic, seasoning, parsley and egg into a bowl and mix well with your hands. Divide the meat evenly into 24, rolling into balls the size of a walnut shell.

3. Heat the oil in a large frying pan over a medium-high heat and carefully brown the meatballs, in batches so as not to crowd the pan, for about 5 minutes per batch, turning until golden all over. Place the browned meatballs into a casserole dish. Once they are all cooked, pour the white wine into the frying pan, stirring and scraping at the base with a wooden spoon to dislodge all the meat essences. Stir in the tomatoes or passata and pour this over the meatballs.

4. Cover the casserole dish and cook in the oven for 45 minutes, stirring once or twice. Serve with ribbon pasta.

Braised Spanish pork with muscatel raisins

Unusually dark and glossy for a pork casserole, but the rich meat, red wine and raisins make a delicious combination that delivers near-perfection at the table. Serve this with creamy mashed potatoes and lightly cooked spinach. A rib-eye and a blade of pork are the same cut; the difference is that a blade is on the bone. Let the dish cool and rest overnight as this improves the flavours of the rich silky sauce, so this is a great meal to make in advance.

Serves 4–6
Takes 3 hours, plus overnight resting

1 tbsp olive oil

1kg (2lb 4oz) rib-eye of pork or 2kg (4lb 8oz) blade of pork

250g (9oz) shallots, peeled

3 garlic cloves, peeled and finely sliced

250g (9oz) seedless muscatel raisins

750ml (1¼ pints) bottle of red wine

3 bay leaves

1 bunch of marjoram

sea salt

freshly ground black pepper

1. Preheat the oven to 170°C/325°F/gas mark 3. In an ovenproof dish that has a lid, heat the olive oil over a medium-high heat, then brown the pork all over. Remove to a plate, then add the shallots to the dish and carefully brown them all over; add the garlic for the last minute of cooking. Return the pork to the pan, add the raisins, wine, herbs and seasoning, then bring to a gentle simmer.

2. Cover and transfer the dish to the oven. Cook for 1 hour, then baste with the juices and cook for a further hour. Remove from the oven and allow to cool, then cover and store in the refrigerator overnight.

3. The next day, preheat the oven to 180°C/350°F/gas mark 4, and bring the chilled pork dish to room temperature. Return the dish to the oven and cook for 40 minutes more.

4. To serve, remove the pork from the dish and carve it into thick slices. Place the meat on warmed plates and spoon over the plump raisins, shallots and sauce.

Spicy pork stir-fry

Pork tenderloin responds superbly to quick cooking and works very well when mixed with all these hot, fresh Asian flavours.

Serves 4
Takes 20 minutes

200g (7oz) vermicelli noodles

1 tbsp vegetable oil

500g (1lb 2oz) pork tenderloin, sliced into rounds

2 garlic cloves, crushed, peeled and finely chopped

1 lemon grass stalk, finely chopped

2 red chillies, deseeded and finely chopped

5cm (2in) fresh root ginger, peeled and finely chopped

2 carrots, peeled and finely sliced

½ Savoy cabbage, cored and shredded

1 tbsp fish sauce

juice of 2 limes

2 tbsp toasted sesame seeds

2 tbsp cashew nuts, chopped

1 bunch of spring onions, finely sliced into matchstick lengths

leaves from 1 bunch of coriander, chopped

1. Cook the noodles according to the packet instructions.

2. Meanwhile, heat the vegetable oil in a large pan or wok on a medium-high heat and add the pork. Seal on each side and cook until just brown, then reduce the heat and add the garlic, lemon grass, chillies and ginger, stirring constantly. Continue to stir-fry for 4 minutes.

3. Add the carrots and cabbage to the wok and toss through, then add the fish sauce and lime juice and quickly heat. Drain the noodles and serve in warmed bowls, add the pork and vegetables and top with the sesame seeds, cashew nuts, spring onions and coriander.

Peasant rabbit paella

The word paella usually conjures up images of exotic seafood delicately tumbled amongst tubby grains of rice. But in central Spain, they make a more rustic style of paella using rabbit, which is easily available there. Do not rush the cooking of the rabbit for this dish, as it's important to cook it slowly so that it falls off the bone when eaten. Ask your butcher to cut each rabbit leg into two and the saddle into four.

Serves 4–6
Takes 2½ hours

115g (4oz) young broad beans

1 tbsp olive oil

1 average size rabbit (1.2–1.3kg/2½–3lb), jointed

2 onions, peeled and diced

2 garlic cloves, crushed, peeled and finely diced

1 bay leaf

2 tsp smoked sweet paprika

sea salt

freshly ground black pepper

1 litre (1¾ pints) chicken or vegetable stock

280g (10oz) short-grained paella rice

1. If you only have later-season broad beans, they will need to be skinned before use: bring a large pan of water to a boil and tip in the beans, after only around 10 seconds, drain and rinse the beans well in cold water – the skins should now slip off easily between your fingers.

2. Heat the olive oil in a large paella pan, large shallow pan or flameproof roasting tin over a medium-high heat, add the rabbit and brown until golden all over; it should take about 10 minutes. Add the onions and garlic and cook for a few minutes, then add the bay leaf, paprika and seasoning, pour in the stock and bring to a gentle simmer.

3. Cover the pan and cook at a gentle simmer for 1 hour 15 minutes. Add the rice and mix well, return to a simmer and cook for 20 minutes (don't stir the rice again before serving). Add the broad beans and cook for a further 8 minutes. Serve.

Braised salmon of beef

A great cut that has been overlooked as a whole braising cut, a 'salmon' of beef has a good texture and lovely flavour. It is the best part of the silverside and a good butcher will know the cut. The beetroot in this recipe adds great depth of colour to the sauce and enriches the dish with a fantastic sweet but earthy flavour.

Serves 4–6
Takes 2½ hours

1 tbsp olive oil

1kg (2lb 4oz) salmon of beef

3 onions, peeled and finely sliced

2 garlic cloves, crushed and peeled

1 litre (1¾ pints) beef stock, plus more if needed

3 bay leaves

3 sprigs of thyme

sea salt

freshly ground black pepper

3 carrots, peeled and halved

2 beetroot, washed, peeled and quartered

2 celery sticks, halved

2 leeks, halved and well washed

1. Preheat the oven to 180°C/350°F/gas mark 4. Heat the olive oil in a large casserole dish over a medium-high heat and brown the salmon of beef all over, then remove the meat and place on a plate. Tip the onions into the pan and sauté for 8 minutes, then add the garlic and cook for a further 2 minutes. Return the beef to the pan and add the stock, herbs and seasoning.

2. Cover the pan and cook in the oven for 1 hour. Add the carrots and beetroot, cover again and cook for a further 45 minutes. Then add the celery and leeks, cover and cook for a further 20 minutes, adding more stock if needed.

3. To serve, remove the salmon of beef from the pan and carve into thick slices. Ladle the vegetables and stock into bowls and top with slices of the beef. Serve with fresh bread and English mustard.

Tasty chilli burgers

If making these for children, don't add the chilli. The feta adds a lovely twist. You must use good-quality minced beef for a superior flavour and texture.

Serves 4
Takes 20 minutes

900g (2lb) lean minced beef

1 tbsp soy sauce

1 tbsp Worcestershire sauce

1 red chilli, deseeded and finely diced

freshly ground black pepper

leaves from ½ bunch of parsley, finely chopped

150g (5½oz) feta, crumbled

1 egg

olive oil, to cook

4 crusty bread buns

1 Little Gem lettuce

4 slices of beef tomato

1. Place the minced beef, soy and Worcestershire sauces, chilli, pepper and parsley in a bowl and mix with your hands until evenly blended. Add the feta and mix it in, then add the egg to bind. Divide the mixture into 4 and shape each portion into burgers.

2. Heat a griddle pan or frying pan, brush it with olive oil, then cook the burgers over a medium heat for 3–4 minutes each side for rare, 5 for medium and 6 for well-done meat (if you must).

3. Serve the burgers in buns with lettuce and sliced tomato.

Game pie

As we sold more and more pies I realized we needed to add variety.
A classic mixed-game pie was missing from our menu, so we came up
with this wonderful recipe.

Makes 1 large (24x12cm/9½x4½in) or 4 small (12x6cm/4½x2½in) pies
Takes 3 hours, plus overnight marinating

For the filling	For the hot water pastry
4 pheasant breasts	700g (1lb 9oz) plain flour
4 pigeon breasts	50g (2oz) icing sugar
300ml (½ pint) Port	pinch of salt
2 tbsp Redcurrant jelly (see page 322)	200g (7oz) lard
1 garlic clove, crushed, peeled and finely diced	For assembly
8 strips of orange zest	25g (1oz) lard, melted
250g (9oz) skinned pork belly, finely diced	1 tbsp plain flour
400g (14oz) venison, finely diced	1 egg, beaten
24 rashers of thinly sliced dry-cured streaky bacon, rind removed	home-made gelatine (see opposite page)
1 free range chicken breast, sliced	50g (2oz) fresh cranberries

1. For the filling, finely slice the pheasant and pigeon breasts. Place them in a bowl,
add the port, redcurrant jelly, the garlic and strips of the orange zest. Season and mix
together, cover and refrigerate for 24 hours. Strain and freeze the marinade to use in
casseroles. Mix the pork and venison in a bowl, cover and refrigerate.

2. To make the pastry, mix the flour, icing sugar and salt in a bowl. Place the lard and
200ml (7fl oz) water in a pan and quickly melt together, then pour this into the flour
and mix as fast as you can until it forms a smooth pastry dough. (If you wait too long,
it sets hard and is very difficult to roll.) What dough you are not working with, seal in
kitchen wrap and cover with a tea towel, to help keep it soft. If making individual pies,
divide the dough into 8 balls, 4 weighing 185g (6½oz) and 4 weighing 115g (4oz). For
one large pie, divide it into 2 balls, one 750g (1lb 10oz) and the other 450g (1lb).

3. Preheat the oven to 170°C/325°F/gas mark 3. Brush the tins or tin thoroughly with
lard and lightly dust with flour. Roll out the larger pastry balls and use them to line the
tins or tin. Lie the bacon in strips to form a layer inside the pastry and allow the excess
lengths of bacon to hang evenly over the rim.

4. Take one-third of the venison and pork mix and place a thin layer at the bottom of the pie case. Top with half of the marinated pheasant and pigeon breast and all of the chicken. Place on another layer of the venison, then another layer of pheasant and pigeon, then the remainder of the venison. Fold the overhanging bacon strips over the top.

5. Brush the edges of the pastry with egg. Roll out the smaller pastry balls and place the sheets on top, crimping the edges with your fingers. Make a 3cm (1in) hole in the centre, then brush all over with egg. Cook in the oven for 1 hour. Remove from the oven and cool. Place a small funnel in the pastry hole and pour in a little home-made gelatine. Top with a few cranberries and again leave to set for 1 hour. Serve.

Home-made gelatine

A wonder ingredient for pies, that not only binds them together but also adds that final richness and great depth of flavour. It's also very nutritious!

Makes 300–400ml (10–14fl oz)

2 pig's trotters, ordered in advance from your butcher

5 peppercorns

2 bay leaves

1. Place the trotters in a saucepan of cold water and bring to a boil. Remove the trotters, discard the water and rinse the pan. Return the trotters to the pan and cover with fresh water, adding the peppercorns and bay leaves. Cover with a tightly-fitting lid and simmer for 4 hours. Check every hour, making sure that the trotters are always just covered with water, adding more if needed.

2. Strain the liquid through muslin and leave to chill. Test the setting density, which should be just like a cube of concentrated fruit jelly. If it's too soft, gently simmer once more to concentrate the setting properties. Cool, chill and use in the game pie (opposite).

Classic roast partridge

Partridge is an excellent choice for those who do not want a bird that is too gamey; it has lovely, tender, slightly sweet-tasting meat with a gentle flavour. It roasts really well and doesn't need more than some good bread sauce and rich, tasty gravy to accompany it.

Serves 2
Takes 50 minutes

25g (1oz) butter

2 plump partridges

vegetable oil, for the tin

25g (1oz) plain flour

125ml (4fl oz) red wine

1 tbsp Redcurrant jelly (see page 322)

1. Preheat the oven to 200°C/400°F/gas mark 6. Smear the butter evenly over the partridge breasts. Lightly oil a small roasting tin, add the partridges and place in the hot oven to roast for 30–35 minutes. Test if the birds are cooked by tearing away a leg: if it comes away easily, it is cooked; if not return to the oven for a further 10 minutes, then check again. (You can also tell if the birds are cooked if, when you pierce the thickest part with a skewer, the juices run clear.)

2. When cooked, remove the birds from the oven, place on a warm plate and keep warm. Add the flour to the roasting tin and mix well, then blend in the red wine and redcurrant jelly. Place the tin over a medium-high heat and mix well, bring to a simmer and allow the liquid to reduce slightly, then serve with the partridge.

Roast Michaelmas goose

Traditionally, farmers enjoyed a well-fattened goose on September 29th.

Serves 8 | Takes 4½ hours

5kg (11lb) goose, with its giblets

1 onion, peeled and roughly chopped

2 bay leaves

2 celery sticks, halved

6 black peppercorns

1 leek, halved and well washed

500g (1lb 2oz) cooked potato, grated

500g (1lb 2oz) minced pork

goose liver, diced

250g (9oz) fresh breadcrumbs

2 red onions, peeled and finely diced

500g (1lb 2oz) Cox apples, peeled and grated, plus 2 extra, quartered and cored

2 garlic cloves, crushed, peeled and diced

1 tbsp dried sage

¼ tsp ground mace

1 egg, beaten with 250ml (9fl oz) water

sea salt

freshly ground black pepper

2 pears, quartered and cored

¼ tsp grated nutmeg

¼ tsp ground cloves

2 tbsp soft light brown sugar

2 tbsp plain flour

100ml (3½fl oz) white wine

1. Place the giblets (except the liver) in a pan with 1 litre (1¾ pints) of water, the onion, bay, celery, peppercorns and leek. Simmer for 1 hour and then strain and reserve.

2. Meanwhile, preheat the oven to 220°C/425°F/gas mark 7. In a bowl mix the potato, pork, liver, breadcrumbs, red onions, grated apple, garlic, sage, mace, egg and seasoning. Prick the goose all over with a fork. Fill the neck and rear of the goose cavity with stuffing and fold over the skin, securing with skewers. Weigh the goose and calculate a cooking time of 30 minutes per 1kg (2lb 4oz). It should take a total of around 3½ hours.

3. Place the goose on a roasting cradle over a deep roasting tin (the cradle will allow fat to drip away). Roast for 30 minutes, reduce the heat to 180°C/350°F/gas mark 4 and cook for a further 3 hours, draining off excess fat throughout.

4. Place the pears and last 2 apples in a bowl, add the nutmeg, cloves and sugar. Toss then add to the goose and cook for 15 minutes. Remove from the oven and transfer the goose to a serving plate. Reserve some of the fat and return the fruit to the oven.

5. To make the gravy, skim the fat from the roasting tin with a metal spoon, add the flour and whisk until smooth. Slowly pour in the giblet stock and wine and bring to a boil, stirring and pouring in juices that have run out of the goose. Carve and serve.

OCTOBER

October on the farm

The weather has grown colder with hard, early-morning frosts. I am surprised and delighted to find some black kittens in residence at Grange Farm still, prancing around and chasing each other on top of the high straw stack in the large barn. I've been so busy with the harvest that I hadn't thought about them for a while. They have been with us for six months and, though Sarah feeds them fresh pig hearts every evening, they are impossible to catch. Word of free food must have travelled as a tabby cat, whom we assume is their mother, appears at feeding time. I like having cats around and they're useful as vermin controllers. Most farmers with sheep have no time for them for fear of their spreading toxoplasmosis, but I'm not so concerned, because it is only one reason for the spread, and the benefits of their keeping rodents at bay are far greater.

The Tamworth pigs I bought last month need to start work now they have settled in, so I introduce my prize boar Turpin to Primrose and Primula, who at 11 months are the two oldest gilts in the new herd. I put them together in a freshly straw-bedded barn but, judging by the squeals from the girls, they are not totally convinced about their new housemate. That Saturday I glance over the stable door and see Primrose has succumbed, and the following Monday Primula is also deflowered. The results of this union will be revealed in 112 to 114 days – or to use the old-fashioned term, three months, three weeks, three days – and I'm hoping each sow will have at least eight piglets. Meanwhile, Turpin has moved in with Dandelion and Burdock.

My plans for a late summer holiday have been dashed as Thanksgiving and Christmas are just around the corner and we have too much to do. The shops' sales are growing, with an ever-increasing stream of orders. Every Monday we gather at the farm to iron out any problems. In one such meeting it dawns on us that we will be receiving orders for more than 1,000 turkeys, 500 geese, 180 pigs, 80 lambs, 30 carcasses of beef and a plethora of pies, sausages, bacons and hams. We have a plan, so I'm quietly confident. David Harrison (the mainstay of the office side of The Ginger Pig) has developed a computer system to replace my old methods, while Amy Fletcher will now take and manage the orders by phone.

The harvest provides me with a pleasant distraction from all this future activity, because I can drive around in my fabulous state-of-the-art tractor listening to music and preparing the soil for the coming season's crops and the fields for the stock.

This month we tup (mate) our largest flock of Mule ewes. My shepherd for the last five years has handed in his notice to take a job working for Natural England. So Chris, the young second shepherd, has taken charge while I look for a new head shepherd.

The Mule ewes have moved into the land around the farm for 'flushing' (grazing on rich feed), which will increase their fertility and condition. While they feed on grass, their proximity to the tups ensures that they all come into season together.

The tups are going mad with excitement at the ewes being back at the farm. Chris prepares them by fitting them with a raddle harness, which has a stick of paint that marks the ewes as they are 'covered' (or mated); yellow ink is used in the first week and blue during the second, and this helps us at lambing time. We mix in each excited tup with 50 ewes and they stay together for three weeks. I'm not sure if I feel sad or annoyed when I find a tup that has turned his feet up through sheer exhaustion and excitement. It's not unusual to lose at least one ram a year through their overdoing it!

I'm not sure if I feel sad or annoyed when I find a tup that has turned his feet up through sheer exhaustion and excitement. It's not unusual to lose at least one ram a year through their overdoing it!

I call in my specialist scanning man, John Barnes, to help me see how many lambs the Dorset ewes (who were covered in July and are due in November) are going to produce, so we can feed them the correct amount in the run-up to lambing. It's an important process, as a ewe carrying one lamb and eating too much may produce an unusually large lamb that needs a Caesarean section, and I prefer the births to be as natural as possible. We round up the ewes and they are passed through a crate, where a scanner is run over their stomachs and the screen instantly shows us how many lambs they are carrying.

While he's here I also get John to look at some of the cows, and it's good news. Of the 20 scanned Riggits and Belted Galloways, 17 are in calf. Another ambitious and more long-term project of mine is to breed red Riggits. I have a fascination for all coloured breeds, but the red gene is recessive, so most Riggits are black with a white line down the back. However, two years ago, during a Riggit meeting on Dartmoor hosted by Anton Coaker, I spotted a young red bull as we walked over the moor looking at Anton's other cattle. A deal was agreed, but it took five months for Anton to lure this bull back to the main farm, at which point I rushed over with my cattle trailer to bring him to Yorkshire. We have named him

Riggity Man. Breeding cattle is a labour of love. I have owned Riggity Man for more than 18 months and Sarah has fed him by hand every day to try and tame his wild moor instincts, with the aim of getting him to work with my herd of black Riggit heifers next spring. Only 285 days (or nine months) after that will I know if any of these females are carrying the red gene. Fingers crossed.

A Riggit heifer (left) with Beauty the cow (centre) and Red Apple (right), all Galloways.

Smoked pork hock
and parsley pasta

Smoked pork hocks have wonderfully sweet, melting meat and a good
flavour that blends perfectly with the simplicity of the rest of these
ingredients to make a tasty sauce.

Serves 6
Takes 1½ hours

2 smoked pork hocks

leaves from 1 large bunch of flat-leaf parsley, roughly chopped

85g (3oz) Parmesan, grated

sea salt

freshly ground black pepper

2 tbsp good olive oil

4 tbsp mascarpone

425g (15oz) linguine

1. Place the hocks in a large pan, cover with cold water and bring to a boil. Reduce the
heat, cover and simmer for 1 hour. Remove from the heat and leave until cool enough
to handle, then peel off the skin and discard along with any excess fat. Pick off all the
meat and roughly chop. Reserve 125ml (4fl oz) of the stock and freeze the rest to make
rich pea or lentil soups.

2. Mix the ham with the parsley, Parmesan, seasoning, olive oil, mascarpone and
reserved stock.

3. Bring a large pan of water to a boil and cook the pasta according to the packet's
instructions. Drain and return to the pan along with the ham mixture, toss well
with two wooden spoons and serve at once.

Sausage and butterbean pot

Good sausages make all the difference to this dish as, while cooking, the juices melt out of them to enrich the sauce that bastes the beans.

Serves 6
Takes 1 hour 45 minutes, plus overnight soaking

500g (1lb 2oz) dried butterbeans

2 tbsp olive oil

2 onions, peeled and sliced

4 red peppers, cored, deseeded and sliced

12 tasty sausages (try chorizo or Toulouse-style sausages)

2 garlic cloves, crushed and peeled

2 bay leaves

2 sprigs of thyme

2 tsp tomato purée

sea salt

freshly ground black pepper

1. Place the beans in a large bowl and cover generously with cold water. Leave to soak for 12 hours. The next day, drain the beans and place in a pan of fresh water. Bring to a boil and boil hard for 10 minutes, then reduce the heat and allow to simmer for 45 minutes to 1 hour, or until tender.

2. Meanwhile, preheat the oven to 180°C/350°F/gas mark 4 and heat the oil in a roasting tin. When hot, add the onions, peppers and sausages and cook for 20 minutes.

3. Drain the beans, reserving 450ml (16fl oz) of the cooking liquid. Remove the sausages from the roasting tin. Add the beans, garlic, herbs, reserved cooking liquor, tomato purée and seasoning, mix well and return the sausages. Cover with foil and return to the oven for 20 minutes. Remove the foil, turn the sausages and cook for a further 10 minutes, then serve.

Navarin of lamb

This dish is traditionally made in spring with the new season's vegetables, but it's very satisfying in autumn as well. It can be made with either lamb or mutton; mutton will deliver a stronger flavour with more depth. Get your butcher to cut the neck of lamb into pieces for you.

Serves 6–8
Takes 2½ hours

1 tbsp olive oil

1.5kg (3lb 5oz) middle neck of lamb on the bone, cut into 6 pieces

1 onion, peeled and roughly diced

2 garlic cloves, crushed, peeled and finely chopped

25g (1oz) plain flour

2 tbsp tomato purée

1 bouquet garni

1 litre (1¾ pints) lamb or chicken stock

200g (7oz) small waxy potatoes, such as Charlotte, peeled

15g (½oz) butter

3 carrots, peeled and roughly chopped

200g (7oz) baby turnips, left whole

115g (4oz) small white onions, peeled

115g (4oz) green beans, trimmed

115g (4oz) peas

1. Heat the oil in a large pan over a medium-high heat, add the lamb and brown. Remove the meat and add the onions and garlic. Cook until soft but not coloured. Remove from the heat and stir in the flour. Mix well, until all the fat has been absorbed into the flour. Return the lamb to the pan, add the tomato purée, bouquet garni and stock and bring to a simmer. Reduce the heat, cover and cook gently for 1½ hours, stirring occasionally.

2. Add the potatoes to the lamb and submerge them in the cooking juices. Cover the pan and return to the heat for 15 minutes.

3. Melt the butter in a saucepan and add the carrots, turnips and white onions. Sauté until just turning brown, then add to the lamb and cook for a further 25 minutes. Finally add the beans and peas and cook for a final 5 minutes, then serve.

Slow-roast shoulder of lamb

This is a recipe that every family should cook. The preparation is so simple and the cooking looks after itself. It needs to be cooked slowly, so pop it in the oven and get on with your day; you'll return to the most succulent of long, slow roasts that melts in your mouth. The flavour is sublime and the dish perfection when served with home-made Quince jelly (see page 322).

Serves 6
Takes 4½ hours

1 head of garlic

3kg (6lb 8oz) shoulder of lamb or hogget

6 onions, peeled

8 carrots, peeled

sea salt

freshly ground black pepper

1. Preheat the oven to 190°C/375°F/gas mark 5. Cut the head of garlic in half and rub it all over the shoulder of lamb, then break it up into cloves in a roasting tin. Add the onions and carrots and place the lamb on top, season and pour on 1.4 litres (2½ pints) of water. Tent the tin with foil and place in the oven for 30 minutes.

2. Reduce the heat to 150°C/300°F/gas mark 2 and cook for a further 4 hours. About 30 minutes before serving, remove the foil and allow the lamb to crisp and brown. The lamb is so tender it doesn't require carving; the blade should just be lifted out, then the lamb spooned from the tin with the vegetables and juices. Great with mashed potatoes.

Spiced and seared goose skirt

The flavour and texture of this cut of beef, also known as bavette, is amazing. The trick for quick cooking is to use a high, searing heat and then to rest the meat before carving, or it will be tough. I can't emphasize enough that you must rest the meat, so do not rush this. However tasty it looks, wait!

Serves 4–6
Takes 20 minutes, plus at least 2 hours marinating

700g (1lb 9oz) goose skirt

2 tbsp harissa paste (see page 324)

2 garlic cloves, crushed and peeled

2 tbsp olive oil, plus more for the couscous

sea salt

freshly ground black pepper

175g (6oz) couscous

200g (7oz) peppery rocket

1. Place the goose skirt in a plastic bag. Mix together the harissa, garlic, oil and seasoning. Spoon the harissa mixture into the bag and rub it all over the beef. Leave this to marinate for 2 hours at room temperature or in the refrigerator overnight.

2. If the meat was chilled, return it to room temperature. Heat a barbecue, grill or large griddle pan and sear the meat on the highest heat for 3 minutes on each side, then remove and allow to rest for 10 minutes.

3. Place the couscous in a large bowl, cover with boiling water, add a dash of olive oil and mix with a fork until all the water is absorbed. Place the couscous on plates and top with a handful of rocket. Thinly slice the rested beef into ribbons and arrange on top of the rocket, pouring on any juices from the carving board as well. Great served hot or warm.

Asian beef curry

Clod of beef is a great cut to use for long, slow cooking, which in this recipe allows the spices and flavours to mingle with the meat. Don't be alarmed by the long ingredients list; this curry is very easy to put together and delivers a wonderfully complex flavour.

Serves 4–6
Takes 3½ hours, plus overnight marinating

For the spice paste

5cm (2in) galangal or fresh root ginger, peeled and roughly chopped

3 garlic cloves, peeled, crushed and finely diced

1 tsp cumin seeds

1 tsp coriander seeds

1 tsp fennel seeds

½ onion, peeled and roughly chopped

1 chilli, deseeded and finely chopped

¼ tsp ground cinnamon

1 lemongrass stalk, finely chopped

3 cardamom pods

4 kaffir lime leaves, chopped

1 clove

sea salt

freshly ground black pepper

For the curry

1kg (2lb 4oz) clod of beef, cubed

1 tbsp vegetable oil

400g (14 oz) can chopped tomatoes

juice of 2 limes

750ml (1¼ pints) beef stock

leaves from 1 bunch of coriander, chopped

1. Place the galangal (or root ginger), garlic, cumin, coriander and fennel seeds, onion, chilli, cinnamon, lemongrass, cardamom, kaffir lime leaves, clove, salt and pepper in a small blender and whizz until everything is chopped. Add 100ml (3½fl oz) water and whizz again, until the mixture resembles a paste. Place the meat in a bowl and add the spice paste. Mix well, cover and marinate overnight in the refrigerator.

2. The next day, remove the beef from the refrigerator and let it stand at room temperature for 1 hour. Preheat the oven to 150°C/300°F/gas mark 2. Heat the oil in a large pan, add the meat and brown. Add the tomatoes, lime juice and stock, bring to a simmer, then cover and cook in the oven for 2½ hours, stirring occasionally.

3. Remove the lid and cook for a further 30 minutes, to allow the sauce to reduce and thicken. Serve with the coriander sprinkled on top and plain steamed or boiled rice.

Chicken in white wine with porcini

The Ginger Pig chickens are between 80 and 155 days old (depending on weight), so they need long cooking, but their age delivers a fantastic depth of flavour. They are superb and also roast well. If using a shorter-lived chicken, reduce the final cooking time by a third.

Serves 6
Takes 1¼ hours

1 tbsp olive oil

2.5–3kg (5lb 8oz–6lb 8oz) Master Gris chicken, jointed

6 shallots, peeled and finely diced

1 garlic clove, crushed, peeled and finely diced

50g (2oz) dried porcini

1 x 750ml (1¼ pints) bottle of white wine

200ml (7fl oz) chicken or vegetable stock

150ml (¼ pint) double cream

1 bay leaf

1 sprig of thyme

sea salt

freshly ground black pepper

25g (1oz) plain flour

3 sprigs of tarragon, roughly chopped

1. Preheat the oven to 200°C/400°F/gas mark 6. Brush the inside of a roasting tin with oil, add the chicken in a single layer and place in the oven to brown for 10 minutes. Put the porcini in a bowl and cover with boiling water, then set aside until they are needed.

2. Add the shallots and garlic to the chicken and return to the oven for 5 minutes. Pour in the wine, stock, porcinis and their water, cream, bay, thyme and seasoning, cover snugly with baking parchment, then seal with foil and return to the oven for 30 minutes. Remove the paper and foil and return to the oven for a further 30 minutes.

3. Lift out the chicken joints into a serving dish with a slotted spoon. Stir the flour into the cooking juices, then whisk it in. Place the tin over a medium heat and bring to a simmer, stirring. Add more flour if you want a thicker sauce. Sprinkle in the tarragon. Pour the sauce over the chicken and serve with ribbon pasta.

The Ginger Pig chicken and ham pie

Originally we made these with leg meat as everyone wanted to buy whole breasts, but now we use whole chickens as the demand for pies is so high.

Makes 1 large (24x12cm/9½x4½in) or 4 small (12x6cm/4½x2½in) pies
Takes 2½ hours

For the filling	For the shortcrust pastry
2kg (4lb 8oz) whole chicken	900g (2lb) plain flour
50g (2oz) butter	350g (12oz) lard
50g (2oz) plain flour	2 large eggs, beaten
125ml (4fl oz) double cream	pinch of salt
pinch of white pepper & pinch salt	For assembly
400g (14 oz) cooked smoked ham, in one piece, chopped	25g (1oz) lard, melted
	1 tbsp plain flour
4 sprigs of flat-leaf parsley, finely chopped	1 egg, beaten

1. For the filling, preheat the oven to 190°C/375°F/gas mark 5. Place the chicken in a large lidded ovenproof dish, cover with water, then with a sheet of baking parchment and the lid. Cook in the oven for 1½ hours, or until the juices run clear when the thickest part is pierced with a skewer. Lift the chicken out of the liquid and leave both to cool. Remove the skin and meat from the bones, roughly chop and place in a bowl.

2. Skim off and discard the fat from the stock. In a pan melt the butter, add the flour and mix to make a smooth roux, then slowly pour in 750ml (1¼ pints) of the stock, stirring. Bring to a boil; it should be good and thick. Remove from the heat and cool, then add to the chicken with the cream, seasoning, ham and parsley, and mix well.

3. Place the flour and lard in a food processor and blitz until evenly blended, then transfer to a mixing bowl. Add the eggs, salt and 125ml (4fl oz) chilled water and mix to a smooth dough ball. If making individual pies, divide the dough into 8 balls, four weighing 185g (6½oz) and 4 weighing 115g (4oz). If making one large pie, divide into 2 balls, one 750g (1lb 10oz) and the other 450g (1lb).

4. Preheat the oven to 190°C/375°F/gas mark 5. Brush the inside of each tin with lard, then dust lightly with flour. Roll out the larger pastry balls and use them to line them. Divide the filling between tins, then brush the pastry edges with egg. Roll out the smaller pastry balls and place the sheets on top, pushing the edges together. Trim off excess with a knife and crimp the edges, decorating with pastry trimmings. Cook in the oven for 50 minutes. Leave to cool for 5 minutes, then turn the pies out and enjoy hot or cold.

Lemon roast guinea fowl

Originally these beautiful birds came from Africa, but they are now bred in France and known as pintadeaux. They are allowed to mature to 94 days old, so they have optimum flavour at the table, and their flesh is tender and golden. Ask for Label Rouge, which will have a superior quality and mean the birds have been reared in the open air.

Serves 4
Takes 1½ hours

1.5kg (3lb 5oz) guinea fowl

zest and juice of 1 unwaxed lemon

50g (2oz) fresh breadcrumbs

50g (2oz) Parmesan, grated

1 tsp capers, rinsed and chopped

2 garlic cloves, crushed, peeled and finely diced

leaves from ½ bunch of parsley, chopped

1 red chilli, deseeded and finely diced

sea salt

freshly ground black pepper

vegetable oil, for the tin

1. Preheat the oven to 180°C/350°F/gas mark 4. In a bowl, mix the lemon juice and zest, breadcrumbs, Parmesan, capers, garlic, parsley, chilli and seasoning. Carefully separate the skin from the meat on the breast of the guinea fowl, starting from the neck end and making sure you don't tear it. Place a layer of the lemon stuffing in between the breast and the skin and pat until smooth and evenly spread.

2. Weigh the bird after you have stuffed it and calculate the cooking time, allowing 20 minutes for each 500g (1lb 2oz), plus 20 minutes extra.

3. Lightly oil a roasting tin and place the guinea fowl in it. Tent loosely with foil and roast according to your calculations. For the last 25 minutes of cooking, remove the foil to allow the skin to become crisp and golden. To check that the bird is fully cooked, the juices should run clear when the thickest part is pierced with a skewer.

NOVEMBER

November on the farm

The first Dorset lambs will be delivered in a few weeks and Chris is still in charge and enjoying his new responsibilities as acting senior shepherd. The barns have never looked more organized, with a brand-new lay-out of lambing pens. Following their scans last month, we've put the ewes into pens according to how many lambs they are carrying and we will feed them different amounts to avoid any oversized lambs that can cause more dangerous births.

Alan is my general helper around the farm and has been assisting Chris with the neverending round of jobs. They are constantly learning skills from each other. It's good to see, as I clearly remember Alan saying back in the summer that, 'There ain't much work in that lad,' as Chris walked quietly across the yard, yet today he is full of admiration for him.

Demand for lamb from the shops in London is relentless and we are butchering around 35 sheep each week. We are trying to introduce our customers to hogget and mutton, which delivers a much deeper and more complex flavour than lamb and comes from animals only a couple of months older. It's a slow process, but we're having some success in convincing people to try it.

A major problem for sheep farmers this year has been the terribly wet weather. Constant, pounding rain means the ewes are always sodden, but we need them to be dry before putting them into the warm barns for lambing. If we bring them in wet and cold they heat up too quickly, which can lead to pneumonia. But the rain is lashing down without a break, so we have to risk moving them anyway or the ewes will start lambing out in the fields.

Most lambs are born at night so that by morning they will be up and running, safe from predators hunting for an easy meal. Chrissie has been coming to Grange Farm for 5 years to help with night lambing. She was previously a local farmer with a flock of milking sheep that produced cheese, but she now spends most of the year in Africa working with children and wildlife, and returns every winter to help me. Sitting in the kitchen in the middle of a cold night listening to her talk about her travels in Africa makes me think farming can be a little mundane.

I always leave Chrissie a bottle of Port on the kitchen table to ward off the worst of the cold night air; in the morning I can estimate how many lambs have been delivered by checking the number of nips she has had. On a busy night 18–20 ewes can lamb, giving us 40–50 lambs; quads are our record from one ewe. I appreciate Chrissie's experience and help as there's nothing worse than finding two ewes who have lambed in the same pen whose young have been mixed up, or a ewe who has not delivered but adopts someone else's lambs. The first few hours of a new lamb's life are crucial for bonding with the ewe and a mix-up is called 'mismothering'. Occasionally it's a real effort to get a lamb fastened to the ewe's teat and they can wander about bleating aimlessly; Chrissie is skilled at quickly spotting these problems, sorting them out and creating a safe and happy lambing barn. With 300 Dorset ewes and the possibility of up to 450 lambs yet to be born, it's a very busy but happy time on the farm.

We also need to organize the tupping (mating) of all the Blackface, Bluefaced Leicester and Mules, so once again more than 550 ewes are brought in from the moor to the fields around the farm for 'flushing', to improve their condition. The raddle harnesses are being put on the tups when Chris rushes into the kitchen saying, 'I've just found one of the Blackface tups dead.' It's hard to fathom the reason – maybe the excitement was too much for him. We desperately need a replacement, and quickly. I get on the phone, but unsurprisingly all the other local farmers need their Blackface tups for their own ewes. After numerous calls I locate one that is available up in the Borders. A real piece of luck.

I point to the back of my car where I have optimistically put some plastic down. Philip is horrified and laughs, informing me that I couldn't possibly put this particular tup in the car: 'He's a nasty bastard and will head-butt out the windows!'

The following morning I leave at 4am to collect the precious tup. Things don't go well for me, as the roads are badly flooded after the rains and the traffic is dreadful, but my Range Rover manages eventually to get me to the farm in Alston. Philip the farmer sells me his healthy and strong-looking tup for a bargain price of £400, and asks how I am going to transport it back to Yorkshire. I point to the back of my car where I have optimistically put some plastic down. Philip is horrified and laughs, informing me that I couldn't possibly put this particular tup in the car: 'He's a nasty bastard and will head-butt out the windows!'

I have no alternative but to return to Yorkshire for the trailer, then drive all the way back up to the Borders once more to collect my tup. For the whole of the journey home the ram kicks and rams the walls in a frenzy, making the trailer weave dangerously all over the road. The next day we get the tup to work and all goes well. He is good with the ewes but, boy, has he got some head-butt. I can promise that he won't be travelling anywhere any time soon.

The butchers on the farm are now working flat-out in preparation for the festivities this month and next month. All the beef needs to be hung in time for Christmas, extra bacon and hams are being cured, and then there are all the turkeys to prepare for Thanksgiving this month. The butchers in the London shops are helping us by trying to plan their orders as well as they can, so that the small farm butchery can react and be as ready as possible for their busiest time of the year.

Near right: Tim, Chrissie and Sarah discussing the night time lambing activity. Far right: a Dorset Ewe.

Slow-roast belly of pork

The trick to this dish is to get good crunchy crackling. It is only produced when the skin has been scored and the pork subjected to prolonged, gentle heat. That's the reason for the long cooking time.

Serves 4–6
Takes 6 hours

1.5kg (3lb 5oz) pork belly

1 tbsp olive oil

4 onions, peeled and cut into wedges

6 carrots, peeled and cut into chunks

4 beetroot, peeled and cut into wedges

6 potatoes, peeled and cut into wedges

sea salt

freshly ground black pepper

6 sage leaves, roughly chopped

1. Preheat the oven to 170°C/325°F/gas mark 3. Get your butcher to score the pork skin, or do it yourself with a thin-bladed sharp knife, taking care not to cut too deeply. Wipe the skin dry with kitchen paper.

2. Brush a roasting tin with the oil and add the vegetables, seasoning and sage. Top with the pork belly, skin side up, place in the oven and cook for 1 hour.

3. Reduce the heat to 150°C/300°F/gas mark 2 and cook for a further 4½ hours. Return the temperature to 180°C/350°F/gas mark 4, or even a little more if needed to reach that final crispy perfection, and cook for a further 30 minutes.

4.Remove the pork to a carving board, cover the meat with kitchen foil and allow to rest for 15–30 minutes. Lift out the vegetables and, using a metal spoon, skim off and discard the excess fat from the juices. Carve the pork and serve with the vegetables and juices.

Venison burgers on toasted ciabatta

Venison makes for a sophisticated take on the burger, but it needs pork fat to add moisture to the meat while cooking, so don't leave it out.

Serves 4
Takes 45 minutes

700g (1lb 9oz) minced venison

280g (10oz) minced pork fat

5 juniper berries

2 garlic cloves, peeled, crushed and finely diced

2 sprigs of sage, leaves stripped and roughly chopped

2 tbsp cranberry sauce

sea salt

freshly ground black pepper

2 tbsp olive oil

1 loaf of ciabatta

1 bunch of watercress

1. Place the venison and pork fat in a bowl and mix well with your hands. Using a mortar and pestle, crush the juniper berries and add to the meat with the garlic, sage, cranberry sauce and seasoning. Mix together, divide into 4 and shape into burgers.

2. Heat the olive oil in a frying pan over a medium-high heat and cook the burgers on each side for 5–8 minutes or until they are cooked through.

3. Meanwhile, slice the ciabatta in half lengthways and then into 4 pieces, or simply slice the loaf thickly. Toast, then scatter one side of each piece with watercress and top with a venison burger. Serve topped with more watercress and mustard, and an array of your favourite sauces.

Wet-cured ham from scratch

Don't be scared – making your own ham is really very satisfying and will give a huge sense of achievement. The best way to test if your brine is strong enough is to add a potato, which should bob on the top; if it sinks, you need more salt. You will need a large plastic box, big enough to take the ham but still fit in your refrigerator, and a large syringe, available from your chemist.

Serves about 20
Takes 5 hours, plus 10 days curing and overnight soaking

For the ham	2.25kg (5lb) curing salt mix
1 cinnamon stick	7kg (15lb 4oz) leg of pork, ideally from a gilt
2 tbsp black peppercorns	For the glaze
1 tbsp cloves	175g (6oz) French mustard
1 tbsp fennel seeds	200g (7oz) soft brown sugar
6 bay leaves	

1. Clean your plastic brining box (see recipe introduction) with boiling water. Place 1 litre (1¾ pints) of water, all the spices and the bay in a saucepan. Bring to a boil and simmer for 30 minutes. Leave until cold.

2. Place 6 litres (10½ pints) of cold water in the box, pour in the curing mix (available from www.sausagemaking.org or The Ginger Pig), stir until dissolved, then mix in the spiced water from the pan. Inject the pork leg in its thickest part with the liquid from the box (the brine), to ensure the cure goes to the centre. Put your brining box in the refrigerator first, or it will be too heavy to lift, then add the pork leg and submerge, meat side down and ensure it is completely submerged. Place a plate on top to hold the pork down. Check the pork every day and cure for 10 days.

3. Remove the meat from the brine and dry, then wrap it in muslin and hang it in a cool place for a minimum of 3 hours. In winter it can be kept in a well-ventilated, dry place for months, but in summer only a couple of weeks. If this worries you, and you have room, store it in the refrigerator. Never cover it with plastic; it must be able to breathe.

4. Soak the ham in cold water overnight, changing it frequently. Place in your largest saucepan, cover with fresh water and bring to a boil. Discard this water and cover with more cold water, cover and simmer gently for 3½–4 hours until cooked through. Remove from the pan and leave until cool enough to handle.

5. Preheat the oven to 170°C/325°F/gas mark 3. Mix the ingredients for the glaze. Trim the skin from the ham and cut a criss-cross pattern through the fat. Spread the glaze generously over the fat and bake in the oven for 1 hour until browned. Serve hot or cold.

Boned and rolled fennel-stuffed chump of pork

Fennel seeds go so well with slow-roast pork. The Italians have been cooking this dish for years; during the winter they eat it hot and in summer, cold and finely sliced.

Serves 4–6
Takes 3½ hours

1kg (2lb 4oz) boned chump of pork	sea salt
1 tbsp olive oil	freshly ground black pepper
1 large onion, peeled and finely diced	2 apples, peeled and grated
115g (4oz) fresh breadcrumbs	1 egg, beaten
2 tbsp fennel seeds	25g (1oz) plain flour
1 tsp chopped oregano	200ml (7fl oz) vegetable or chicken stock, or 100ml (3½fl oz) white wine
1 tsp chopped sage	

1. Preheat the oven to 150°C/300°F/gas mark 2. Cut the skin from the meat in one piece and reserve. Cut into the middle of the meat until you can open it out into a fairly even, flat shape. Set aside.

2. Heat the oil in a frying pan over a medium heat, fry the onion until soft but not coloured, then add the breadcrumbs, fennel, herbs, seasoning and apple. Mix well. Remove from the heat, add the egg and mix; it will start to bind together.

3. Spread the stuffing over the chump, then carefully roll it up and place the skin back on the meat. Tie with string at 1.5cm (generous ½in) intervals to hold the joint together.

4. Place in the oven and roast for 3 hours, then increase the oven temperature to 190°C/375°F/gas mark 5 and roast for a further 20 minutes, or until the pork is cooked through, ensuring that the crackling crisps up. Remove the pork from the roasting pan and leave it to rest in a warm place. Skim off and discard the excess fat from the juices, sprinkle in the flour and mix until smooth, season and add the stock or wine and 100ml (3½fl oz) of water. Mix well, return to a medium heat and bring to a boil, stirring constantly until thickened. Serve with the carved pork.

Mutton shepherd's pie

Made with mutton as was originally the case, this pie has far more depth of flavour than the more usual version made with lamb. Mutton was, until recently not seen as fashionable, but I urge you to return to this classic recipe as it's simply much better.

Serves 6–8
Takes 1¼ hours

olive oil

2 onions, peeled, cut into 1cm (½in) dice

4 carrots, peeled, cut into 1cm (½in) dice

4 celery sticks, cut into 1cm (½in) dice

½ small swede, peeled, cut into 1cm (½in) dice

1kg (2lb 4oz) minced hogget

1 bay leaf

200ml (7fl oz) red wine

600ml (1 pint) chicken or lamb stock

1 tbsp tomato purée

1 tbsp Worcestershire sauce

sea salt

freshly ground black pepper

2kg (4lb 8oz) potatoes, peeled

100ml (3½fl oz) milk, warmed

85g (3oz) butter

1. Heat a little oil in a frying pan placed over a medium heat, add the onions, carrots, celery and swede and gently sauté until soft but not coloured. Remove the vegetables and add the minced hogget to the pan, stirring well to break the meat up, and cook until it is all sealed and browned. Return the vegetables to the pan with the bay leaf, wine, stock, tomato purée, Worcestershire sauce and seasoning, cover and simmer gently for 30 minutes, stirring occasionally.

2. Meanwhile, preheat the oven to 180°C/350°F/gas mark 4. Cut the potatoes into even-sized pieces and simmer in a saucepan of boiling water for 20 minutes, or until soft. Drain the potatoes and return them to the pan, place on a low heat and toss well to drive off any excess moisture. Remove from the heat and mash thoroughly until smooth, then add the milk, butter and seasoning and mix well.

3. Transfer the hogget mixture to an ovenproof dish and spoon on the mashed potato, spreading inwards from the rim and evening it out with a fork on top. Place in the oven and cook for 30 minutes, until the potato is just browning and some of the juices are bubbling around the edge.

Mexican braised blade of beef

Blade of beef is a great cut of meat that works really well with long, slow cooking. The recado de achiot (from www.coolchile.co.uk) and red wine add deep, spicy flavours. I realize I have been very specific with my chilli requirements so if you can't get hold of that blend, substitute a Mexican adobo spice rub. It will taste different, but still very good.

Serves 8
Takes 4¼ hours

1.5kg (3lb 5oz) round or square blade of beef

50g (2oz) recado de achiot

200ml (7fl oz) red wine

1. Preheat the oven to 150°C/300°F/gas mark 2. Place the beef in a roasting tin and rub all over with the recado de achiot; pour in the wine. Cover with foil, carefully sealing the edges. Place in the oven and cook for 4 hours.

2. Remove the meat to a carving board and keep warm. Meanwhile, rapidly heat the cooking juices in the roasting tin over a high heat, stirring in all the sticky bits around the edge, and boil to reduce the liquid by half and make a rich sauce.

3. Carve the beef into slices and serve topped with a little sauce.

Pheasant pot

Try this variation on pot au feu with a tasty wild pheasant – farm-reared pheasants do not have as much flavour as their diet is bland. Hen pheasants are best, as they have more breast meat and are more tender.

Serves 4
Takes 1 hour 20 minutes

2 plump hen pheasants

2 bay leaves

sea salt

freshly ground black pepper

1 onion, peeled and halved

1 garlic clove, crushed and peeled

4 celery sticks, chopped

2 carrots, peeled

6 medium waxy potatoes, peeled

1. Place the pheasants in a casserole dish and just cover with water, then add the bay leaves, seasoning, onion and garlic. Cover and bring to a boil over a medium heat, then reduce the heat and simmer for 40 minutes.

2. Add the celery, carrots and potatoes, making sure the potatoes are submerged in the cooking liquid. Replace the lid and simmer for a further 20 minutes, or until the vegetables are tender. Serve the pheasants with the vegetables and cooking liquor.

Tim's roast chicken

The chickens that are sold by The Ginger Pig are Master Gris (a French breed known for their excellent flavour) and our birds live for between 80 and 155 days (depending on weight), far longer than most supermarket birds. That's why this recipe has a longer than usual cooking time as it's needed to tenderize this tasty meat. By wrapping the chicken in foil, it steams in its own juices, which intensifies the flavour and keeps the meat moist.

Serves 4–6
Takes 2½ hours

1 head of garlic

2 bay leaves

1 red onion, peeled and cut into wedges

sea salt

freshly ground black pepper

2.5kg (5lb 8oz) Master Gris chicken, or other chosen variety

50g (2oz) butter

25g (1oz) plain flour

200ml (7fl oz) vegetable or chicken stock, or 100ml (3½fl oz) white wine

1. Preheat the oven to 170°C/325°F/gas mark 3. Lay 2 large sheets of foil on top of each other at right angles, making a cross. Cut the garlic in half widthways and snip the bay leaves into pieces. Put the garlic, bay, onion and seasoning into the cavity of the chicken. Rub it all over with butter and place the chicken in the centre of the foil cross. Fold the foil up around the bird, sealing well.

2. Place the chicken in a roasting tin and cook for 2 hours. Remove from the oven and increase the oven temperature to 180°C/350°F/gas mark 4. Peel away and discard the foil and return the chicken to the oven for 20 minutes to crisp up the skin. Check the chicken is cooked, by piercing the thickest part of the leg with a skewer; if the juices run clear it is ready but, if not, return to the oven and check after 15 minutes.

3. Remove the chicken from the roasting pan, tipping it to allow juices to run free from the middle of your bird, and leave it to rest in a warm place. Skim off the excess fat from the juices with a metal spoon, sprinkle in the flour and mix until smooth. Season, add the stock or wine and 100ml (3½fl oz) of water, mix well and return the roasting pan to a medium heat. Bring to a boil, stirring constantly, and serve with the chicken.

DECEMBER

December on the farm

Mickey, my new dog, has arrived. He's a handsome 20-month-old Border Collie from Scotland, and he is part-trained. Unfortunately, we have a slight communication problem, as he doesn't understand my Yorkshire accent and keeps giving me puzzled looks. When my last head shepherd left I decided to get re-involved with my sheep. I used to go out in the Land Rover to check them, but now I want to go out on to the moor in the traditional way, with my own dog, as it's a much better and far more thorough method. Dogs round up the sheep, driving them towards me, so I can see how they move and spot any problems more easily.

Back in 1999, when I moved to Grange Farm, my Berkshire sows came with me, but they did not flourish. Kevin, who's in charge of the pigs, gleefully told me that they don't do as well this far north as it is too cold, so for 10 years we've been without them. But I've recently been dreaming of breeding the traditional but rare Plum Pudding pig, a cross between a Berkshire and a Tamworth. So it's with a rebellious feeling that I ring Vic, a pig breeder, just to see if he has any Berkshire gilts for sale. 'Well I am cutting back but I could try and find you one,' he tells me. He comes back later with a suggestion. 'You can buy my granddaughter's favourite gilt, Claire, but she's won lots of shows, so you'll have to pay well.' We agree a fairly stiff price and the next day I leave early with my cattle trailer for Skegness, arriving at Vic's in time for breakfast. His wife makes her own bacon, hams and sausages in their farmhouse kitchen and her sausages are the best in the world. Over time, and many meals with Vic, I've worked out her recipe and use something similar for my own sausages. After breakfast, Vic sells me two other Berkshire gilts as companions for Claire (strangely, at the same high price), but I happily return to Yorkshire with my three pigs.

This winter is the coldest since we have been in Yorkshire and Kevin has just reminded me that Berkshires don't like cold weather. I'm worried, but also desperate to have them on the farm, so every morning I dutifully take armfuls of straw into their little house to make sure they are as snug as possible. I will rear Berkshires at Grange Farm and make Kevin eat Berkshire ham in Yorkshire. Vic rings me later in the month to say he is retiring, but wants to keep four sows. Real pig breeders never retire.

He then asks 'Would you take all the litters?' 'Yes,' I respond without thinking. So I'm pretty sure the Berkshire breed is here to stay in Levisham, and that I'm now a step closer to my dream of breeding the spotty-coated Plum Pudding pig.

At Blansby Farm, Kevin is struggling with the pigs in the snow and sub-zero temperatures. The pipes are frozen, so there's no running water, but the bowser (a big water tank on wheels) is too large and heavy to get up the remote icy lane.

At Blansby Farm, Kevin is struggling with the pigs in the snow and sub-zero temperatures. The pipes are frozen, so there's no running water, but the bowser (a big water tank on wheels) is too large and heavy to get up the remote icy lane. Kevin has to come to Grange Farm to collect a smaller one, but as he drives away a tyre blows, so he has to abandon his car and take one of our tractors. It's a real challenge to look after the stock in these awful conditions.

Getting around the roads in the vans is also proving dangerous and difficult. We're now loading them with meat and driving them to Lockton during the day, from where they can get away more easily at 1am for the London shops. This decision was brought on by a van getting stuck one night on the notoriously steep Levisham Hill. I had to get my tractor to drag the van, loaded with five tons of meat, to the other side of the hill. With still no sign of the snow abating, a real worry is that people won't be able to get to work. This would be a major problem, as it's our busiest time and we need all hands on deck. Steve, one of my butchers, comes to the rescue and is now driving one of the Range Rovers as a sort of work bus, collecting everyone from their homes and returning them after a day in the office, butchery, bakery and farm.

Orders from London are coming thick and fast. It's Amy's first Christmas at The Ginger Pig and it's going to be a challenge for her. She is great on the phone but her knowledge of meat is limited and, with the orders flying in, she's at my side every 10 minutes with a new question. By next year, she'll know everything there is to know.

The butchery classes that run at Moxon Street are flourishing and we've sold more than 600 vouchers as Christmas gifts. On Christmas Eve, everyone has left the farm and it is beautifully quiet when the phone rings with a lady requesting a voucher for her husband. This is not a problem, but can I work the computer to email a voucher so she can put it in her husband's stocking on time? No. Instead, I have to wait for Sarah to return from checking the stock, so that she can electronically magic the voucher over. This way, at 8pm on Christmas Eve, we do our last bit of business.

Christmas is very strange at Grange Farm, as it has been hectic all month, with phones ringing, sausages being made, game pies prepared, meat being butchered, vans being towed and some 400 lambs being born. Now everything has come to a standstill I feel a little sad and deflated. For a few minutes, the farm seems very empty and quiet.

On Christmas Eve I cook a delicious free-range goose from a friends' poultry farm in Lincolnshire, and Sarah and I enjoy this in front of the Aga with a bottle of fine wine. Now there's only one job left to do. At midnight, the van rolls into the yard returning from London. The last turkey I have left weighs 8kg (18lb), and I'm looking forward to tucking into this tomorrow with Sarah, Anne (my ex-wife) and my Mum. We are exhausted but well fed, and it's the end of another busy Christmas at The Ginger Pig.

Early morning on the farm.

Lamb 'Henrys' with beans

Lamb shanks can seem trendy and wasteful, as there are only four on every lamb and the cut doesn't make good use of the whole carcass. So we have created a cut that we call Henrys or trunks, from the less fashionable but far tastier and sweeter shoulder. Go on, get your butcher to do the same.

Serves 5
Takes 2½ hours

750g (1lb 10oz) cooked cannellini beans

2 onions, peeled and roughly diced

2 garlic cloves, crushed, peeled and finely diced

3 sprigs of rosemary

2 sprigs of thyme

1 shoulder of lamb, cut into 5 pieces by a butcher

450ml (¾ pint) white wine

150ml (5fl oz) chicken stock (optional)

1. Preheat the oven to 180°C/350°F/gas mark 4. Place the beans, onions, garlic, herbs, lamb and wine into a roasting tin, cover with baking parchment, then seal tightly all around with kitchen foil.

2. Place the roasting tin in the oven and cook for 2 hours. Remove the foil and paper and cook for a further 30 minutes until the lamb is cooked through, brown and crisp. Add a little stock or water if the tin threatens to dry out.

3. Serve the beans and liquor topped with the lamb.

Slow-baked, herb-crusted leg of mutton

Good meat cannot be rushed and the slow cooking of this leg of mutton and all these vegetables (with the addition of a whole bottle of red wine, naturally) makes this a dish that is most fitting for a celebratory meal.

Serves 6–8
Takes 5 hours

1 red onion, peeled and cut into 6 wedges

2 carrots, peeled and cut into 3cm (1in) pieces

2 celery sticks, chopped into 3cm (1in) pieces

2 beetroot, peeled and cut into 6 wedges

2 parsnips, peeled and cut into 3cm (1in) pieces

1 head of garlic, plus 2 garlic cloves

1 sprig each of sage, thyme and rosemary

sea salt

freshly ground black pepper

2kg (4lb 8oz) leg of mutton

750ml (1¼ pints) bottle of red wine

200g (7oz) toasted or stale white bread

leaves from 1 small bunch of parsley

2 tbsp olive oil

1½ tbsp Dijon mustard

1. Preheat the oven to 150°C/300°F/gas mark 2. Put all the vegetables in a roasting tin, break up the head of garlic and scatter the cloves throughout, along with the herbs and seasoning. Place the leg of mutton on top and pour over the red wine. Cover with foil, sealing tightly around the edges. Place in the oven and roast for 4½ hours.

2. Break up the bread and place in a food processor with the parsley, remaining 2 garlic cloves, seasoning and olive oil, and blitz. Remove the mutton from the oven and smear it with the Dijon mustard, then sprinkle the herb crumbs on top.

3. Return to the oven and cook for a further 30 minutes, until cooked through and a lovely golden brown.

Roast rib of beef

Buy a rib of beef on the bone – it really does look impressive, and carving is not a problem if you cut the meat from the bone before slicing. If you prefer a boned and rolled rib, ask the butcher to give you the bones and then roast them in the oven with the meat, as they add depth to the flavour of your dish.

Serves 10
Takes 2¼ hours

3kg (6lb 8oz) rib of beef on the bone

2 tbsp plain flour

2 tsp mustard powder

2 tsp freshly ground black pepper

25g (1oz) flour

300ml (½ pint) beef stock, red wine or vegetable cooking water

1. Preheat the oven to 220°C/425°F/gas mark 7. Weigh the beef to calculate the exact cooking time (see page 327). Mix together the 2 tablespoons of flour, mustard powder and pepper and rub all over the beef. Place the joint on a rack over a roasting tin and put in the oven. Cook for 25 minutes to seal the meat.

2. Reduce the oven temperature to 170°C/325°F/gas mark 3. For rare beef, continue to cook for 30 minutes per 1kg (2lb 4oz); for medium give it 55 minutes and for well done (if you must) 65 minutes. When cooked, remove from the roasting tin and keep warm, saving all the juices that flow out for adding to the gravy.

3. Carefully pour or spoon off all the fat from the roasting tin, add the second measurement of flour and blend in to make a smooth paste. Place on a low heat while constantly stirring, then slowly pour in the stock, wine or water and bring to a boil. Add any juices from the meat and serve, with Yorkshire pudding (see page 327), Horseradish sauce (see page 320) and mustards.

Pork and Madeira pâté

If possible ask your friendly butcher to mince the pork belly for you or do it yourself by chopping, then blitzing it in a whizzer. I like to do it myself as there is something satisfying about seeing the pork belly in its complete state, then processing it at home. There are also two ways you can prepare your chosen ovenproof dish. Traditionally it would be lined with bacon, but this doesn't appeal to me. If you line the dish with baking parchment it will always turn out without any fret or worry.

Serves 10–12
Takes 3 hours, plus overnight chilling

625g (1lb 6oz) pork belly

280g (10oz) lean minced pork

200g (7oz) pig's liver

sea salt

1 tsp freshly ground black pepper

17 juniper berries, crushed

3 garlic cloves, crushed, peeled and finely diced

½ tsp mace

25g (1oz) plain flour

150ml (5 fl oz) Madeira

1 egg, beaten

3 bay leaves (these must be fresh, not dried)

1. Preheat the oven to 170°C/325°F/gas mark 3. Line a 900g (2lb) loaf tin or terrine with baking parchment. Chop the pork belly, then blitz in a food processor. Place it in a large bowl with the minced pork. Chop and blitz the liver, then add it to the meat with the seasoning, juniper, garlic and mace. Whisk the flour into the Madeira until smooth, then add to the meat with the egg. Mix with your hands.

2. Fill the loaf tin or terrine with the meat, taking care to get into the corners and pressing the mix down, then top with the bay leaves. Cover with foil and place in a roasting tin filled with hot water. Cook in the oven for 2½ hours.

3. When cooked, place a weight on top to compress the meat, leave to cool, then place in the refrigerator overnight. The next day, ease it out and peel away the paper.

Braised oxtail

This is a bold, rich, dense dish that needs long, gentle cooking for the meat to melt and tenderize, creating a rich, unctuous sauce. Oxtail can't be rushed.

Serves 6–8
Takes 3 hours

2.5kg (5lb 8oz) oxtail (about 2 oxtails), chopped

1 tbsp olive oil

3 carrots, peeled and cut into 1cm (½in) dice

2 onions, peeled and cut into 1cm (½in) dice

4 celery sticks, cut into 1cm (½in) dice

2 tbsp soy sauce

450ml (¾ pint) red wine

600ml (1 pint) beef or vegetable stock, plus more if needed

2 bay leaves

2 sprigs of thyme

sea salt

freshly ground black pepper

25g (1oz) plain flour, plus more if needed

4 sprigs of parsley, roughly chopped

1. Preheat the oven to 190°C/375°F/gas mark 5. Place the oxtail and olive oil in a roasting tin and toss well to coat all the pieces of meat, then cook in the oven for 20 minutes, until browned. Add all the diced vegetables and mix with the meat, then return to the oven for a further 10 minutes.

2. Reduce the oven temperature to 150°C/300°F/gas mark 2. Add the soy sauce, wine, stock, herbs and seasoning, cover with baking parchment, then with foil, and seal lightly around the edge. Return to the oven and cook for 2½ hours, checking halfway through and adding more stock if needed.

3. When cooked through, lift out the oxtail with a slotted spoon and put it into a warmed serving bowl, then skim off any excess fat from the top of the juices. Sift over the flour and mix it in, then place the roasting tin on a medium heat and bring to a simmer, stirring constantly, until the consistency of the sauce is to your liking (you can add more flour if you want, but always remove the tin from the heat before adding it). Return the oxtail to heat through, then scatter with parsley and serve.

Coq au vin

A properly reared, long-lived chicken requires more cooking than inferior quality birds, which is why this recipe needs more time in the oven than you might expect. If you are tempted (and tut-tut on you) to use a quickly reared chicken, cut the cooking time by one-third, or all the meat will fall off the bone and spoil this wonderful dish.

Serves 6–8
Takes 1¾ hours, plus overnight marinating

2.5–3kg (5lb 8oz–6lb 8oz) Master Gris chicken, jointed

1 garlic clove, crushed, peeled and finely diced

750ml (1¼ pints) bottle of red wine

1 tbsp olive oil

16 shallots, peeled

280g (10oz) smoked bacon, diced

400g (14oz) mushrooms, sliced

600ml (1 pint) chicken or vegetable stock

1 bay leaf

1 sprig of thyme

sea salt

freshly ground black pepper

25g (1oz) plain flour, plus more if needed

small bunch of parsley, finely chopped

1. Place the chicken, garlic and wine in a shallow bowl; try to make sure all the chicken is covered by the wine or rotate it during marinating. Cover and refrigerate overnight.

2. The next day, bring the chicken to room temperature and preheat the oven to 190°C/375°F/gas mark 5. Oil a roasting tin, add the shallots, then roast for 10 minutes. Drain the chicken, reserving the red wine, add to the shallots and cook for 15 minutes until the chicken browns, then add the bacon and mushrooms, mix them into the juices and cook for a further 5 minutes. Pour in the marinade, stock, herbs and seasoning, then cover with baking parchment and a layer of foil, and tightly seal around the edges. Reduce the oven temperature to 170°C/325°F/gas mark 3 and cook for 1 hour, or until the juices run clear when the thickest part of the chicken is pierced with a skewer.

3. With a slotted spoon, lift out the chicken and shallots and place into a warmed serving dish. Sift the flour over the cooking juices and whisk it in, then place on a medium heat and bring to a simmer, stirring constantly. Add more flour if you want a thicker sauce (see opposite), removing the pan from the heat before adding. Sprinkle in the parsley. Pour the sauce over the chicken and serve. Lovely with rice.

Citrus roast festive turkey

Take the strain away from the kitchen and prepare the turkey on Christmas Eve. Then you simply have to put it in the oven on the big day. Work out cooking times in advance, adding the weight of stuffing to that of the bird.

Serves 12
Takes 6 hours

6kg (13lb) free range turkey, with giblets

1 onion, peeled and roughly chopped

6 bay leaves

2 celery sticks, chopped

6 black peppercorns

1 leek, roughly chopped and well washed

175g (6oz) fresh breadcrumbs

1kg (2lb 4oz) pork sausage meat

zest and juice of 3 unwaxed lemons

4 garlic cloves, crushed, peeled and finely diced

2 red onions, peeled and finely diced

200g (7oz) black olives, chopped

6 sprigs of rosemary

sea salt

freshly ground black pepper

1 egg, beaten with 200ml (7fl oz) cold water

18 rashers of streaky bacon, rind removed

60g (2¼oz) plain flour

100ml (3½fl oz) red wine

1. Place the giblets in a saucepan with 1 litre (1¾ pints) of water, the onion, 2 bay leaves, the celery, peppercorns and leek. Bring to a boil and simmer over a low heat for 1 hour; you should end up with 600ml (1 pint) of liquid. Strain.

2. Preheat the oven to 220°C/425°F/gas mark 7. Place the breadcrumbs, sausage meat and lemon juice and zest in a bowl. Dice the remaining bay leaves and add them, the garlic, red onions and olives. Remove the rosemary needles from the sprigs and finely chop. Add them to the bowl with the seasoning and egg. Mix well with your hands.

3. Stuff the turkey, placing two-thirds in the large cavity and the rest in the neck end. Weigh the stuffed bird and calculate the cooking time, allowing 40 minutes per 1kg (2lb 4oz). Place the turkey on a roasting cradle over a large tin. Weave the bacon over the breast, cover with foil and place in the oven. Cook for 40 minutes, reduce the heat to 170°C/325°F/gas mark 3 and cook for 3 hours 40 minutes. Increase the heat to 180°C/350°F/gas mark 4, uncover and cook for 40 minutes, basting. Insert a skewer into the thickest part of the leg; if it is cooked, the juices should run clear.

4. Remove from the roasting tin, keep warm and allow to rest for 20 minutes. Skim off excess fat from the juices, whisk in the flour until smooth, then slowly stir in the stock and wine. Bring to a boil. Adjust the seasoning and pour in any extra juices. Serve.

JANUARY

January on the farm

It's New Year at Grange Farm and the land is still covered in snow. It may look beautiful, but boy, does it make work hard. We have all trudged miles through the deep snow-filled fields and we're physically and mentally exhausted. Morale has sunk to an all-time low. On our daily rounds we look after 140 chickens, 58 pigs, 320 ewes, 400–500 baby lambs in the barns, more than 1,000 sheep in the fields, two Riggit bulls, 10 cows and 2 baby calves, not forgetting my dog Brisket, a Grand Basset Griffon Vendeen, my sheepdog Mickey and the kittens.

The conditions are the worst I've seen in more than 20 years as a farmer, with a fiercely strong and biting easterly wind, sub-zero temperatures and snowdrifts that make getting near the moor almost impossible. Others, who are older and wiser than me, say it's the worst winter since 1947, a year when the snow was deeper than the houses. The animals are completely reliant on us, as there still isn't a blade of grass and all the water troughs and pipes are frozen solid. Added to all this, we have to fend off starving foxes and badgers who are on the lookout for food.

Kevin, who is in charge of the pigs, has arrived from Blansby Farm to tell me that they are really struggling. The pigs are out in the fields, but each sow has her own house, in which they are sheltering from the often freezing conditions. The little piglets are snuggling up to mum for warmth so closely that, when she moves, some are getting suffocated. Every day, dead piglets are collected from the pig houses, which is so sad and disheartening. Kevin reckons that out of the 120 piglets we had, we will probably be left with only about 75 when it comes to weaning them and, being a skilled stockman, he was almost spot on – he weaned 74, which is a huge loss of 46 piglets.

With everyone at the farm struggling, my exhausted mind wanders and I think of visiting a Bonham's sale in Chester, as I've spotted a handsome grandfather clock in their new catalogue. (Prior to becoming to a farmer I was an antique oak-furniture dealer.) However, my end-of-year tax bill is hanging over me heavily, the floorboards have not yet been laid on my landings and the roof is leaking, so that puts a stop to any more such wishful thinking. I must not spend any money I don't need to and, most importantly, I need to stay here and look after the stock the best I can.

The Dorset ewes and lambs, born the week before Christmas, are still holed up in the warm barns. They need much more space and should ideally be out in the fields, but it's not possible because of the very cold weather, so my general helper Alan is having to constantly housekeep and lay down plenty of fresh bedding straw for them. I spend all morning clearing the snow on two lanes just to get some hay to the other sheep, and tomorrow I'll do it all over again as snow is forecast once more.

The tups' work has finished for this season and now we finally separate them from the ewes. With their departure, I always think of exhausted soldiers leaving a battlefield: some are limping, others leaning against each other and the odd one has a bleeding head, earned from fighting over the last few females. Oh well, it's back to a life of grazing and the boys living together until it all kicks off again in July.

The tups' work has finished for the season, and now we finally separate them from the ewes. With their departure, I always think of exhausted soldiers leaving the battlefield: some are limping, others leaning against each other, and the odd one has a bleeding head, earned from fighting over the last few females.

We have received a couple of unusual requests. One is from Susie, a bride-to-be and customer at our Hackney shop, who wants us to make her a savoury wedding pie to replace the traditional cake. Les, who makes all the pies at the farm, is thrilled and sets about planning this three-tiered masterpiece. He gathers cake tins from his mum, which were used to make her own wedding cake, and Anne sets about locating a freestanding cake-stand strong enough to take the considerable weight of Les's creation. Each pie has a different meat filling: at the base sits our classic pork pie; chicken and bacon goes in the middle; and mixed game sits triumphantly on top, crowned with glowing cranberries set in farm-made gelatine. This architectural feat is then carefully driven to London and delivered to the delighted couple. I think our meat-pie cake may overtake the fashion for cupcake wedding cakes!

The other request is from Jeremy, who recently did a lamb butchery course at our shop in Moxon Street. He so enjoyed our meat that he wants to serve Ginger Pig racks of lamb at his wedding reception. It's wonderful to get calls like this as it tells me we're doing something right.

We're moving things around at the farm office. David Harrison and I are busy swapping computers, there are wires everywhere and now there's a loss of internet connection. Chaos ensues. I decide to take a tactical visit to the bakery and reappear when calm and organization has returned. All I use my computer for is searching for tractor parts, the weather, antiques and facts when I'm trying to win an argument.

Burns Night is approaching, so we need to make haggis for the shops. I speak to the abattoir to get the sheep's pluck (lungs, liver and heart) returned with the carcasses to the farm butchery. Les's haggis recipe is a mix of pluck and mutton legs simmered slowly with onions, herbs and oatmeal. I pride myself on always using as much of the whole animal as possible, and this is a great way to do that.

The ewes and lambs are at last out in the fields and, though the snow is melting, we now have a mud bath and a tractor is stuck up to its axle. Kevin brings another over from Blansby to pull it out. The muddy mess also means the grass will take far longer to recover in the spring. The cattle are being kept in the barns because otherwise they will damage the grassland further. This is inevitable as they are heavy but have small feet. We call it 'poaching the land' when, in wet weather, cattle turn grass into a big, muddy, squelchy mess. Since they are being kept in a closed environment we have to keep a close eye on their health, because germs spread more easily in a hot, steamy barn.

One good thing to come out of this month is my new venture of making pure beef and chicken stock for the shops. It is so reduced and of such a good quality that, when cool, it sets solid. Again I feel satisfied that very little of my animals is being wasted.

Meat pie tins and other things in the farm bakery.

Hungarian pork goulash

It's important to add some pork belly to this dish, as the fat is needed to add moisture and richness to the sauce.

Serves 6
Takes 3 hours

1 tbsp olive oil

1.25kg (2lb 12oz) shoulder of pork, cut into 3cm (1in) dice

280g (10oz) pork belly, skinned and cut into 3cm (1in) dice

1 onion, peeled and finely diced

2 garlic cloves, crushed, peeled and finely diced

2 tsp sweet smoked paprika

½ tsp cayenne pepper

2 tsp caraway seeds

sea salt

freshly ground black pepper

2 cans chopped tomatoes, each 400g (14 oz)

320g (11 oz) jar of peeled, roast peppers (or 3 peppers, chargrilled and peeled)

2 tbsp soured cream

1 bunch of chives, snipped

1. Preheat the oven to 180°C/350°F/gas mark 4. Heat the olive oil in a large ovenproof pan over a medium heat and fry the meat until brown on all sides, then add the onion and garlic and sauté for 3 minutes. Add the paprika, cayenne, caraway and seasoning, mix well and cook for a further 4 minutes. Pour in the tomatoes and top up with just enough water to cover the meat. Bring to a boil, then cover with a lid and place in the oven to cook for 2 hours.

2. Drain the jar of peppers (or prepare them, if using fresh), cut the peppers into thin strips and add them to the goulash. Stir through and cook for a further 30 minutes. Serve topped with the soured cream and chives, on bulgur wheat or rice.

Rillettes of pork

In the past, a whole pig would be killed by a smallholding and all the meat butchered, cooked or cured. Rillettes are a great way of using some of the belly. Compressed into a jar, covered and sealed with hard fat, they keep for months. Before refrigeration, this was a popular method of preserving.

Serves 4–6
Takes 5 hours

50g (2oz) pork or goose fat

1kg (2lb 4oz) skinless pork belly, cut into 3cm (1in) dice

300ml (½ pint) white wine

2 garlic cloves, crushed, peeled and finely diced

2 sprigs of thyme

sea salt

freshly ground black pepper

1 onion, peeled and finely diced

1. Melt the fat in a heavy-based saucepan, add the pork and cook over a very low heat for 15 minutes; do not allow the meat to brown. Drain off and reserve the excess fat. Add the wine, garlic, thyme, seasoning and onion to the pan, cover and simmer very gently for 4½ hours, stirring occasionally and adding a little water as needed.

2. Cool a little, then mash with a fork, breaking up all the meat and the garlic cloves (if you prefer a smoother result, blend the mixture in a food processor). Taste and adjust the seasoning. Spoon and compress very tightly into an earthenware or glass pot that has been scrupulously cleaned with boiling water. Melt the reserved fat and pour it over the top, completely sealing the meat beneath it.

3. These rillettes are best left covered in the fridge for at least a week to improve in flavour and can be kept for up to 6 months if the pot is well sealed with fat, contains no air pockets and is kept refrigerated. Enjoy with crusty bread, piquant cornichons and crunchy lettuce.

Ginger Pig sausage roll

A good British sausage roll is hard to find, so we decided to make our own. We sell an awful lot of them at lunchtime.

Makes 8
Takes 2 hours, plus chilling and overnight resting

For the filling

700g (1lb 9oz) minced pork

175g (6oz) pork fat, minced

115g (4oz) fresh breadcrumbs

2 tsp dried mixed herbs

1 tsp chopped sage

sea salt

freshly ground black pepper

For the puff pastry

600g (1lb 5oz) very strong white flour, preferably '00', plus more to dust

450g (1lb) chilled butter

pinch of salt

2 tbsp white wine vinegar

1 egg, beaten

1. Place the minced pork and pork fat in a bowl and mix together, then add the breadcrumbs, 125ml (4fl oz) water, the herbs and seasoning. Mix with your hands until evenly blended. Set aside.

2. Sift the flour into a large bowl. Melt 50g (2oz) of the butter and mix with the salt, vinegar and 230ml (8fl oz) ice-cold water. Add to the flour and mix to a smooth dough. Place in the refrigerator to chill for 1 hour.

3. Place the remaining butter between 2 sheets of plastic wrap and roll out to the thickness of your finger. Roll the pastry out into a rectangle just over twice the size of the flattened butter. Unwrap the butter and place it in the middle of the pastry. Folding over the pastry edges like an envelope, totally encase the butter. Roll this out again to a rectangle the same size as it was before the butter was added, then fold three times, like you would a letter. Roll out once more, turn 90 degrees and fold three times again. Seal in plastic wrap and chill in the refridgerator for 1 hour. Repeat the rolling and folding four more times, adding a light dusting of flour each time, and chilling after each repetition. (In total, the process should be performed five times.) Wrap and leave to rest in the refrigerator overnight.

4. Preheat the oven to 180°C/350°F/gas mark 4. Roll the pastry out to approximately 41x26cm (16x10in). Work the sausage meat into an even, long roll and place along the length of the pastry. Brush the exposed pastry with egg, then roll over and crimp the join together with a fork. Cut into 4 sausage rolls. Brush the outside of each with egg, place on a baking sheet and cook for 50 minutes. Serve warm.

Clod of beef stew
with herb dumplings

Clod is a tender, melting cut of meat when cooked slowly. With dumplings to mop up all the delicious juices, this stew makes a great one-pot meal.

Serves 6
Takes 3 hours, plus overnight chilling

For the stew

2 tbsp olive oil

1.5kg (3lb 5oz) clod of beef,
cut into large pieces

2 onions, peeled and finely sliced

1 tbsp chopped oregano leaves

4 bay leaves

sea salt

freshly ground black pepper

200ml (7fl oz) red wine

1.2 litres (2 pints) beef stock

1 tbsp plain flour

4 carrots, peeled and sliced

4 celery sticks, sliced

4 parsnips, peeled and sliced

For the dumplings

200g (7oz) self-raising flour

115g (4oz) suet

leaves from 1 small bunch of parsley, chopped

1. Preheat the oven to 150°C/300°F/gas mark 2. Heat the olive oil in a large ovenproof pan over a medium-high heat, add the meat and brown well all over. Remove the meat from the pan and add the onions. Sauté gently until soft but not coloured. Return the beef to the pan and add the herbs, seasoning, wine and stock. Gently bring to a boil. Cover and cook in the oven for 2 hours. Remove, cool and refrigerate overnight.

2. The next day, bring the casserole to room temperature and preheat the oven to 150°C/300°F/gas mark 2. Put the stew in the oven and gently warm through. When the stock has just melted into liquid again, remove from the oven, sift in the flour and stir. Mix in the carrots, celery and parsnips, cover and place in the oven for 10 minutes.

3. Meanwhile, make the dumplings. Place all the ingredients in a bowl and mix well, adding just enough water to bind the dough without its becoming sticky. Divide into 12 and roll each piece into a ball. Remove the casserole from the oven and arrange the dumplings in a single layer on top. Cover and cook in the oven for a further 30 minutes or until the dumplings and the stew are piping hot.

Salt beef from scratch

All too often we are mystified by salt beef, which is a dish that makes one think of the delicious sandwiches of New York. You can now bring that glamour into your own home with ease. Serve the salt beef whole and hot with horseradish and mustards, in rye-bread sandwiches or cold. You can buy curing salts from www.sausagemaking.org or The Ginger Pig.

Serves 20
Takes 4½ hours, plus 8 days curing and overnight soaking

475g (1lb 1oz) salt	1 tsp whole cloves
750g (1lb 10oz) curing salt mix	3 bay leaves
100g (3½oz) soft brown sugar	1 tsp ground mace
2 tbsp black peppercorns	1 tsp ground ginger
2 tbsp coriander seeds	4kg (8lb 13oz) boned beef brisket or silverside
12 juniper berries	

1. You will need a scrupulously clean brining crock, plastic bowl or bucket (never use metal as it reacts). Start by cleaning the chosen pot with household soda, then rinse with boiling water to sterilize. Place 600ml (1 pint) of water into a saucepan and add the salt, curing mix and sugar. Bring to a boil, stirring until everything is dissolved. Roughly crush the whole spices and add along with the bay, mace and ginger. Pour into the prepared brining vessel and top up with enough boiled water to cover the beef (you will have to give this your best guess). Mix and leave to cool.

2. When the brine is cold, add the brisket, cover tightly with a double layer of plastic wrap and store in a cool place for 8 days.

3. Remove the beef from the brining pot and soak in fresh water overnight. Rinse and place the beef in a large pan. Cover with fresh water and bring to a gentle simmer. Spoon off and taste a little of the cooking water and, if it's too salty, discard it and start again. When the water is simmering, skim off any foam that rises to the surface, cover and simmer very gently for 4 hours. Check it every hour and add more water if required.

4. When tender and cooked, remove the beef and allow it to rest in a warm place for at least 10 minutes. Slice and serve in sandwiches or with vegetables, mustards and Horseradish sauce (see page 320).

Lamb's liver with sage

Only ever use lamb's liver that is really fresh – one-day old is the maximum age you should buy. If you have a good butcher, he will know the liver's age. Lightly seared, as in this recipe, lamb's liver is delicious and tender, and at only a fraction of the price of calves' liver.

Serves 4
Takes 15 minutes

500g (1lb 2oz) lamb's livers, finely sliced

50g (2oz) butter

12 sage leaves

150ml (¼ pint) red wine

150ml (¼ pint) double cream

sea salt

freshly ground black pepper

1. Trim any membrane or large tubes from the livers. Melt the butter gently in a frying pan over a medium-low heat and, when it foams, add the sage. Cook for just 30 seconds, then remove the sage. Turn the heat up slightly to medium-high and add the liver to the pan in batches, so as not to crowd the pan, and sear it quickly for 2 minutes on each side. Remove and keep warm while you cook the remaining liver.

2. Working quickly, add the wine to the pan and simmer to reduce by half, then add the cream. Season, bring to a boil and cook until thick enough to coat the back of a spoon.

3. Serve the liver with the sauce spooned over and sprinkled with the crisp sage leaves. Creamy mashed potato goes really well with this quick but tasty dish.

Lancashire hot pot

Mutton is almost essential for this recipe; it adds far more flavour and is perfect for the long slow cooking this classic British peasant dish requires. Get your butcher to cut the mutton into chop-sized pieces.

Serves 6
Takes 2¾ hours

1kg (2lb 4oz) King Edward or Marfona potatoes

25g (1oz) butter

2 onions, peeled and cut into 1cm (½in) dice

3 carrots, peeled and finely sliced

200g (7oz) pearl barley

2 sprigs of thyme

1 bay leaf

1.5kg (3lb 5oz) middle or scrag end neck of mutton, sliced into 3cm (1in) chops

4 lamb's kidneys

sea salt

freshly ground black pepper

2 tsp Worcestershire sauce

750ml (1¼ pints) lamb stock

1. Preheat the oven to 180°C/350°F/gas mark 4. Peel the potatoes and slice to a thickness of 5mm (¼in). Rub the inside of a casserole dish with half the butter, then place one-third of the potato slices over the base. Add the onions, carrots, barley, thyme and bay leaf. Place the mutton on top.

2. Cut the kidneys in half, peel away the membranes and snip out the white cores with scissors. Discard the cores and tuck the kidneys in amongst the mutton. Season. Add the Worcestershire sauce to the stock and pour it over the dish.

3. Top with the remaining sliced potatoes, in a neat layer, cover and cook in the oven for 2 hours. Remove the lid, and dot the potatoes with the remaining butter. Return the dish to the oven for a further 30 minutes, until the potatoes are crisp and golden.

Roman lamb fillet

Lamb fillet taken from the neck used to be great value. Sadly though, as with all lamb, it has crept up in price. It is a small cut packed with great flavour and texture and a great favourite of mine.

Serves 4
Takes 40 minutes

500g (1lb 2oz) neck of lamb fillet

4 sprigs of rosemary

2 tbsp olive oil

2 garlic cloves, crushed, peeled and finely diced

juice of 1 lemon

175g (6oz) pitted black olives, roughly chopped

sea salt

freshly ground black pepper

125ml (4fl oz) red wine

leaves from 1 bunch of parsley, roughly chopped

1. Cut the lamb into 4 even lengths. Spear a sharp, thin knife through the centre of each piece along its length and insert a sprig of rosemary into the resulting slits. Heat the oil in a pan, over a medium-high heat add the lamb and brown it on all sides for about 15 minutes.

2. Add the garlic and reduce the heat to low, then cook for a further 4 minutes. Remove the lamb and let it rest in a warm place. Add the lemon juice, olives, seasoning and wine to the pan, and simmer to reduce by half.

3. Slice the lamb. Add the parsley to the sauce, bring back to a simmer, then spoon over the lamb. This is excellent served with creamed polenta, mashed potatoes or tagliatelle.

Roast duck with Puy lentils

Duck legs are great value, with sweet-tasting, tender meat. When cooked with Puy lentils, they make a tasty, simple, one-pot, mid-week kitchen supper that is good enough to impress guests.

Serves 4
Takes 45 minutes

4 duck legs and thighs

1 tbsp olive oil, plus more for the tin

4 banana shallots, peeled and chopped

280g (10oz) Portobello mushrooms, sliced

250g (9oz) Puy lentils

600ml (1 pint) chicken or game stock, plus more if needed

300ml (½ pint) red wine, plus more if needed

sea salt

freshly ground black pepper

3 sprigs of thyme

2 bay leaves

1. Preheat the oven to 200°C/400°F/gas mark 6. If not already separate from each other, cut the duck thighs and legs apart and trim them of excess fat. Place in a lightly oiled roasting tin and cook in the oven for 15 minutes.

2. Meanwhile, heat the 1 tbsp oil in a large ovenproof pan over a medium-high heat and sauté the shallots for 2 minutes. Add the mushrooms and cook for a further 5 minutes, then tip in the lentils, stock, wine, seasoning and herbs. Bring to a boil.

3. Remove the duck from the oven and place on top of the lentils. Cover the pan and cook in the oven for 20 minutes, then remove the lid and cook for a further 10 minutes until the juices run clear when the thickest part of the duck is pierced with a skewer or until the duck is crispy. If a little more liquid is needed while cooking, add a splash more stock or red wine.

FEBRUARY

February on the farm

Andy Holmes, a butcher at the farm, carrying a lamb carcass.

I woke up this morning to another six inches of snow. Arthur, my new senior shepherd, has just started with us; he must have brought the snow down with him from Northumberland. He will be living in a tied cottage at Thorton Dale with his wife Lesley, sheep, dogs, geese and chickens. Mickey, my collie, will be pleased as he finds Arthur's Scottish accent more to his liking than my Yorkshire lilt. Arthur is a highly experienced shepherd and I hope he works well with Chris and Alan. Chris has done such a good job looking after things while we've been without a senior shepherd and I want him to continue to flourish as he has done over the last few months. The three of them will now need to find a routine that works to their different strengths and qualities.

Three years ago my cousin Alex, who lives in London, decided he wanted a country home and we discussed his buying something with land that I could use for my stock. He found Park Farm and, while going through the negotiations to buy it, East Moor Farm (next door) came up for sale, so, true to form, Alex bought both. To be fair, I had a lot to do with it, as Park Farm is a beautiful, grand building with land on the side of a valley, but without barns, while East Moor Farm, on the other side, has a working dairy that could easily be adapted for beef stock. By buying both we can use the wood that runs along the valley for game shooting.

Alex also decided that Park Farm would benefit from handsome cattle wandering its 380 acres. I already had 40 Longhorns, but we needed to add to the herd. I discovered some stock that I had always admired was coming up for sale, so I let Alex know that we had to visit Holsworthy Market in Devon and asked him to bring his cheque book. I hired a large articulated lorry. On seeing it, a sceptical Alex commented, 'We'll never fill it.' 'Oh yes, we will, as there's a lot of land back at East Moor and Park Farm,' I replied. The sale began with me standing under the auctioneer's nose with a long list of the 40 cattle I hoped to buy. It's rare for a herd of quality Longhorns to come on the market together, so I excitedly started bidding without conferring with Alex. He began to worry when I bought number 10, but by the 20th his panic had shifted to concern about how we'd fit our new cattle in the wagon. I stopped at the 35th Longhorn, as these animals each weigh a ton and cost about £1,400.

Today the Longhorns look very graceful around Park Farm and Alex is delighted. I have also continued to increase my herd to keep up with the ever-growing demand for quality air-hung beef. We now have more than 500 Longhorns and, just this month, my builders completed a new large barn to house the herd in the winter months.

My bulls, Jupiter and Dynamo, both produce splendid calves and I'm fairly confident in my claim that Dynamo is the best Longhorn bull in the country. I bought him when he was nine months old, four years ago, from a breeder in Cockermouth, and carefully reared him in a barn. He used to wave his head aggressively at me, trying to assert himself, but I persevered with daily feeds of the best barley and hay. I like to calm a bull with constant human contact, because I believe he will then learn to be kinder to the cows. Dynamo sometimes still tries to show me who's boss; he has once charged me and made contact and another time he blasted straight through the barn wall, but he seems to be growing up and leaving his teenage wild days behind. He is handsome, with perfect horns, a thick, dappled deep mahogany-and-white coat and a white line running down his back. He spends his days wandering the fields surrounded by his beautiful harem and this seems to suit him very well.

Dynamo still sometimes tries to show me who's boss; he has once charged me and made contact and another time he blasted straight through the barn wall.

Running the large herd at East Moor and Park Farm became too much for me alone, so I employed Mike three years ago as my stockman, and today he lives at East Moor looking after the beef stock on 380 acres used for grazing and arable farming. The herd have a lovely, gentle life and I believe this contributes to the quality of the meat; we are also one of the few butchers to hang beef for a minimum of four to five weeks. We supply many restaurants, including Hawksmoor steak restaurant in London, which has been buying its meat from me since it opened. Will and Hugh, the proprietors, have been discussing a brand-new restaurant venture, which will increase their orders and mean we need to supply more beef.

With the growing demand for beef, I'm spending a lot of time with Mike and we're slowly working out which Longhorn heifers to keep back for our breeding herd. We also plan how much arable land we can take out of production to replace with grass, to cater for the extra cattle. The cows will be covered (mated) in July 2010, so calves will be born in April 2111 and won't be ready for the butchers until summer 2013. That means I may need to find some good-quality stock for sale to help increase my herd more quickly. We have to think several years ahead to respond to any increase in demand at the butchery shops and restaurants.

Primrose has given birth to nine healthy piglets, the first to be born at Grange Farm for four years. Turpin is terribly proud, while Primula looks fit to burst, though she's not showing any of the other classic signs of a pregnant gilt. I am beginning to think she may not actually be pregnant as it was her first time being covered; perhaps she's just been eating a little too well and growing a bit tubby. If, by the end of this month, nothing has happened I will put her back in with Turpin.

A handsome Longhorn cow at East Moor Farm.

Spiced lamb pilaf

Quick, tasty, full of different flavours and textures and, best of all, it's made from the leftover meat from yesterday's roast.

Serves 2
Takes 30 minutes

1 tbsp vegetable oil

1 onion, peeled and finely diced

1 garlic clove, crushed, peeled and finely diced

1 cinnamon stick

2 cloves

4 cardamom pods, crushed

1 tsp turmeric

200g (7oz) basmati rice

350g (12oz) cooked lamb, chopped

600ml (1 pint) vegetable or lamb stock

leaves from 1 bunch of flat-leaf parsley, chopped

3 spring onions, roughly diced

2 tomatoes, roughly diced

leaves from 1 bunch of coriander, chopped

1. Heat the oil in a large, shallow pan over a medium heat and add the onion. Gently sauté for 5 minutes then stir in the garlic and spices and cook for a further 3 minutes. Add the rice, stir well, add the lamb and stock and bring to a boil.

2. Reduce the heat to achieve a gentle simmer, cover the pan and cook for 12 minutes. Mix in the parsley, spring onions, tomatoes and coriander. Serve with mango chutney.

Lamb's kidneys in rich red-wine sauce

Traditionally kidneys were sold in a jacket which was a parcel of natural fat and this helped retain their fresh flavour and rich colour. If you see a butcher displaying kidneys like this you know that you are onto a fine butchers.

Serves 2
Takes 20 minutes

8 lamb's kidneys

25g (1oz) butter

1 tbsp olive oil

115g (4oz) button mushrooms

2 shallots, peeled and diced

150ml (¼ pint) red wine

1 tsp Dijon mustard

sea salt

freshly ground black pepper

150ml (¼ pint) double cream

3 sprigs of tarragon, roughly chopped

1. Cut the kidneys in half, peel away the membranes and snip out the white cores with scissors. Discard the cores. Heat the butter and olive oil in a large frying pan over a high heat and add the kidneys and mushrooms. Fry for 5 minutes, then add the shallots and cook for 2 minutes more.

2. Pour in the wine; take care, as it will steam and splatter a little. Boil until you have reduced the liquid by half; this should take about 5 minutes on a high heat.

3. Add the mustard and seasoning, pour in the cream and simmer for 5 minutes, until thickened. Finally add the tarragon, stir through and serve on rice or couscous.

Fragrant lamb kebabs

Minced lamb isn't just for shepherd's pie – here's a delicious alternative use for lamb mince that is just as economical.

Serves 4
Take 15 minutes

625g (1lb 6oz) lean minced lamb

2 shallots, peeled and finely diced

50g (2oz) fresh breadcrumbs

leaves from 1 bunch of parsley, finely chopped

leaves from 1 bunch of mint, finely chopped

1 egg, beaten

½ tsp cinnamon

½ tsp allspice

½ tsp cumin

½ tsp mace

4 flat breads

½ cucumber, finely sliced

4 tomatoes, finely sliced

¼ iceberg lettuce, shredded

leaves from 1 bunch of coriander, chopped

4 tbsp natural yogurt

1. Place the lamb, shallots, breadcrumbs, parsley, mint, egg and spices in a bowl and use your hands to blend everything together. Shape into 8 sausages and spear each lengthways on a metal skewer.

2. Heat the grill to high and grill the kebabs on each side until cooked through, which, in total, should take about 12 minutes. Meanwhile, toast the flat breads and cut them open. Fill each with the cucumber, tomatoes, lettuce and coriander.

3. Remove the kebabs from the skewers and place in the flat breads. Serve with a small bowl of yogurt for dipping.

Cassoulet

A warming feast, with different meats immersed in a sea of beans. The time difference I give for cooking the haricots is due to age; old beans need longer.

Serves 6–8
Takes 4 hours, plus overnight soaking

500g (1lb 2oz) dried haricot beans, soaked overnight

1 onion, peeled and quartered

3 garlic cloves, crushed and peeled

3 large tomatoes, quartered

1 bouquet garni

250g (9oz) pork rind, in one piece if possible

½ tsp ground cloves

3 confit goose or duck legs from a jar

400g (14oz) boned shoulder of lamb, cut into 3cm (1in) cubes

350g (12oz) pork belly, cut into 3cm (1in) cubes

400g (14oz) Toulouse sausages

4 sprigs of thyme

sea salt

freshly ground black pepper

250g (9oz) fresh breadcrumbs

1. Drain the beans and place them in a large pan of fresh water. Bring to a boil with the onion, two of the garlic cloves, the tomatoes, bouquet garni, pork rind and cloves. Boil for 5 minutes, then simmer for 1–2 hours, until soft. Drain, reserving the liquor.

2. Meanwhile, preheat the oven to 180°C/350°F/gas mark 4. Melt 2 tbsp fat from the confit in a roasting tin, then add the lamb and pork belly, toss to coat and cook in the oven for 1 hour. Add the sausages and cook for a further 15 minutes.

3. Rub the inside of a large casserole with the remaining garlic and leave it in the pot, then add half the beans. Arrange the lamb, pork, sausages, cooking fats and juices and confit on top, sprinkle with the thyme and seasoning and top with the remaining beans. Pour on the reserved cooking water, to come just to the top of the beans.

4. Sprinkle with half the breadcrumbs and place in the oven to cook for 1½ hours, stirring occasionally. Sprinkle with the remaining breadcrumbs and return to the oven for a further 30 minutes. Serve this rich meal with a crisp green salad.

Aromatic melting pork

This dish is very simple to prepare and cook, but it delivers tender pork and vegetables with a succulent sauce all from one pot.

Serves 8
Takes 2¼ hours

900ml (1½ pints) milk

1.5kg (3lb 5oz) boned and rolled shoulder of pork

6 onions, peeled and quartered

6 carrots, peeled and halved

4 garlic cloves, crushed and peeled

4 celery sticks, halved

3 bay leaves

2 sprigs of marjoram

3 sprigs of thyme

5 strips of unwaxed lemon zest

sea salt

freshly ground black pepper

1. Preheat the oven to 170°C/325°F/gas mark 3. Heat the milk in the oven in a ovenproof casserole that has a lid. Just before it boils, add all the other ingredients. Cover with a circle of baking parchment, then with a tightly fitting lid.

2. Cook in the oven for 1 hour, reduce the temperature to 150°C/300°F/gas mark 2 and cook for a further hour until cooked through and tender. Carve the pork and serve with tagliatelle, spooning over the juices and vegetables.

Pork fillet with new season rhubarb

Think of this as a more exciting twist on pork with apple sauce. The tangy, sharp flavours of the rhubarb perfectly complement the sweet pork to make a delicious and very simple dish.

Serves 4
Takes 45 minutes

1 tbsp olive oil

sea salt

freshly ground black pepper

650g (1lb 7oz) pork fillet

1 sprig of rosemary

175g (6oz) new season rhubarb

1. Preheat the oven to 190°C/375°F/gas mark 5. Put the oil in a roasting tin and place in the oven for 3 minutes. Season the pork, place in the hot oil, roll to coat, add the rosemary, then cook in the oven for 20 minutes. Turn and cook for 10 minutes more.

2. Cut the rhubarb into 4cm (1½in) lengths, then add it to the roasting tin with 100ml (3½fl oz) water. Cook for a further 10 minutes until the pork is cooked through and the rhubarb is tender. Remove from the oven, keep warm and leave to rest for 5 minutes. Slice the pork into chunky, juicy rounds and spoon over the soft rhubarb and its juices.

Spare ribs

Ask your butcher to cut ribs from the belly of pork. If you want larger ribs you can ask for those from the chine, but I prefer smaller ribs in one length for each person.

Serves 4
Takes 2 hours, plus marinating

4 sheets of 6-rib belly of pork, each approximately 800g (1lb 12oz)

2 tbsp honey

juice and zest of 1 unwaxed lemon

2 tbsp Japanese soy sauce (for example, Kikkoman)

3 garlic cloves, crushed and peeled

50g (2oz) muscovado sugar

2 tbsp tomato purée

2 tbsp Worcestershire sauce

1 tbsp balsamic vinegar

2 tsp Dijon mustard

sea salt

freshly ground black pepper

1. Heat a large pan of water, add the ribs and gently simmer for 30 minutes. Remove from the heat and leave to cool in the water. Mix together all the remaining ingredients until smooth and blended.

2. Remove the ribs from the water and pat them dry with kitchen paper, then rub them all over with the marinade and leave, covered, at room temperature for at least 1 hour, or overnight in the refrigerator if possible.

3. When ready to cook, preheat the oven to 180°C/350°F/gas mark 4. Place the ribs in one layer on a roasting tray and roast for 40 minutes or until cooked through, basting them frequently with the marinade. Serve them whole to be cut at the table.

Quick-roast salmon of beef

This cut of beef is wonderful for a high heat blast in the oven. Allowed to relax and tenderize, it will always deliver a rosy pink centre and is perfect with home-made Horseradish sauce (see page 320).

Serves 6–8
Takes 1 hour 10 minutes

1 tbsp beef dripping or olive oil

1.5kg (3lb 5oz) salmon of beef

sea salt

freshly ground black pepper

2 tbsp Japanese soy sauce (for example, Kikkoman)

1 tsp English mustard

1. Preheat the oven to 220°C/425°F/gas mark 7. Heat the fat in a large roasting tin. Rub the outside of the beef with seasoning, soy sauce and mustard, add it to the hot roasting tin carefully and cook in the oven for 45 minutes. This quick, high heat cooking makes the meat brown on the outside and soft when pressed.

2. Remove from the oven, keep warm and allow to rest for 15 minutes before carving. Serve with a selection of mustards and Horseradish sauce (see page 320).

Sticky shin rounds with cipollini onions and balsamic vinegar

This is a great-value cut that needs long, gentle cooking. It makes a really tasty sauce, because all the connective tissue in the shin breaks down to become a really good, sticky casserole.

Serves 6–8
Takes 3½ hours

2 tbsp olive oil

1.5kg (3lb 5oz) beef shin, cut into rounds

12 cipollini onions, peeled

3 tbsp balsamic vinegar

sea salt

freshly ground black pepper

1 litre (1¾ pints) beef stock

115g (4oz) button mushrooms or 25g (1oz) dried porcini mushrooms

25g (1oz) butter

leaves from 1 large bunch of parsley, chopped

1 large bunch of chives, snipped

1. Preheat the oven to 150°C/300°F/gas mark 2. Heat the oil in a large ovenproof pan over a high heat, then add the meat and cook until browned. Remove the meat, add the onions and cook until just brown, then return the meat, add the vinegar, seasoning and stock, and bring to a boil. Cover and cook in the oven for 3 hours.

2. Meanwhile, if you are treating yourself by using porcini mushrooms, soak them in hot water for 30 minutes, then strain their soaking water into the beef. If you are using button mushrooms, gently melt the butter and sauté them for 8 minutes. Add whatever type of mushroom you're using to the casserole along with the herbs, stir well and serve.

Pan-roast pigeon stuffed with spinach

A young, quickly roasted wood pigeon can be surprisingly good. Most of the meat is on the breast and it should be cooked rare so that it is a beautiful rosy pink inside.

Serves 2–4
Takes 45 minutes

½ small red onion, peeled and finely diced

½ celery stick, finely diced

50g (2oz) bacon, chopped

2 tbsp olive oil

280g (10oz) fresh spinach

4 sage leaves, finely chopped

sea salt

freshly ground black pepper

2 medium pigeons

150ml (¼ pint) red wine

3 tbsp Redcurrant jelly (see page 322)

1. Heat half the oil in a frying pan over a low heat, add the onion, celery and bacon and sauté for 5 minutes; do not brown. Add the spinach and sauté for 2 minutes, until it just wilts. Now add the sage and the seasoning, remove from the heat and leave to cool.

2. Preheat the oven to 230°C/450°F/gas mark 8. Stuff the pigeons with the cooled spinach mixture. Heat the remaining olive oil in a roasting tin and then add the pigeons, baste with a little of the oil, season and roast in the oven for 20 minutes.

3. Remove from the oven, transfer the pigeons to another pan and keep warm. Place the roasting tin directly over a medium heat, add the wine and Redcurrant jelly and simmer until the liquid is reduced by half, stirring occasionally. Serve a whole or half pigeon per person, pouring over the juices.

Mediterranean guinea fowl

The slightly gamey flavour of guinea fowl marries well with all the fresh, clean vegetable flavours here. Everything is gently simmered in white wine before the final addition of a burst of citrus from lemon zest, that goes so brilliantly with the garlic.

Serves 4–6
Takes 1½ hours

1 tbsp olive oil

115g (4oz) pancetta, cut into 2cm (¾in) dice

1 guinea fowl, jointed into 8

2 red onions, peeled and sliced

8 garlic cloves, crushed and peeled

1 red pepper, cored, deseeded and chopped into 1cm (½in) chunks

1 yellow pepper, cored, deseeded and chopped into 1cm (½in) chunks

3 tbsp black or green olives

2 bay leaves

sea salt

freshly ground black pepper

1 tsp chopped oregano

300ml (½ pint) white wine

finely grated zest of 2 unwaxed lemons

leaves from 1 bunch of parsley, chopped

1. Preheat the oven to 190°C/375°F/gas mark 5. Place the oil, pancetta and guinea fowl in a roasting tin and toss to coat everything in the oil. Put the tin in the oven and cook for 15 minutes. Remove and add the onions, garlic and peppers. Return to the oven and cook for a further 15 minutes.

2. Add all the remaining ingredients except the lemon zest and parsley, cover tightly with foil and return to the oven for a further 30 minutes until cooked through. Mix together the lemon zest and parsley and sprinkle over the top of the dish just before serving.

MARCH

March on the farm

The 500 Blackface sheep are in the barns for lambing and Chrissie is once again on hand for night duty. It's a tiring job, walking between the two barns aiding ewes with delivery. Once the lambs are born, they need to be put into a pen with the ewe to bond. We want the lambs to stay with their natural mothers, but unfortunately a ewe can sometimes struggle with triplets or quads, so we might have to remove one and place it with another ewe who has delivered a stillborn. We rub the lamb with the other ewe's afterbirth to try and get her to accept it as her own. If this doesn't work, the stillborn is skinned and the skin placed over the living lamb like a jumper, so after one lost life another life happily continues. In the morning, Arthur, Alan and Lesley take over. Lesley has created a nursery at one end of the barn, where the healthy ewes and lambs roam more freely, feeding well, before being moved back out to the fields. This is a happy place as the lambs start to run with that characteristic bounce and kick of their long springy legs.

However, we are losing too many lambs. It may be to do with the very hard winter; the dreadful conditions made the stock so hungry that the ewes jostled each other to get near the hoppers. I've never had a year like this, and all of us are dispirited and saddened. It's distressing to see a ewe deliver a dead or mummified lamb; it's not what nature intended. Sarah took a foetus to the DEFRA (Department of Environment, Food and Rural Affairs) lab to run a check but it came back clear, and just this morning she has taken another. Chrissie has taken to reading up to try to discover the reason for the loss of life. But in the meantime we must soldier on and hope for a turn in fortunes.

Since November I have been lifting fodder beet, which originates from the wonderfully named mangle wurzle. It's a sweet, crisp winter food that supplements the ewes' diet and encourages lactation. By the middle of March it has all been gathered and the sheep have stripped the fields of stubble turnip. I need to think about preparing the fields for the next crop, which is spring barley. The land needs to be ploughed and covered with farm muck, but the hideous weather has made a mud bath of the heavy clay we have on Blansby and East Moor. I live in hope of a dry day with wind and I'm glued to the weather reports on Metcheck.com.

The soil on Grange Farm needs some extra help, so I am considering what nutrients to add. I decide to get soil samples assessed, as looking after soil is quite an exact science. At Grange we have a mix of limestone and reclaimed moorland, which is sandy and short of lime (lime is key to growing crops). Blansby is clay on limestone and East Moor loam over clay and reclaimed moorland, so all the farms need individual treatment. This will be expensive, but worthwhile for my long-term plans.

When I arrived at Grange Farm ten years ago, I built a butchery, fulfilling a long-held dream to breed, farm and butcher my stock for my own shop. Now I have six butchers, each of them a character that reminds me of *Dad's Army*. Steve is Corporal Jones, getting into a flap about every aspect of the farm and butchery, and needing to know the whys, whats and wheres of each wagon that passes his door. Les, who trained as a butcher but now runs the bakery, is Captain Mainwaring. He never panics, gets everything done his own way and comes up with great new ideas, his latest being the large meat pies topped with latticed pastry and fruits. Stevie B is Sergeant Wilson, as perfectly turned out for work as he is for the York races, always with a bit of a twinkle in his eye. Andy is Private Walker, a very conscientious butcher, but away from work he's busy with eBay and has an amazing in-depth knowledge of everyone else's business. Michael is Private Pike, tall, quiet and focused on making excellent sausages. Ian is Private Godfrey, a bit of a fruity character who retires this year to exchange his butcher's knife for some golf clubs. And I suppose I am Colonel Pritchard, as I like to think that I'm right all the time and that I am the best butcher on the farm and at the shops in London!

With Easter coming we have been selecting Dorset lambs for the shops. We usually choose 80, but poor weather means we do not have as many at the ideal weight, and I refuse to kill an animal before it is ready.

Alongside all the laughter and fun, there is a lot of work to be done at the butchery. With Easter coming we have been busy selecting Dorset lambs for the shops. We usually choose 80 animals, but poor weather means we do not have as many as that at the ideal weight, and I refuse to kill an animal before it is ready.

The butchery has a large walk-in cold room that is used for hanging the carcasses after they return from the abattoir. It takes organization, as meat needs to be sold in order. The beef hangs for three weeks or more, lamb for five days but pork can be dealt with immediately. Leaner pork carcasses are sent to London to be sold as fresh meat. Larger, fattier ones are butchered at the farm to make sausages, pies, sausage rolls, bacon and hams. In one week, Michael can make up to one ton of sausages, Les more than 1,000 pies and Andy 30 hams and 40 sides of bacon.

We are interviewing for a new butcher to join our small army, and the best applicants are sent to Andy for a test. They have a shoulder of pork to bone and roll, which should take 10–15 minutes. Out of the three lads, only one knows what he's doing and produces a piece of meat just about fit to sell in the shop.

Four years ago I went to Valance in France with Patrice, who manages my shops in London, to visit a pig farm where he used to work. On the farm they produce boudin noir, salami and ham, and they open a shop nearby each afternoon which attracts people from all around the region. Patrice has been asking me for months if he could start making salami and his persistence and enthusiasm finally won me over (or wore me down). I am investing £30,000 in our old shop in Thornton Dale to fit in the necessary de-humidifying rooms, and at the end of this month Patrice starts salami production. We will also cure hams; I have been inspired by the cookery book, *Farmhouse Fare*, a collection of recipes from country housewives published in *Farmers Weekly* in the 1930s. With Patrice's expertise we will be able to experiment and perfect our hams, adapting and bettering the original recipes to a new 2010 style. In London we're always getting requests for maple-cured bacon, pancetta, sweet-smoked bacon – the list is endless, and I'm getting excited at the idea of producing some of the country's finest ham and salami.

Gone to lunch.
The working block
in the cold room.

Rump of beef pot au feu

This can be made with a variety of cuts, depending on your budget. Starting with the most expensive, the cuts you could use are rump, topside, silverside, brisket or shin. I like rump as it is really tasty, comes in one piece and has a beautiful texture. But see what your butcher is offering and have fun playing around with this great, simple recipe.

Serves 4–6
Takes 3½–4 hours

1.8kg (4lb) rump of beef (or topside, silverside, brisket or shin. See recipe introduction)

4 onions, peeled and quartered

4 garlic cloves, crushed, peeled and diced

5cm (2in) fresh root ginger, peeled and sliced

8 peppercorns

1 cinnamon stick

sea salt

1 bunch of parsley

1 bunch of thyme

3 bay leaves

350g (12oz) new potatoes

4 carrots, peeled

4 celery sticks, cut in half

1 head of spring cabbage, cut into wedges

1. Place the beef in a large pan (the bigger the better) and cover with water. Bring to a boil and simmer for 5 minutes, then remove the beef and discard the water. Return the beef to the pan and cover with fresh water, adding the onions, garlic, ginger, peppercorns, cinnamon and salt. Bring back to a gentle simmer. Tie together the parsley, thyme and bay leaves and add to the pan. Cover and simmer very gently for 3 hours, checking the water level occasionally and topping it up if necessary.

2. Remove the beef and vegetables from the pan and keep warm. Skim the fat from the top of the liquor with a metal spoon. Return the meat and vegetables to the pan with the potatoes and carrots. Simmer, lid on, for a further 15 minutes. Add the celery and cabbage to the pot, pushing down so they are submerged. Cook, covered for 8 minutes.

3. To serve, remove the beef and carve in slices. Serve a selection of the vegetables in individual bowls, topped with slices of meat and a ladle or two of the cooking liquor.

Steak tartare

This wonderfully simple and healthy meal is totally reliant on the quality of the beef you use. Only ever make this dish with top-quality, single-breed, air-hung beef so that you can ensure your steak tartare delivers perfection. There are two ways of making this dish: the first is to mix all the ingredients together as I do; the second has all the ingredients served separately, to be mixed at the table by the diner.

Serves 2
Takes 30 minutes

200g (7oz) fillet of beef (ask for tail as it should be cheaper)

200g (7oz) rump of beef

2 shallots, peeled and finely diced

6 drops of Tabasco sauce

1 tsp tomato ketchup

½ tsp English mustard

1 tsp Worcestershire sauce

1 tsp salted baby capers

3 small gherkins, diced

2 tsp chopped parsley

2 tsp snipped chives

sea salt

freshly ground black pepper

2 eggs

2 tsp very good-quality balsamic vinegar or balsamic syrup

1. Trim both the beef fillet and rump of any fat and sinew, then chop finely by hand with a sharp knife. Place in a mixing bowl. Add the shallot, Tabasco, ketchup, mustard, Worcestershire sauce, capers, gherkins, parsley, chives and seasoning (easy on the salt; remember the capers are already salty).

2. Mix well by hand to ensure an even distribution of flavourings. Shape the mixture into 2 patties and place on plates. Make an indentation in the middle of each.

3. Crack the eggs and pour out the egg white (reserve it to make meringues for your pudding course). Place the half of the shell containing the egg yolk in the indentation on top of the steak. Garnish the plate with a swirl of balsamic and a twist of pepper. Serve.

Peruvian pork

This recipe has travelled far to make it into the book. It comes via a friend of Tim's in France, though it takes its original inspiration from Pamela Westland's book *The Encyclopedia of Spices*. It is an unusual and tasty treat. The cumin and orange deliver a twist and I love the use of sweet potatoes. Serve it in bowls with bread for dipping or with rice.

Serves 4
Takes 3 hours 10 minutes

1 tbsp vegetable oil

1.25kg (2lb 12oz) pork shoulder, diced

2 onions, peeled and sliced

1 garlic clove, crushed, then peeled

½ tsp red chilli flakes

3 tsp cumin seeds, crushed

400g (14 oz) can sweetcorn

400g (14 oz) can tomatoes

zest and juice of 2 large oranges

sea salt

freshly ground black pepper

550g (1lb 4oz) sweet potatoes, cut into 3cm (1in) dice

1. Preheat the oven to 190°C/375°F/gas mark 5.

2. Heat the oil in a flameproof roasting tin, add the pork and cook, turning, for 15 minutes, until browned on all sides. Mix in the onions, garlic, chilli and cumin.

3. Put the pork in the oven and cook for 5 minutes. Add the sweetcorn, tomatoes, orange zest and juice and seasoning. Cover with baking parchment, then seal with a sheet of kitchen foil. Return to the oven and cook for 15 minutes.

4. Reduce the oven temperature to 150°C/300°F/gas mark 2 and cook for a further 1½ hours, stirring halfway through.

5. Add the sweet potatoes with 100ml (3½fl oz) of water, stir and cook for a further 40 minutes, until the pork is cooked through and the sweet potatoes are tender.

Mid-week meat loaf
with spiced tomato sauce

This staple dish of the USA is rather overlooked here, but meat loaf is so easy to make and great value. Serve it hot with the sauce as a supper dish and enjoy it cold with bread and salad the next day – if there is any left.

Serves 6
Takes 2 hours

50g (2oz) butter

2 onions, peeled and finely diced

1 garlic clove, crushed, then peeled

100ml (3½fl oz) red wine

24 thin rashers of streaky bacon

200g (7oz) chicken livers, trimmed and chopped

400g (14oz) shoulder of pork, finely diced

350g (12oz) minced chicken or turkey

2 eggs, beaten

3 bay leaves, torn

leaves from 1 bunch of parsley, finely chopped

sea salt

freshly ground black pepper

1. Melt the butter in a frying pan over a low heat and sauté the onions and garlic gently for 4 minutes, then add the wine and simmer for another 2 minutes. Remove from the heat and allow to cool. Meanwhile, line a 1kg (2lb 4oz) loaf tin with plastic wrap and line with the bacon, allowing it to hang over the sides so you can wrap it over the top of the meat loaf later. Preheat the oven to 170°C/325°F/gas mark 3.

2. Tip the chicken livers into a large bowl and add the pork, chicken or turkey, eggs, bay, parsley and seasoning. Mix with your hands to get an even blend, then add the wine mixture. Fill the prepared tin with the meat, flatten the top and wrap the overhanging bacon over. Cover with kitchen foil, seal well and bake in the oven for 1 hour 15 minutes.

3. Remove the meat loaf from the oven and allow to rest for 10 minutes. Turn out the meat loaf, slice and serve with Tomato sauce (see page 325).

Smoked roast gammon in cider

Most smoked gammon will need soaking in water overnight. Traditionally, if people were unsure how long to leave it in water, they would dip their finger in and test it. If the water was salty, they would continue to soak the meat; if it was just sweet, it should be perfect to cook. However, this is no longer considered safe. A good butcher will tell you how long your chosen piece of gammon needs to soak.

Serves 8
Takes 3 hours, plus overnight soaking

2kg (4lb 8oz) piece of gammon

2 litres (3½ pints) dry cider

1 bouquet garni

½ tsp ground cloves

200g (7oz) fresh breadcrumbs

50g (2oz) soft brown sugar

1 tbsp Dijon mustard

1. Soak the gammon overnight or for the time advised by your butcher. Place it in a large pan, cover with fresh water and bring to a boil. Boil for three minutes, then carefully drain off all the water.

2. Add the cider to the pan with the bouquet garni, bring to a boil, reduce the heat and simmer very gently for 2 hours. Leave the gammon in the stock, removing it only when cool enough to handle. Cool the stock, then freeze: it can be reused if it is not too salty, or used as a base for a wonderful pea soup.

3. Preheat the oven to 170°C/325°F/gas mark 3. Carefully trim away the skin from the gammon, leaving a good layer of fat. Mix together the cloves, breadcrumbs and sugar. Smear the gammon fat with Dijon mustard, wash and dry your hands, then sprinkle on the breadcrumbs evenly, patting down to secure. Bake in the hot oven for 25 minutes, until golden, and serve hot or cold.

Spring roast lamb with oregano

This dish is a perfect late-spring or early-summer meal. It is enhanced by the herbs and deliciously enriched with olive oil, so I like to serve it simply with steamed new potatoes and greens (especially with Jersey Royals and asparagus as the season moves on). Ask your butcher to cut around the aitchbone and hip bone for ease of carving.

Serves 8
Takes 1½ hours, plus 24 hours marinating

450ml (16fl oz) olive oil, plus 3 tbsp

leaves from 2 bunches of oregano, roughly chopped

4 shallots, peeled and finely chopped

sea salt

freshly ground black pepper

2.7kg (6lb) leg of spring lamb, chump on

1. Mix together the olive oil, oregano, shallots and seasoning. Place the leg of lamb in a large, shallow dish and rub with this marinade. Cover and leave in the refrigerator for 24 hours, turning occasionally.

2. The next day, preheat the oven to 190°C/375°F/gas mark 5. Heat the 3 tbsp olive oil over a medium-high heat in a large flameproof roasting tin, then brown the leg on all sides. Place in the hot oven with the marinade and roast for 1 hour 10 minutes for rare meat, adding 10 minutes for medium. Please do not overcook spring lamb; buy hogget or mutton instead.

3. When cooked, cover and rest the meat in a warm place for 10 minutes before carving.

Lamb or hogget stew with capers and olives

This recipe can be made with lamb or hogget shoulder cut into cubes, or you could always ask your butcher to roll and tie the shoulder, then slice it into 6–8 rounds. This is a meal that I think does not need much to go with it. Serve it on its own but you could also serve it with pasta or mashed potatoes.

Serves 6–8
Takes 2½ hours

1 tbsp olive oil

1.5kg (3lb 5oz) boned and rolled shoulder of lamb or hogget, sliced into 6 or 8 rounds, or cut into 3cm (1in) cubes

4 onions, peeled and quartered

4 garlic cloves, peeled and sliced

25g (1oz) plain flour

2 cans chopped tomatoes, each 400g (14 oz)

leaves from 1 bunch of oregano, chopped

2 sprigs of rosemary

350g (12½oz) black olives, stoned

25g (1oz) small capers, rinsed

600ml (1 pint) white wine

leaves from 1 bunch of coriander, chopped

1. Preheat the oven to 190°C/375°F/gas mark 5.

2. Heat the olive oil in a large roasting tin in the oven, then add the lamb and turn to coat in the hot oil. Return to the oven and cook for 10 minutes, then add the onions and garlic and return to the oven for a further 10 minutes.

3. Now reduce the oven temperature to 170°C/325°F/gas mark 3. Sprinkle in the flour and mix with all the cooking juices, then stir in the tomatoes, oregano, rosemary, olives, capers and wine. Cover with a sheet of baking parchment, pressed down on to the mix, then seal with a sheet of kitchen foil all the way around.

4. Place in the oven and cook for 1 hour. Uncover and turn the meat, then reseal the foil and cook for a further hour. Finally, add the chopped coriander and serve.

Spatchcocked poussins with sticky Thai sauce

A poussin is a young chicken that is usually less than 28 days old. I do not farm poussins but buy them from a reliable source. They are very popular for entertaining, due to the speed of cooking and ease of serving. If you leave out the chilli, you'll find children love to eat them with their fingers.

Serves 4
Takes 40 minutes, plus overnight marinating

85g (3oz) sugar

1 tsp fish sauce

2 red chillies, deseeded and finely diced

2 garlic cloves, peeled and finely diced

2 lemongrass stalks, trimmed and finely sliced

5cm (2in) fresh root ginger, peeled and diced

juice of 3 limes

4 poussins, each approximately 500g (1lb 2oz)

1. Mix the sugar with 75ml (2½fl oz) water in a saucepan and gently simmer until dissolved. Remove from the heat, add the fish sauce, chillies, garlic, lemongrass, ginger and lime juice. Stir and leave to cool.

2. Cut the backbone from each bird with poultry shears, then flatten each bird using the palm of your hand (don't worry if you hear the crack of a bone or two).

3. Place the poussins in a strong plastic bag (check there aren't any holes) and pour in the cooled marinade. Tie a knot in the bag and knead it with your hands to coat the birds all over. Place in the refrigerator overnight, turning occasionally to baste.

4. Remove the poussins from the marinade and insert two metal skewers diagonally, forming a cross, across the flesh side of each, to keep them flat. Put the marinade in a small saucepan and cook over a low heat. Place the poussins under a medium-hot grill (or on a barbecue at a similar heat) and cook for 12–15 minutes each side, turning the birds frequently and basting with the marinade. To check they are cooked, insert a knife into the thickest part. If the juices run clear, they are ready, if not cook for a little longer and check again.

5 Meanwhile, pour any cooking juices from the grill pan into the marinade and bring to a boil. Simmer for 2 minutes, then spoon this sauce over the poussins to serve.

Olive-stuffed chicken leg

This recipe is very therapeutic to make. It's wonderful hot or cold, sliced and served with summer salads. You will be able to ask a good butcher for caul fat. If you really can't find it, wrap the stuffed legs in Parma ham.

Serves 6
Takes 1½ hours

6 boned large chicken legs (make sure you keep the bones)

3 small boneless chicken breasts

1–2 egg whites

sea salt

freshly ground black pepper

85g (3oz) green olives, pitted and chopped

zest of 1 unwaxed lemon

leaves from 1 bunch of parsley, finely chopped

3 tbsp olive oil, plus more for the tin

6 sheets of caul fat (or Parma ham)

1. Place the chicken leg bones in a saucepan and cover with water. Bring to a boil and simmer for 45 minutes. Drain, skim off the fat with a metal spoon, then boil the stock again to reduce it by half.

2. Meanwhile, lie the chicken legs on a work surface, skin side down. Remove the skin from the chicken breasts, then chop the skin and place it in a food processor with the egg whites and seasoning. Blitz until smooth, then add the olives, lemon zest, parsley, 1 tbsp of the olive oil and a little more seasoning. Mix by hand until evenly blended.

3. Preheat the oven to 180°C/350°F/gas mark 4. If using caul fat, rinse it in water, then lay out the sheets (Parma ham will not need rinsing). Place the chicken legs, open, on top, skin side down. Divide the filling into 6 and shape each into a sausage. Place each portion of stuffing on the open legs, then roll the leg meat around it and wrap with the caul fat or ham to secure.

4 Heat the remaining oil over a medium-high heat in a frying pan and add the stuffed chicken, laying the join in the caul fat on the pan to cook first. Turn to brown all over, then transfer to a lightly oiled roasting tin, place in the oven and cook for 40 minutes. Serve whole or sliced, with a few spoons of the leg-bone stock.

APRIL

April on the farm

Mike Jenkins – the chief sausage maker at Grange Farm.

The clocks have gone forward and spring has arrived. Unfortunately this also means my working day has just increased by four hours. But it's good to have the extra time to prepare the land for crops, which have to be in by the end of the month, and to give the cattle extra attention, as they will soon be delivering their calves. On top of this we also need to repair the damage inflicted by the harsh winter and deliver the last of the lambs.

Primrose's piglets have now grown to a good size and are strong enough to be weaned, so we have set up a large pen with a new pig ark by the farm. Trying to round the piglets up into the trailer causes a rebellion, with lots of squeals and squeaks, but eventually we catch all the rascals and quad bike them over to their new home. At first they are not so happy or confident and scurry into the ark to hide, but eventually the bolder ones pop out to investigate and start to settle in. After a couple of days they have turfed up the grass and made a real muddy mess, which is a sign of contentment. My cousin Alex has given us five pudgy Gloucester Old Spots and I have put all the piglets together. Sarah has affectionately nicknamed this the nursery. An exhausted Primrose is finally enjoying some peace and quiet and indulging in long hours of uninterrupted sleep.

Gemma, our speciality pig vet, spends the day with us at Grange Farm and Blansby. We discuss our long-term breeding plan as, although we only had a few Tamworths last July, we now have over 35 with even more on the way. Dandelion struggled with her litter, so we had to act quickly and hand-rear them for a few days before they were fostered by another sow. It's not unusual for this to happen with a first-time mother. Gemma and I agree to cover Dandelion again, as we are confident she will make a good mum second-time round. Two other Tamworth gilts are pregnant and Gemma advises that my Berkshires are ready to be covered by Turpin, to establish my Plum Pudding line of pigs. Inspecting the pig stock with Gemma is fascinating, as she provides a fresh outlook and makes some useful comments, bringing to our attention the better-shaped animals: pigs with good strong legs for handsome hams and straight backs for quality bacon. On Gemma's authoritative advice we mark a few pigs that do not meet the required standard for breeding – though will still make excellent eating – and these will be fattened up for the shops.

The first calves of the year are born at Grange Farm: two little Riggits and one Belted Galloway. When the Galloway was born we were there to keep a watchful eye on his mother, Tosca. All went well with the delivery, but as she slowly turned around she was startled to discover her baby, still in his bag. I have never seen a cow look so shocked, so I felt we needed to stay around. My instincts were right as Tosca, an unprepared first-time mother, was not keen on helping her calf; we had to get her in the crush to hold her still for the calf to suckle. I can happily report that Tosca has calmed and both are now doing well. We have had nine little Galloway and Riggit calves at Grange Farm, and the Longhorn cattle at East Moor have had many more young.

I make a flying visit to London, as the shop in Moxon Street is running without a manager. It needs a strong character to run the counter. I'd like to find a skilled butcher who is good with the customers, someone who can engage them in conversation, whether it's about a cut of meat and how best to cook it or a discussion of the new political 'leaders' debates' on television. My best butchers, Borut, Daniel and Steve, all work together in Hackney, but after a crafty conversation I manage to convince them that Steve should move over to Moxon Street to run the shop. He requests a meeting with me as he has plans for the shop and wants to make some changes. I feel it's best to do this straight away, so I jump on the train to King's Cross. Steve is Australian, so I need to check his changes aren't going to include the addition of kangaroo burgers or crocodile steaks. All goes well. Steve has great suggestions and transfers to Moxon Street the next day. It's been a long journey to London, but it's time well spent, as I'm confident Steve will inject more enthusiasm into the way the shop is run.

My instincts were right as Tosca, an unprepared first-time mother, was not keen on helping her calf; we had to get her in the crush to hold her still for the calf to suckle.

I'm passionate about our sausages, although I ventured into sausage-making by accident 10 years ago. I used to sell slaughtered pigs to other butchers, but they were notoriously slow payers. I decided the only way to reduce my stress levels would be to start selling my own jointed pork. A butcher owed me money and I knew he might never be able to pay, so I suggested that he taught me how to make sausages in lieu. He showed me how to cut the meat, which seasonings he favoured, and the all-important best consistency to aim for. He did me a great turn. One afternoon he took me five miles up the road from his shop and introduced me to a butcher who had just retired, and I bought his equipment: a 1950s mincer, a cast-iron enamelled sausage filler and a burger press, all setting me back the incredible bargain price of £40.

The following day I set to work in my kitchen to make my first sausages. It was tricky getting the pressure right on the sausage filler and I ended up firing 14lb of sausage meat across the kitchen and up the ceiling and walls. But I didn't give in and after much practice and experimentation, I came up with a sausage I liked. It is the same recipe that we use today.

The remaining ewes are brought in from the moor for lambing – and happily this time, we don't suffer the complications we had last month. The results on the lamb foetus come back from DEFRA and they haven't found anything wrong, but we have had the vet out, who has suggested that the very hard winter did not help matters. Next year we plan to give the sheep an anti-abortion jab to try and cut down on losses, and together with the vet and Arthur we are putting together a programme that will track all the different breeds of sheep and record all occurrences, so we can get the flock back into top condition. Lambing has been tough this year: Arthur, Alan, Lesley and Chrissie are exhausted. Both Arthur and Lesley have been working seven days a week since they arrived a couple of months ago, so Lesley wants to finish off her unpacking, sort out hers and Arthur's new home in Thornton Dale and make some friends. Chrissie is packing her bags: she is heading to Australia, then sailing via some Pacific islands and visiting Africa – before lambing starts again.

Sheep grazing on the moor.

Mint-crusted roast rack of lamb

A rack of lamb will vary in size, so you need to adjust the cooking time accordingly. Don't be scared: use your hands to judge when your meat is ready. Rare meat is soft, medium is firmer and well-done is hard.

Serves 6
Takes 45 minutes

2 tbsp olive oil

6 x 3-chop French-trimmed racks of lamb, each approximately 450kg (1lb)

leaves from 1 bunch of mint, finely chopped

1 bunch of chives, finely snipped

leaves from 1 bunch of parsley, finely chopped

sea salt

freshly ground black pepper

6 tsp Dijon mustard

1. Preheat the oven to 220°C/425°F/gas mark 7. Heat the oil over a medium-high heat in a thick-based frying pan and brown each of the lamb racks in turn on all sides until golden. This should take 6–8 minutes in total. Place in a roasting tin, put into the hot oven and cook for 8–10 minutes for pink meat; 10–12 minutes for medium.

2. Mix together the herbs and seasoning in a small, shallow dish. Remove the lamb from the oven, brush the skin side of each rack with the mustard, then dip and press in the chopped herbs.

3. Return to the oven to cook for a further 3 minutes. Remove the meat and leave it to rest for 5 minutes, before slicing and serving with gratin dauphinois.

Lamb kofta kebabs

The marriage of the spices with the lamb makes these kebabs genius in flavour and texture and much enjoyed by all generations.

Serves 4
Takes 30 minutes

800g (1lb 12oz) minced lamb (shoulder or neck deliver great flavour)

2 shallots, finely diced

1 garlic clove, crushed

zest and juice of 2 unwaxed lemons, plus more to serve

4 tsp ground cumin

leaves from 1 bunch of thyme

2 red chillies, deseeded and finely chopped

sea salt

freshly ground black pepper

½ cucumber

1 lettuce (tender young leaves are best here)

leaves from 4 sprigs of coriander

leaves from 4 sprigs of flat-leaf parsley

2 tbsp olive oil

4 flat breads

2 tomatoes, sliced

4 tbsp Greek yogurt

4 tbsp houmous

1. Take a large bowl and tip in the lamb, shallots, garlic, all the lemon zest and half the juice, the cumin, thyme, chilli and seasoning. Mix with your hands to blend evenly.

2. Divide the meat into 4 and shape each into a sausage around a long metal skewer, making sure they are of an even thickness along the length.

3. Heat the grill to high and cook the kebabs, turning, until browned on all sides. This will take about 15 minutes, depending on the ferocity of your grill.

4. Meanwhile, using a mandolin, finely slice the cucumber into ribbons or very thin rounds. Put into a bowl, add the torn lettuce leaves, coriander, parsley, olive oil and remaining lemon juice. Toss. Warm the flat breads under the grill for 20 seconds.

5. This is the sort of meal that is best self-assembled at the table so take the green salad, tomatoes, yogurt and houmous to the table with the kebabs. Give each person a warm flat bread; they can then top these with yogurt and houmous, scatter them with salad and tomato, squeeze over lemon juice and finally place the kebabon the top. Then they just have to remove the skewer, roll up and enjoy.

Seared rump of beef
with papaya and bean-sprout salad

Rump is the steak that delivers the best depth of flavour. It works well
with this salad, which is packed with Oriental herbs and tastes.
Halve the recipe to serve as a lovely starter for a special occasion.

Serves 4
Takes 45 minutes

2 papayas, the firmer and greener the better

115g (4oz) bean sprouts

½ cucumber, peeled

5cm (2in) fresh root ginger, grated and mixed into a paste

1 garlic clove, crushed and peeled

1 red chilli, deseeded and very finely diced

leaves from 1 bunch of fresh coriander, chopped

2 limes

sea salt

freshly ground black pepper

1 tsp vegetable oil

4 rump steaks, weighing a total of 350g (12oz)

1. Peel the papayas, cut in half and scoop out and discard all the seeds. Slice the papaya
then cut it into equal-sized matchsticks. Place these in a large bowl and add the bean
sprouts. Cut the cucumber in half lengthways, scoop out the seeds with a teaspoon and
discard. Cut the flesh into matchsticks and add to the bowl.

2. Mix the ginger, garlic, chilli and coriander in a bowl. Juice one of the limes, add to the
bowl and season. Pour this dressing into the papaya salad and carefully toss to mix.

3. Heat the oil over a high heat in a frying pan and, when smoking, add the steaks. Cook
for 2 minutes each side for rare, or 3 minutes each side for medium. Remove and allow
to rest for 1 minute.

4. Slice the steaks with a sharp knife. Divide the papaya salad between four plates and
arrange the steak on top. Cut the remaining lime into wedges and serve with the salad.

Royal fillet of beef

Ask your butcher for the middle of the fillet, which I call the 'royal' cut. It is even in shape and therefore easy to cook. It is expensive but, for a special occasion, it's worth it. This dish goes really well with asparagus, which is abundant from now until the middle of June.

Serves 6 as a main course or 12 as a starter
Takes 45 minutes

1.3kg (3lb) middle fillet of beef

leaves from 2 bunches of curly parsley

leaves from 1 bunch of thyme

1 bunch of chives

1 tsp sea salt

1 tbsp coarsely cracked black pepper

1 egg white

3 tbsp Dijon mustard

2 tbsp olive oil

1. Preheat the oven to 220°C/425°F/gas mark 7. Trim the fillet of any fat and sinew.

2. Chop all the herbs together very finely, adding the salt and pepper. Mix well, then shape the herby mass on your chopping board into a neat rectangle the length and width (of all sides) of your fillet.

3. Whisk the egg white until just stiff, add the mustard and whisk it in. Smear this over the fillet, then firmly roll it in the herb mix, coating all over except for the ends.

4. Heat the olive oil over a medium-high heat in a large, heavy-based ovenproof frying pan or flameproof roasting tin and seal the beef all over. Transfer to the oven and roast for 8 minutes, then turn and roast for 8 minutes more for beautifully rare beef, which I believe is the only way to eat this superb cut. Add another 8 minutes for medium. If you must, you can roast the meat further, but be warned it will be a total waste of such a tender cut.

5. Remove the meat from the oven and allow it to stand for 5 minutes before carving. Serve with Horseradish sauce (see page 320).

Toad-in-the-hole

After a hard day spent farming in the fresh spring weather your appetite is enormous, and this is what Tim calls a 'proper' toad-in-the-hole for hungry workers. Have fun and play around with using different sausages to make a new variety of flavours in this classic dish.

Serves 4
Takes 45 minutes

For the toads

4 skinless chicken breasts

4 sausages

4 rashers of streaky bacon

1 tbsp olive oil

For the batter

3 eggs

200ml (7fl oz) milk

175g (6oz) plain flour

1. Preheat the oven to 170°C/325°F/gas mark 3. On the underside of each chicken breast, cut a lengthways incision large enough for a sausage. Stuff the chicken breasts with the sausages, then wrap a strip of bacon around each breast to secure the sausages in place.

2. Brush a metal roasting tin all over with the olive oil, place in the toads and cook for 20 minutes. Meanwhile, make the batter: blend together the eggs, milk and flour with a hand-held blender until smooth, then set aside to rest for 10 minutes.

3. Increase the oven temperature to 190°C/375°F/gas mark 5, and pour the batter into the tin with the toads. Place the tin in the top half of the oven and bake for 40 minutes.

Spring beef pasta

This method of lightly poaching a sirloin steak is truly wonderful and also very simple. Cook it to your liking and make sure that you carve it as thinly as possible; it will just melt among all the other flavours.

Serves 4
Takes 20 minutes

175g (6oz) spaghetti

200g (7oz) sirloin steak

140g (5oz) sugarsnap peas

140g (5oz) cherry tomatoes

½ red onion, peeled and finely diced

2 tbsp olive oil

2 tbsp black olives, pitted and roughly chopped

leaves from 1 bunch of flat leaf parsley, roughly chopped

1 red chilli, deseeded and finely sliced

140g (5oz) rocket

freshly ground black pepper

sea salt

leaves from 1 bunch of basil

50g (2oz) Parmesan cheese

1. Plunge the spaghetti into a large pan of boiling water, stir and simmer for 8 minutes. During this time, put the steak on top of the spaghetti, cover, and cook for 2 minutes for rare, 4 minutes for medium. If you really must have your steak cooked all the way through, cook for 6 minutes.

2. Add the sugarsnap peas, tomatoes and onion, cover and cook for a further minute, then remove the steak and place on a carving board to rest for 2 minutes.

3. Drain the pasta, return to the pan, add the oil, olives, parsley, chilli and rocket, season and mix well on a low heat. With a sharp knife, slice the steak into ribbons, then add to the pasta, tear in the basil and sprinkle over the Parmesan. Toss and serve.

Sticky citrus-marinated pork chops

If using pork loin chops, ask the butcher to cut into the fat every 5cm (2in) as this will allow the meat to stay flat while cooking, giving a better result.

Serves 4
Takes 25 minutes, plus up to 24 hours marinating

4 pork loin chops (or chump chops if you want to be thrifty)

3 tbsp dark Kikkoman soy sauce

4 tbsp grain mustard

zest and juice of 1 unwaxed lemon

zest and juice of 1 orange

100ml (3½fl oz) maple syrup

½ tsp dried thyme

2 garlic cloves, crushed, then peeled

sea salt

freshly ground black pepper

vegetable oil, for the grill pan

1. Place the pork chops in a large, strong plastic bag (make sure there are no holes in it first). Whisk together the soy, mustard, lemon and orange zest and juice, maple syrup, thyme, garlic and seasoning, pour into the bag and seal well. Shake to coat the chops in the marinade and leave in the refrigerator for 1 to 24 hours (overnight is best).

2. The next day, allow the chops to return to room temperature. Heat the grill to high and lightly oil the grill pan. Place the chops on the grill pan in a single layer and grill for 8 to 10 minutes, basting regularly with the marinade. Turn the chops and grill for a further 8 to 10 minutes, again basting to ensure a really golden and sticky coating. (The cooking time will vary according to the thickness of your pork chops.)

3. Pour the remaining marinade into a small saucepan and carefully bring to a boil. Gently simmer for 3 minutes. Serve the chops with this hot sauce at the table.

Braised pork with red peppers

Chump of pork is an economical but tasty cut and needs gentle cooking in a moist atmosphere to get the best from it. The flavours of the sweet smoked paprika and peppers add to the richness of this great recipe.

Serves 4
Takes 2½ hours

1kg (2lb 4oz) boneless chump of pork, sliced into 4

2 tbsp olive oil

4 shallots, peeled and diced

2 garlic cloves, crushed and peeled

leaves from 4 sprigs of oregano, chopped

1½–2 tsp smoked sweet paprika

sea salt

freshly ground black pepper

300g jar of roasted, peeled red peppers (or 3 red peppers, chargrilled and peeled)

200ml (7fl oz) white wine

1. Preheat the oven to 180°C/350°F/gas mark 4.

2. Place the pork and olive oil in a flameproof roasting tin and cook in the oven for 15 minutes, to brown on all sides. Now add the shallots and garlic, return to the oven and cook for a further 10 minutes.

3. Add the oregano, paprika and seasoning. Drain the peppers, slice into strips (if they're not in strips already), and mix in well with the wine. Reduce the oven temperature to 150°C/300°F/gas mark 2. Cover the tin with baking parchment, then with a sheet of kitchen foil, taking care to seal it around the edges. Return to the oven and cook for 2 hours.

4. When cooked, skim off and discard any excess fat with a metal spoon. Serve the pork with the vibrant pepper sauce and juices spooned over.

Spiced quail

Small, farmed quail are a little richer than chicken, and this recipe adds
a deliciously sticky marinade.

Serves 4
Takes 40 minutes, plus 2 hours marinating

1 tbsp sunflower oil

3 garlic cloves, crushed

1 red chilli, deseeded and finely chopped

2cm (¾in) fresh root ginger, peeled and grated

juice and zest of 1 unwaxed lemon

2 tbsp Kikkoman soy sauce

4 tsp grainy mustard

sea salt

freshly ground black pepper

4 quail

1. Whisk together the oil, garlic, chilli, ginger, lemon juice and zest, soy sauce, mustard
and seasoning. Place into a strong plastic bag (check it doesn't have any holes) and add
the quail. Seal the bag firmly, then shake and knead to coat the birds all over in the
marinade. Store in the refrigerator for 2 hours.

2. Bring the quail to room temperature. Preheat the oven to 220°C/425°F/gas mark 7.
Place the birds and their marinade in a roasting tin and cook for 15 minutes, then baste
with the juices and cook for a further 10 minutes.

3. To serve, encourage your friends to start eating with their knives and forks. They will
soon revert to their fingers to get to every last morsel of meat and tasty sauce.

May

May on the farm

Arthur Ramage,
the shepherd,
with two young
Texel-cross lambs.

We have some new additions to the farm: six white Sussex chickens to join our expanding flock. David Howard, a multi-talented gardener (he designed the gardens at Highgrove), Riggit breeder and native poultry rearer, brought them to us from Gloucestershire on his way to his new home in Northumberland. He also sent us a selection of traditional English fruit trees (apple, plum and greengage), which we've planted to create an orchard. The thought of an orchard fills me with immense pleasure and anticipation. The chickens and pigs will eventually be able to forage the windfalls while clearing the ground of nasty bugs that might destroy the trees. And I'm hoping the bakery will start making seasonal fruit chutneys and the shops will sell apples alongside pork joints. I have just been in touch with my beekeeper friend, who has many hives on the moor, and he is going to move some of them into the orchard so the bees will be able to enjoy the spring blossom. I'd love to start producing honey. It's amazing to think we could be sustaining three types of agriculture – fruit, eggs and honey – simply by planting a small orchard.

Around the farm the dry stone walling is being replaced, for the first time in 150 years, by Andrew Fordham-Brown. He is slowly working his way around the farm, as my cash flow allows, and has just told me that it will take three to four years to repair all the walls. Andrew arrives in his old 1977 Army ambulance Land Rover, which he has refitted, and he often sleeps in there with his dog Jess. Andrew has found a lot of adders among the stones. He says there are more this year than he has seen in a long time, which is surprising considering the very hard winter we've had.

Dry stone walling is a craft that goes back thousands of years. It is a method of building a wall without mortar, the stones being selected so that they naturally interlock. Dry stone walls can be found throughout the world but it is a technique common in Yorkshire. Stones were originally found widely around the local farmland, and this walling technique allowed these to be put to good use while also clearing the fields.

Sarah, my shepherd Arthur, his wife Lesley and I head off to the annual Dorset sheep fair in Exeter. The evening before the sale, we pop in to check the stock quality and spot a couple of handsome tups, lots number 126 and 127, which we mark down as possible purchases.

We arrive at the sale with plenty of time for a thorough inspection. Arthur and I walk round individually marking up the superior-looking stock for which we are interested in bidding. Arthur is not convinced about those we first selected the night before and spots lot number 152, whom I agree looks rather tempting and deserves a bid. I settle in the ring ready to go, but it's sluggish going. On average the tups sell for 500–600 guineas, but I buy lot 126 for 850 guineas and lot 127 for 1,100 guineas. I know these two brothers will make an excellent pair in the fields around the farm and serve the ewes very well. We now have to wait for lot 152 to come up and, as the sale is plodding along rather slowly, we amuse ourselves in the meantime with a bit of retail therapy, buying waxed jackets, leather boots, wellies and a warm jumper from the stalls at the fair.

Eventually, lot 152 arrives in the ring looking really good, and the bidding commences at 800 guineas, which is very high. I join in at 1,100 guineas

Eventually, lot 152 arrives in the ring looking really good, and the bidding commences at 800 guineas, which is very high. I join in at 1,100 guineas and eventually seal the deal at 3,000 guineas, the most I have ever paid, and perhaps a record price for a Dorset tup. His full name is Bally Taggart Nirvana from Ireland, but I decide we can't call him this back in Yorkshire, so rename him Golden Balls.

and eventually seal the deal at 3,000 guineas, the most I have ever paid, and perhaps a record price for a Dorset tup. His extravagant full name is Bally Taggart Nirvana, and he comes from Ireland, but I decide we can't call him that back in Yorkshire, so I rename him Golden Balls. After sorting out the paperwork, we load the trailer with our new sheep and leave Exeter at 5.30pm, arriving back at Levisham way past midnight, where we put our expensive new stock in barns for the night. The next morning, the sheep are properly introduced to their surroundings and turned out into the fields around the farm. I am extremely pleased with them and, as Arthur was the one who smartly spotted Golden Balls, my confidence in him continues to grow.

We have pulled forward the tupping of the Dorsets from August to June so that they will lamb in October instead of early December. The weather is not as harsh in the autumn so the lambs will be both stronger and better able to withstand another hard winter, and they will also be bigger in time for the Easter trade. The sheep fair has boosted our interest in the Dorset breed, and Arthur is going to go through our 400 ewes to select some of the best to be covered by Golden Balls, which will hopefully produce some really top-quality lambs. I may even start showing and selling stock, as it would be good to sell some Dorsets into other flocks to help to strengthen the quality of this fine breed across the country.

Finally, the Dorsets have all been sheared, by the two local lads from Thirsk. They can shear 402 of these sheep in a day, which is good going, as the Dorsets have wool on their belly, legs and the crown of the head. Next month they will shear the Mules and Blackfaces (who have less wool). Once again I sell the fleeces to the Wool Marketing Board, and it works out at about £1 a fleece. If I wanted to sell them directly I would have to process the fleeces into spun wool, which would be much more lucrative but also a lot of hassle.

Dorset tups in spring fields anticipating the great pleasures to come in July.

Spiced Jacob's rib, or short ladder American-style

These ribs are not for the faint-hearted as they are big. Ask your butcher to cut them individually, both to make them more manageable and to give a bigger surface area for that all-important crunchy coating.

Serves 1
Takes 2 hours, plus overnight marinating

For the ribs	For the glaze
¼ tsp cayenne pepper	25g (1oz) butter
½ tsp paprika	25g (1oz) sugar
½ tsp ground cumin	2 tbsp white wine vinegar
½ tsp garlic powder	1 tbsp Worcestershire sauce
½ tsp black pepper	juice of ½ lemon
½ tsp salt	2 tbsp ketchup
500g (1lb 2oz) beef ribs (about 2 ribs per person)	1 tsp mustard
vegetable oil, for the baking tray	2 tbsp honey

1. Mix together all the spices, garlic powder and seasoning, place in a resealable plastic bag, add the ribs and shake the bag to coat the ribs. Leave them in the bag to marinate overnight in the refrigerator.

2. Melt the butter for the glaze in a small saucepan, over a low heat, add the sugar and vinegar and stir until dissolved. Mix in the remaining ingredients until smooth and blended.

3. If cooking on a barbecue, the ribs will need a good 1½ hours with constant turning. If cooking in the oven, preheat to 170°C/325°F/gas mark 3, place the ribs on a lightly oiled baking tray and cook for 1½ hours until cooked through. Both methods of cooking require the ribs to be frequently basted with the glaze; use a brush to paint it on evenly, delivering a wonderful sticky finish. Serve with kitchen towel to clean up your sticky hands.

Pork hash

Cook a large pork roast on Sunday and get a quick meal from the cold meat on Monday. Add a kick with chopped chillies, if you like, when adding the tomatoes. This recipe can also be made with lamb (use thyme instead of sage), beef (use flat-leaf parsley) or chicken (use tarragon).

Serves 1
Takes 30 minutes

½ tbsp olive oil

175g (6oz) potatoes, peeled and cubed

1 onion, peeled and sliced

175g (6oz) cooked pork, finely shredded

1 firm tomato, roughly chopped

3 sage leaves

1 egg

1. In a large frying pan, heat the oil and fry the potatoes over a medium heat for 12 minutes, until just golden. Add the onion and cook for a further 5 minutes.

2. Check the potatoes are cooked, then add the pork, tomato and sage and mix.

3. Make a nest-shaped space in the middle of the pan's contents, crack in the egg and cover the pan. Cook for 2 minutes, until the yolk is just opaque and the white cooked.

Boiled collar of ham with parsley sauce

The choice between smoked and green ham is a matter of personal taste. Think which kind of bacon you prefer, then buy accordingly. This is a very simple dish, but the classic parsley sauce makes it a firm favourite of mine.

Serves 4
Takes 3½ hours

1.5kg (3lb 5oz) rolled collar of gammon, green or smoked

2 bay leaves

10 black peppercorns

2 juniper berries

2 onions, peeled and halved

2 celery sticks, halved widthways

2 carrots, peeled and halved widthways

2 leeks, trimmed and halved widthways, well washed

1 small head of spring cabbage

1. Place the gammon in a large saucepan, cover with water and bring to a boil. Remove the gammon and discard the water. Add fresh water to the pan and return the gammon with the bay, peppercorns and juniper. Bring to a boil, cover and simmer over a low heat for 2 hours.

2. Add the onions, cover and cook for a further 20 minutes. Add the celery, carrots and leeks and cover and cook for 20 minutes. Cut the spring cabbage into wedges, trim away the core and add to the pot; cover and cook for 4 minutes.

3. Remove the gammon from the pan and carve. Serve in bowls with the vegetables, moistened with a little of the cooking stock and Parsley sauce (see page 325).

Rolled and stuffed breast of lamb

This is a good use for a frequently overlooked cut. There is not a lot of meat on a breast but it is flavoursome and, when slow-cooked, the fat runs from the meat. This is the perfect cut for students: when Tim first left home and lived on his own, he would buy a breast of lamb, lie it over a bed of potatoes and parsnips and slow-roast it for up to four hours. It provided supper for two days and soup on the third.

Serves 4
Takes 2½ hours

1 tbsp olive oil	sea salt
1 onion, peeled and finely diced	freshly ground black pepper
2 garlic cloves, crushed, then peeled	1 breast of lamb, boned (keep the bones)
175g (6oz) mushrooms, finely chopped	1 tbsp plain flour
175g (6oz) spinach, finely chopped	1 tbsp Redcurrant jelly (see page 322)
140g (4oz) Cheddar cheese, grated	100ml (3½fl oz) red wine
1 egg, beaten	

1. Preheat the oven to 170°C/325°F/gas mark 3. Heat the oil in a frying pan, add the onion and garlic and cook until lightly brown. Tip in the mushrooms and cook for 5 minutes, then add the spinach to wilt. Leave to cool, then mix in the Cheddar, egg and seasoning.

2. Lie the lamb skin side down on a large sheet of kitchen foil, spread evenly with stuffing, then tightly roll up the breast and wrap in the foil, twisting each end to seal. Place the bones and the lamb in a roasting tin and roast for 1½ hours, then remove the bones.

3. Place the bones in a shallow saucepan and just cover with water. Cover, bring to a boil, then simmer for 35 minutes. Strain. Meanwhile, roast the meat for a further 30 minutes. When cooked, remove from the oven and discard the foil, but retain the cooking juices.

4. Add the flour to the roasting tin and mix well, place over a medium-high heat and slowly pour in the roasted bone stock, mixing until smooth. Add the Redcurrant jelly and wine, bring to a boil and reduce by half. Carve the lamb and serve with the sauce and a rosemary sprig, to garnish.

Ginger Pig beef bourguignon pie

We started making meat pies around eight years ago as we had a lot of off-cuts of meat that were too good to make into mince. After finding a classic recipe in an old cookery book, I adapted it to be more interesting.

Makes 1 large (24x12cm/9½x4½in) or 4 small (12x6cm/4½x2 ½in) pies
Takes 2 hours, plus overnight chilling

For the filling

1.3kg (3lb) chuck steak, cut into 2cm (¾in) dice

350g (12oz) cooked dry-cured bacon, diced

200g (7oz) button mushrooms, chopped

1 onion, peeled and finely chopped

1 small garlic clove, crushed, then peeled

1 tbsp soy sauce, preferably Kikkoman

350ml (12fl oz) red wine

2 tbsp cornflour

leaves of 4 sprigs of flat-leaf parsley, roughly chopped

For the suet pastry

700g (1lb 9oz) plain flour

350g (12oz) suet

½ tsp salt

For assembly

25g (1oz) lard, melted

1 tbsp plain flour

1 egg, beaten

1. Preheat the oven to 180°C/350°F/gas mark 4. Place the beef and bacon in a roasting tin and brown in the oven for 15 minutes, then stir and cook for 15 minutes more. Add the mushrooms, onion, garlic, soy sauce and wine. Cover with baking parchment, pushing it down over the ingredients, seal with kitchen foil, and cook for 1½ hours.

2. Drain off all the liquid into a saucepan. Blend the cornflour with a little water and mix into the cooking juices, then place on the heat and stir until boiling and thickened. Return the liquid to the meat, add the parsley, mix, and leave to cool completely.

3. Place the flour, salt and suet in a food processor and blitz. Transfer to a mixing bowl, add 300ml (½ pint) water and mix until smooth. If making individual pies, divide the dough into eight balls, four weighing 185g (6½oz) and four weighing 115g (4oz). If making one large pie, divide it into two balls, one 740g (1lb 10oz) and the other 460g (1lb).

4. Preheat the oven to 190°C/375°F/gas mark 5. Brush the inside of the tin or tins thoroughly with lard, then dust lightly with flour. Roll out the larger pastry balls and use to line the tin or tins. Divide the filling between them. Brush the pastry edges generously with egg, roll out the smaller pastry balls and place the pastry sheets on top, pushing the edges together. Trim off the excess with a knife and crimp around the edge. Brush with egg, and decorate with pastry trimmings. Cook for 50 minutes. Leave to cool for 5 minutes, then turn out of the tins and enjoy hot or cold.

Slow-roast chilli beef

Top rib is a really tasty, juicy cut of meat that can either be cooked quickly and served rare, or cooked long and slow as in this recipe. It's an underused joint that deserves a place in everyone's kitchen.

Serves 6
Takes 3½ hours

1 tbsp olive oil

1.5kg (3lb 5oz) rolled top rib

4 red onions, peeled and quartered

4 garlic cloves, crushed, then peeled

1–2 red chillies, deseeded and finely chopped

500ml (18fl oz) red wine

sea salt

freshly ground black pepper

1½ tbsp plain flour

½ head of cauliflower, broken into small florets

leaves from 1 bunch of coriander, chopped

1. Preheat the oven to 150°C/300°F/gas mark 2. Heat the oil in a large casserole over a medium-high heat and brown the beef all over. Set aside. Add the onions to the pan and cook for 5 minutes, then add the garlic and chilli and cook for a further minute. Return the beef to the pan and add the wine and seasoning. Cover with a layer of baking parchment, then a layer of kitchen foil and a tight-fitting lid.

2. Place in the oven and cook for 3 hours. Remove the beef and leave to rest in a warm place. Sieve in the flour and mix well with the cooking liquor. Add the cauliflower and place the casserole on the heat. Bring to a boil, reduce the heat and simmer for 4 minutes, then add the coriander.

3. Carve the beef and serve with the sauce.

Duck and pistachio pâté

In the summer months, if you have this in your refrigerator you will always have something to eat, either with hot toast or with a lovely seasonal lettuce and herb salad. The duck fat and skin help to keep the meat moist here, so do not remove them.

Serves 12
Takes 2 hours 40 minutes

1.3kg (3lb) duck meat, including skin and fat

200g (7oz) minced pork

350g (12oz) chicken livers, trimmed

50ml (2fl oz) brandy

200g (7oz) shelled pistachios, plus more, chopped, to serve

leaves from 1 bunch of thyme

sea salt

freshly ground black pepper

115g (4oz) caul fat, ordered from your butcher

1 tbsp duck fat, melted, for brushing

1. Preheat the oven to 180°C/350°F/gas mark 4. Place the duck and pork in a mincer or blender and whizz until chopped. Separately mince or chop the chicken livers. Place all the meat in a bowl, adding the brandy, pistachios, thyme and seasoning.

2. Line a 2kg (4lb 8oz) terrine dish with caul fat, making sure it overhangs the edges, and fill with the duck mixture. Wrap the overhanging fat over, then cover with foil.

3. Place the terrine in a large roasting tin, then add boiling water to come halfway up the sides of the terrine. Bake in the oven for 2 hours or until the juices run clear when the centre is pierced with a skewer. Remove, brush the top with the melted duck fat and sprinkle with chopped pistachios. Cool, then chill in the refrigerator before serving.

Poached chicken and noodle pot

The lightly poached chicken breast is perfectly complemented by the fresh and vibrant flavours that result from the simple cooking style of this dish.

Serves 4
Takes 40 minutes

1 tbsp vegetable oil

4 skinless chicken breasts

2 garlic cloves, crushed, peeled and very finely chopped

5cm (2in) fresh root ginger, peeled and very finely chopped

1 onion, peeled and very finely chopped

1 chilli, deseeded and finely chopped

1 lemongrass stalk, trimmed and very finely chopped

1 litre (1¾ pints) chicken stock

400g (14oz) noodles

350g (12oz) broccoli, broken into florets

leaves from 1 small bunch of coriander, chopped

50g (2oz) toasted sesame seeds

1. Heat the oil in a large saucepan over a medium-high heat and brown the chicken on each side. Reduce the heat and add the garlic, ginger, onion, chilli and lemongrass and cook for a further 2 minutes, but do not brown. Add the stock, bring to a boil, then gently simmer for 12 minutes, until the chicken is cooked. Remove the chicken and keep warm.

2. Add the noodles to the saucepan, submerging them in the stock, and cook according to the packet instructions. Add the broccoli and cook for just 2 minutes.

3. Slice the chicken finely, divide the noodles and broccoli between 4 warmed bowls, then top with the chicken, coriander and sesame seeds. Ladle over the hot chicken broth from the pan and serve.

JUNE

June on the farm

The bakery is busy making pies, including large speciality creations for various celebrations. We made a three-tiered monster the other day for the retirement party of a gentleman who used to eat one of our pork pies for lunch every day. Many years ago, I supplied a butcher in St Peter Port, Guernsey, and I recently received a surprise phone call from the owner. After a much-needed catch-up, he declared that he wished to order meat from us again. I thought I'd tempt him with our other produce and put together a sample box of pies and hams. I heard from him a week later, when he blamed me for his putting on a stone in weight, but he has now ordered a Longhorn from me and asked that it be hung for three weeks before we send it. He plans to order some pies, but they'll be for his customers this time, not himself. I like supplying other good butchers if we have the stock, and have for many years supplied The Hawksmoor restaurant in London. After a successful meeting last month we are now supplying Sophie's Steak House in Chelsea, too. The restaurants order different cuts, so we make better use of the carcass, which is pleasing.

It seems that my two little Galloway Riggit bulls are out to cause me trouble. Last summer they were across the village in a field and we could hear one of them mooing in a very discontented way. It was Mr Riggity Man, my prize-bull-in-the-making. After finding no obvious reason for his discomfort we called the vet out and needed to move both bulls into the farmyard for inspection. We had no crush or handling system at Grange Farm to enable us to do this, but luckily Kevin (who runs Blansby Farm, home to most of our pigs) had also turned up and we had the co-author of this book, Fran, staying with her sons, so we did it the old-fashioned way, with people power, and slowly walked them along the lanes into the pens at the farm.

The vet arrived and, after a few interesting moments involving halters, bent gates and broken rails, Kevin and Mick managed to hold Mr Riggity Man in place. The bull had his temperature taken, was given an antibiotic jab and finally a drench, as it was concluded that he had an upset stomach. A drench involves putting a tube that resembles a vacuum cleaner pipe down the bull's throat, then pouring a solution down the tube into his rumen (one of his stomachs) to settle it.

Just this weekend, my shepherd Arthur reported that the two Riggit bulls were not in their field. We all went out to search for them, as usually when a bull escapes there are tell-tale signs – broken fences, hedges or cow pats – or you can hear them. But there was nothing to be seen. Arthur's wife Lesley thought they had been stolen, but I thought not, as we would have noticed a lorry on a Sunday in these quiet lanes. Eventually we found them three-quarters of a mile away, in a field full of Belgium Blue heifers, doing what nature intended – my two little bulls had lost their virginity.

The journey they'd taken to reach these cows was almost incredible. They had jumped fences, without leaving any evidence of destruction, walked down the extremely steep-sided Levisham valley, swum the river and jumped over more fences. I imagine that the south-easterly wind had blown over the sweet scent of the heifers, enticing my teenage bulls.

The journey that they'd taken to reach these cows was incredible: they had jumped fences, without any evidence of destruction, walked down the extremely steep-sided Leviham valley, swum the river and jumped more fences before arriving.

I needed to talk to Chester Brown, the farmer, to apologize for my unruly lads' behaviour and organize their collection. Luckily, Chester, whose wife Sandra happens to work in our bakery, was very understanding. Collecting them was a challenge, as we had to return with our handling system and build a corral to round all the cattle up so we could extract my two bulls. Once done, we returned home, where I grounded the bulls in a shed for a day before putting them out in a field with two heifers to keep them happy and busy.

Mr Riggity Man is my pedigree bull but the other one, Little Riggity Man, will be going to the abattoir in about six weeks as he is non-pedigree. I bought them together, as Mr Riggity Man needed a companion in the fields, but now he has come of age and is surrounded by heifers I have no worries about his being lonely.

Alan, my all-important handyman who does everything and anything, and me, and anyone else prepared to take a spanner and climb under tractors, are busy checking all the equipment for hay-making, because we will need to have everything in good working order when the sun comes out.

I am pretty exhausted as the days are long and gruelling; I am out on the land at 4.30am and walk in at around 10pm, but I must admit nothing looks better than the dew on the fields at five in the morning, with the sunlight twinkling across the land, cock pheasants scurrying away into hedges and the stock happily grazing on lush grass. In a couple of hours the dew burns off and the image disappears. At least until the next day.

More Tamworth piglets have been born, although only four out of the seven survive. I never expected it to be easy breeding my own herd, and we are getting off to a pretty slow start, but this is farming the old-fashioned way, which takes time, care and patience. I have put my boar Turpin in with four Berkshire gilts, but it seems the girls don't really like him and they are acting rather stroppily. This could be my fault as I don't like to put a boar in with the gilts until the gilts are at least 12 months old and strong enough to take his weight. The problem with this is that they're also bigger and able to stick up for themselves. In commercial farming, gilts are usually put with the boar at eight months and, being smaller, they have no choice about being mounted.

In any case, I have been shopping for new pig arks and water butts as we now have about 75 pigs at Grange Farm. This time last year we had none.

A newly planted meadow at Grange Farm, sown using native seeds.

Oriental pan-fried goose skirt with crunchy salad

This cut is usually cooked slowly, but can also work well cooked as below. Remember to allow the meat to rest, so the muscles can relax. Goose skirt (also called onglet) is a very textured cut of beef that is known for its flavour and can be a little tough for some, but after searing on a high heat, relaxing and slicing thinly, it never seems to fail my family.

Serves 6
Takes 1 hour, plus overnight marinating

For the goose skirt marinade

4 garlic cloves, crushed, then peeled

100ml (3½fl oz) soy sauce

5cm (2in) fresh root ginger, peeled and finely chopped

1–2 red chillies, deseeded and finely diced

freshly ground black pepper

900g (2lb) goose skirt

For the dressing

2 tbsp sesame oil

1 tbsp soy sauce

juice of 2 limes

1 red chilli, deseeded and finely diced

1 garlic clove, crushed, then peeled

For the salad

115g (4oz) bean sprouts

½ Iceberg lettuce, shredded

1 red pepper, cored, deseeded and finely sliced

1 cucumber, peeled, deseeded and sliced

6 spring onions, sliced

leaves from 1 bunch of coriander, roughly chopped

85g (3oz) cashew nuts, roughly chopped

1. Mix all the ingredients for the marinade together and marinate the goose skirt in the fridge for 24 hours, or for as long as possible, turning and basting frequently.

2. Barbecue or griddle on a high heat for 4 minutes on each side for rare, 5 to 6 minutes for medium, or 6 to 8 minutes for well done. Brush with the marinade while cooking. Remove, keep warm and rest for 8 to 10 minutes.

3. Meanwhile, place the bean sprouts, lettuce, red pepper, cucumber and spring onions in a large bowl and toss. Sprinkle with the coriander and cashew nuts.

4. In a bowl, whisk the sesame oil, soy sauce, lime juice, chilli and garlic for the dressing. Cut the beef into ribbons and arrange over the salad, drizzle with the dressing and serve.

The ultimate burger

For a real treat, ask your butcher for some beef legs sawn in half lengthways, so you can scoop out the marrow and mix it with the minced beef.

Makes 4
Takes 30 minutes

1kg (2lb 4oz) minced rump and sirloin

115g (4oz) beef marrow, chopped (optional, but wonderful)

leaves from 1 bunch of parsley, finely chopped

sea salt

freshly ground black pepper

1 egg, beaten

1 tbsp olive oil

4 slices sourdough bread, toasted

115g (4oz) mixed leaves

2 beef tomatoes, sliced

mustards and relishes, to serve

1. Place the minced beef in a bowl and add the beef marrow (if using), parsley, seasoning and egg. Mix well and shape into four burgers.

2. Grill, barbecue or fry the burgers in a little olive oil over a medium-high heat for 3 minutes on each side for rare, 4 minutes for medium and 5 minutes for well done.

3. Plate up the toasted sourdough, top with a handful of leaves, the tomato and the burger. Serve with mustards and relishes.

Seared feather of beef

This is an almost unknown, secret steak. There are only two small feathers on each carcass, and they come from the inside of the shoulder blade. They are good value and deliver a depth of flavour with a good texture. They really only need quick flash-cooking, otherwise they toughen, so take care.

Serves 2
Takes 5 minutes

beef dripping or olive oil

2 feather steaks

mustards or Horseradish sauce (see page 320), to serve

1. Heat the fat in a frying pan or griddle over a medium-high heat and, when hot, sear the steaks for 2 minutes on each side. No longer, please.

2. Remove and rest the steaks for 2 minutes in a warm place. Serve with your favourite mustards or with Horseradish sauce (see page 320).

Barnsley lamb chops
with garlic and anchovies

Barnsley lamb chops are a treat as they are from the best part of the lamb, the saddle. Do not be worried by the use of anchovies in this recipe; it's a combination that works really well and has been used since Roman times. Anchovies cut through the richness and reveal new flavours in the lamb.

Serves 4
Takes 40 minutes

1 head of garlic, cloves separated and peeled

leaves from 4 sprigs of rosemary

4 salted anchovy fillets

freshly ground black pepper

4 tbsp olive oil

4 Barnsley lamb chops, approximately 375g (13 oz) each

1. In a small blender, or with a mortar and pestle, mix the garlic, rosemary, anchovies, pepper and olive oil.

2. Heat the grill to high. Smear the paste all over the chops and grill for 6 to 8 minutes on each side. Serve with Redcurrant jelly (see page 325).

Lamb moussaka

This dish takes a little time to prepare, but the blend of lamb with aubergines makes a great meal that can be prepared in advance, covered and refrigerated, then just put in the oven after a hard day's work. Always make sure you cook it until it is golden and bubbling.

Serves 6
Takes 2 hours

olive oil, for frying

2 onions, peeled and chopped

2 garlic cloves, peeled and finely chopped

900g (2lb) minced lamb

2 tbsp tomato purée

125ml (4fl oz) red wine

1 tsp thyme leaves

1 tsp cinnamon

leaves from 1 bunch of parsley, chopped

sea salt

freshly ground black pepper

2 large aubergines

85g (3oz) butter

85g (3oz) plain flour

500ml (18fl oz) milk

140g (5oz) Cheddar cheese, grated

¼ tsp grated nutmeg

2 egg yolks

1. Heat a little olive oil in a pan over a medium heat, add the onions and garlic and cook until soft. Add the lamb and mix well, breaking up any lumps. Cook for 5 minutes, until browned. Add the tomato purée, wine, thyme, cinnamon, parsley and seasoning. Mix well, cover and simmer gently for 35 minutes.

2. Meanwhile, slice the aubergines finely and sprinkle with salt. Place in a colander, put a plate on top, then a heavy weight. Leave for 30 minutes to drain off excess moisture.

3. Heat a large frying pan over a medium-high heat with a little more oil and fry all the aubergine slices until golden on each side; remove and place on kitchen paper to absorb the excess oil. Take an ovenproof shallow dish and arrange a layer of aubergines over the base. Top with half the lamb, another layer of aubergines, the remaining lamb and a final layer of aubergines. Preheat the oven to 180°C/350°F/gas mark 4.

4. Melt the butter in a saucepan, add the flour and mix to a smooth roux; cook for 1 minute. Remove from the heat and whisk in the milk little by little to make a smooth sauce. Return to the heat and gently bring to a boil, stirring, then simmer for 1 minute. Remove from the heat and add half the cheese, a little seasoning and the nutmeg. Mix in the egg yolks and quickly whisk through the sauce. Pour the sauce over the moussaka, sprinkle with the remaining cheese and bake in the oven for 1 hour until golden. Serve straight from the oven.

Italian slow-roast shoulder of pork

This is a wonderful dish for a large gathering or celebration, as all the work is done in advance and it just needs to be served with a huge salad of all the best seasonal vegetables topped with a good dressing (see page 326).

Serves 20
Takes 8½ hours

1 head of garlic, cloves separated and peeled

5 bay leaves

2 tbsp chopped rosemary, plus a few more sprigs

2 tbsp fennel seeds, ground

2 tsp chilli flakes

1 large onion, peeled and chopped

sea salt

freshly ground black pepper

8kg (18lb) shoulder of pork, skin well scored

4 unwaxed lemons

750ml (1¼ pint) bottle of white wine

1. Preheat the oven to 200°C/400°F/gas mark 6. Place the garlic, bay, rosemary, fennel, chilli, onion, seasoning and 2 tablespoons of water in a blender and whizz to a coarse paste. Rub this generously all over the underside of the meat, avoiding the skin. Slice the lemons and place them and the rosemary in a roasting tin large enough for the pork.

2. Place the pork, skin side up, in the roasting tin. Add the wine, cover with a layer of baking parchment, then a layer of foil, sealing the edges tightly. Cook in the oven for 40 minutes. Reduce the oven temperature to 150°C/300°F/gas mark 2 and cook for a further 7 hours. Do check and baste the pork every couple of hours.

3. Remove the pork from the oven and lift it from the roasting tin. Pour the juices off into a saucepan. Return the pork to the roasting tin. Increase the oven temperature to 180°C/350°F/gas mark 4 and cook the pork uncovered for a further 30 minutes to crisp up the skin. Keep an eye on it at this stage, as it can overcook very easily.

4. Skim the fat from the juices with a metal spoon and discard. Bring the juices to a boil, then simmer and reduce by half. The pork should be so soft that it will not need carving; you just need a fork to scrape the meat from the bone. Serve with the juices.

Jambon persillé

The meat on gammon hocks has a wonderful sweet flavour and a really rosy colour. This simple but delicious dish is very good for a picnic.

Serves 6
Takes 4 hours, plus overnight soaking and chilling

3 gammon hocks

2 pig's trotters

4 sprigs of thyme

2 carrots, peeled and halved

2 onions, peeled and halved

leaves from 1 large bunch of flat-leaf parsley, finely chopped

freshly ground black pepper

1. Put the hocks in a bowl of cold water and soak overnight in the refrigerator, checking and changing the water a couple of times.

2. Place the hocks, trotters, thyme, carrots and onions in a large saucepan, cover with water and bring slowly to a boil. Reduce the heat, cover and simmer for 3 hours. Remove the hocks and trotters and strain the stock through a sieve lined with muslin.

3. When the hocks are cool enough to handle, pull off and discard the skin and any gristle, then remove all the meat, roughly shred it and place it in a bowl. Add the parsley, season with pepper and toss.

4. Line a 1kg (2lb 4oz) terrine tin or bowl with plastic wrap and tightly pack with the ham. Carefully pour in the cooking liquor, cover, refrigerate and chill overnight to set. It will keep in the refrigerator for at least a week. Serve in the sunshine.

Scotch eggs

These giant and very handsome Scotch eggs are a staple at The Ginger Pig and, as usual, the secret of their success is all in the quality of the meat.

Makes 4
Takes 50 minutes

4 eggs, plus 1 egg, beaten, to coat

50g (2oz) plain flour, plus more to dust

700g (1lb 9oz) minced pork

115g (4oz) minced pork fat

2 tsp roughly chopped sage

sea salt

freshly ground black pepper

175g (6oz) Panko (Japanese breadcrumbs)

1 litre (1¾ pints) vegetable oil, for deep-frying

1. Place the 4 eggs in a saucepan of cold water and bring to a boil. Simmer for 6 minutes, then plunge into cold water and peel. Dry the peeled eggs with kitchen paper and dust with flour, which will help the meat to stick to the eggs.

2. In a large bowl, mix the pork, pork fat, sage and seasoning with your hands until well blended. Divide this sausage meat into 4 equal portions. Shape each into a ball. Now insert your thumb into the middle, creating a pocket large enough to fit the egg. Place the egg in the hole and work the sausage meat around it.

3. Put the flour, remaining beaten egg and Panko on three separate plates. Roll the sausage balls in flour, dip into the egg, then roll in the Panko to get an even coating. Now dip again in both egg and Panko to give the outside a thicker crispy layer.

4. Heat the oil in a pan to 170°C/325°F. Cook the Scotch eggs for 13 minutes each, turning them to get an even golden colour. Remove with a slotted spoon and place on kitchen paper to absorb the excess oil. These can be eaten hot or cold.

Roast duck with cherries

When cherries are in season make this with fresh fruit. If they are out of season – or too expensive – don't be ashamed of using a tin of cherries to add a juicy sauce to this simple but delicious roast duck.

Serves 4
Takes 2½ hours

2kg (4lb 8oz) duck

sea salt

freshly ground black pepper

200g (7oz) cherries, stoned

50ml (2fl oz) Port

75ml (3fl oz) chicken stock

4 sprigs of thyme

2 tbsp Redcurrant jelly (see page 325)

1. Preheat the oven to 180°C/350°F/gas mark 4. Trim the duck of any excess skin and remove the fat from the inside cavity at the neck end. Jab the duck all over with a fine-pronged fork to help release the excess fat while cooking. Season well and place the duck on a roasting cradle over a roasting tin. Cook in the oven for 1¼ hours.

2. Increase the oven temperature to 220°C/425°F/gas mark 7 and roast for a further 20 minutes until the juices run clear when the thickest part of the leg is pierced with a skewer and the skin is crispy. Remove the duck from the oven and leave it to rest in a warm place for 15 minutes.

3. Remove the excess fat from the roasting pan with a metal spoon and pour the cooking juices into a saucepan with the cherries, Port, stock, thyme and Redcurrant jelly. Bring to a boil and simmer to reduce by half. Add any juices that have come from the resting duck. Carve the duck and serve with the cherries and juices.

Venison casserole
with prunes and pickled walnuts

Venison is very lean and the biggest challenge to the cook is that of keeping it moist. The most successful way to do this is to make a casserole. This will be full of rich flavours and the prunes and walnuts add texture. If possible, make it a day in advance and then reheat it to get the best-tasting juices.

Serves 6
Takes 3 hours

sea salt

freshly ground black pepper

1.3kg (3lb) venison, cut into 3cm (1in) cubes

1 tbsp olive oil

3 onions, peeled and thickly sliced

2 tbsp plain flour

500ml (18fl oz) of stout, preferably Guinness

3 bay leaves

1 bunch of thyme

250g (9oz) pickled walnuts, drained

8 prunes, stoned

leaves from a handful of flat-leaf parsley, finely chopped

1. Preheat the oven to 180°C/350°F/gas mark 4. Season the venison and place in a large roasting tin with the oil. Toss, then cook in the oven for 20 minutes until browned. Tip in the onions and cook for a further 10 minutes.

2. Remove from the oven, sprinkle in the flour and mix with all the cooking juices, then slowly stir in the Guinness. Add the bay leaves, thyme, walnuts, prunes and more seasoning. Mix well, cover with baking parchment, then secure tightly with kitchen foil.

3. Reduce the oven temperature to 170°C/325°F/gas mark 3 and cook the venison for a further 2 hours until cooked through and tender. Sprinkle with parsley just before serving.

Moroccan chicken with preserved lemons

It is the flavours of the preserved lemon and spices that make this dish sing, while the gentle cooking method adds moisture and gives you really tender chicken, packed with taste.

Serves 4–6
Takes 2 hours

2 onions, peeled and finely chopped

2 tbsp olive oil

4 garlic cloves, crushed, then peeled

1 tsp ground ginger

1 tsp ground cinnamon

2 tsp ground cumin

1 red chilli, deseeded and chopped

2 pinches of saffron strands

freshly ground black pepper

2kg (4lb 8oz) whole chicken

1 litre (1¾ pints) chicken stock

200g (7oz) kalamata olives

2 preserved lemons

leaves from 1 bunch of parsley, roughly chopped

leaves from 1 bunch of coriander, roughly chopped

1. In a casserole big enough to hold the chicken, heat the olive oil over a medium heat and gently cook the onions until soft, then add the garlic, ginger, cinnamon, cumin, chilli, saffron and pepper and cook for 1 minute. Cool, then smear the resulting paste all over the inside and outside of the chicken.

2. Put the chicken into the casserole, add the stock and bring to a gentle simmer. Cover with a lid and simmer for 1½ hours, turning the chicken twice, until the juices run clear when the thickest part of the leg is pierced with a knife. Remove the chicken from the pan and keep warm.

3. With a metal spoon, skim the excess fat from the top of the stock. Boil rapidly over a high heat to reduce its volume by half.

4. Return the chicken to the pot with the olives. Chop the whole preserved lemons into slim wedges and add them with the parsley and coriander. Bring back to a simmer for 2 minutes, then serve with couscous.

JULY

July on the farm

Sarah, our stock-
woman, checking
and feeding the
Galloways.

For the past few years I have promised myself I will organize the garden
at Grange Farm and – at last – I am happy to say that it is done, so as a
much-deserved treat I went to the Hampton Court Festival as one final
addition is needed for my garden: a Victorian greenhouse. After much
looking and investigating I am introduced to Robert Jamison, who I think
will be up to the job. He is going to visit next month to look at the site, as
I want to build the greenhouse on the back bakery wall. It will be 18 feet
long and 10 feet deep and I will be using it to propagate English herbs for
our sausages, vegetables for the farm kitchen and country flowers. I also
purchased some lovely old gardening tools. These are usually hard to find
as I only collect those with the original manufacturer's label and name.
It was a great day, although very hot and crowded, which I am not used
to with all the open space up here on the moors.

I returned home to the sad discovery that my chickens had been greatly
diminished in numbers by a fox. The foxes are wretches and will watch
us all year just waiting for one mistake, and then they jump in for the kill.
The annoying thing is that they only kill for enjoyment and not for food,
so in this one evening we lost over 100 of the chickens that we have been
bringing on for the last 11 months. The working days are long and
strenuous at this time of year. We work by daylight, from the crack of
dawn at 4.30am to 10.30pm, so exhaustion and fatigue are our constant
companions. It is impossible to put the chickens away before sundown
and, on this one evening, someone fell asleep and the fox was waiting,
ready to pounce. Obviously I am furious, so the next night I lie in the field
and take my revenge on the fox with a single gunshot. But still I am at a
loss over my chickens and not sure if I can bring myself to replace them.

Every two years the cattle need to be tested for tuberculosis. Kate, the
local young partner vet with red hair and a large collection of earrings,
arrives to do the job. We round them up and run the tests, but I have
another problem for Kate. I had been watching one of my Belted Galloways, Tatiana, who was in calf when scanned, but has not given birth.
So I ask Kate to examine her, as something's definitely wrong. Kate
sadly finds a mummified calf that Tatiana seems to be trying to abort.

She tries to remove it; but in doing so, the wall of Tatiana's uterus tears. Kate is very upset and feels that she has failed. She suggests we shoot Tatiana, as her chances of surviving an operation are only 50:50. Kate also points out that at this stage we could still use Tatiana for private butchery, which isn't possible once the cow has been given antibiotics.

Steve from the butchery got ready to shoot Tatiana with the humane killer; everyone was ready but very sad and quiet. I went for a walk into the other Galloways field and just looked at how beautiful they were and thought: no, I can't do this.

Steve from the butchery got ready to shoot Tatiana with the humane killer; everyone was ready but very sad and quiet. I went for a walk into the field where the other Galloways were grazing and just looked at how beautiful they were and thought: no, I can't do this. So I quickly ran back to the farm and told them to stop. Arthur, my senior shepherd, walked off in a huff, saying I was going mad, but I asked Kate to go ahead and operate. I felt I had to try; I needed to put the health of the cow first, rather than to think about the health of my bank account.

After the operation, Tatiana is looking a little worse for wear and the next few days are critical. Kate phones constantly to check the cow's progress and comes to have a look three days later. Obviously Tatiana is scared and does not want to enter the crush, so we attempt to entice her in with some oats. After chasing the cow round the barn for 40 minutes, we finally secure her. Kate is happily surprised to find that Tatiana doesn't have a high temperature, all feels fine inside and the wound is healing well. She suggests we put Tatiana out into the field by the farm with the sheep.

Two weeks later all is still going well. I am so very grateful to Kate. As she saved my Galloways, I took a bunch of flowers to the practice for her. I do realise that a hefty bill will arrive soon, but I'm so relieved that Tatiana is still with us and remind myself that my animals' wellbeing comes first.

Alan, my adaptable handyman, is frantically going over the fields with the thistle cutter. This is the best time for it and there is an old saying that I firmly believe about these horrible weeds:

Cut in May and they are here to stay
Cut in June and it's a month too soon
Cut in July and they will wither and die

I have been watching the weather forecast like a hawk to find a good, dry window during which to cut the hay. One day, the prediction is that it will be dry and sunny, so I cut a field of 35 acres, and then it rains. Oh, well. I spun the hay out to dry and a few days later we had turned it into 300 bales of good-quality hay, which is very pleasing.

Another field that I planted with new grass in September and that has had no stock on it was just cut, and we made some beautiful haylage (a feed that is halfway between hay and silage). I do get so much joy out of the productivity of nature. I will again leave this clean ungrazed grass to grow – it is known as 'fog' due to the beautiful colour that it has in the early morning mists. Come the end of September I will put the ewes on it for 'flushing' in preparation for tupping. This wonderful new rich grass will add vitality, increase their fertility and give them a higher chance of conceiving twins. I always say that putting sheep on fog is similar to sending one's wife to Claridges.

A John Deere
tractor in the yard
of Grange Farm.

Rump steak with salsa verde

Rump steak is considered to be the most flavoursome cut by some, but it does need a little extra cooking due to its firmer texture. The salsa verde makes a great addition and brings this simple dish into the summer season.

Takes 15 minutes
Serves 4

olive oil

4 rump steaks, each 200g (7oz) in weight

sea salt

freshly ground black pepper

Salsa verde (see page 324)

1. Heat a griddle pan over a medium-high heat and lightly brush with oil. Cook the steaks for 3 minutes on each side for rare, 4 for medium and 5–6 minutes for well done. Remove and season. Keep warm and allow to rest for 4 minutes.

2. Serve with generous spoonfuls of Salsa verde.

Beef and black bean chilli

This is chilli with a difference. Black beans work far better than kidney beans as they are slightly smaller and give a more velvety texture. I love chilli made with chopped beef instead of minced as it adds texture and makes for a more sophisticated meal.

Serves 8
Takes 3 hours, plus overnight soaking

For the chilli

200g (7oz) dried black beans

4 tbsp olive oil

1.3 kg (3lb) skirt or chuck of beef, cut into 1cm (½in) dice

2 onions, peeled and roughly chopped

2 garlic cloves, crushed, then peeled

1 red chilli, deseeded and finely chopped

2 cans chopped tomatoes, each 400g (14 oz)

100ml (3½oz) red wine

sea salt

freshly ground black pepper

For the guacamole

2 avocados

juice of 1 lime

1 green chilli, deseeded and finely chopped

4 spring onions, finely chopped

leaves from 1 bunch of coriander, chopped

1. Soak the beans overnight in cold water. The next day, drain off the water and put the beans in a large pan. Cover with fresh water and bring to a boil. Rapidly boil for 10 minutes, reduce the heat and simmer for 30 minutes, until soft. Drain and set aside.

2. Meanwhile, preheat the oven to 180°C/350°F/gas mark 4. Heat half the oil in a large roasting tin. Add the meat and brown on all sides, then put in the oven and cook for 20 minutes. Add the onions, garlic and red chilli and cook for a further 5 minutes, then add the tomatoes, wine, 200ml (7fl oz) water and seasoning. Cover the roasting tin with baking parchment and seal with kitchen foil, then cook in the oven for 2 hours.

3. Remove the chilli from the oven, add the beans and stir through, cover again and return to the oven for 30 minutes.

4. Remove all the flesh from the avocados, add the lime juice, green chilli, spring onions, coriander, remaining olive oil and seasoning. Mix well.

5. Serve the chilli in bowls and top with the guacamole and a spoonful of soured cream. Make sure you have lots of toasted flat bread for dipping.

Tortilla
with smoked bacon and cheddar

A good butcher usually has a bowl of bacon offcuts, which you should always buy as they are really useful for pasta sauces, salads, casseroles or for this tortilla. You can use whatever cheese you like instead of Cheddar.

Serves 4
Takes 30 minutes

1 tbsp olive oil

1 onion, peeled and finely sliced

200g (7oz) smoked bacon offcuts, roughly chopped

200g (7oz) cooked potatoes, peeled and sliced

6 eggs

3 tbsp milk

sea salt

freshly ground black pepper

115g (4oz) Cheddar cheese, grated

1. Preheat the oven to 180°C/350°F/gas mark 4. Heat the olive oil in an ovenproof frying pan over a medium heat, add the onion and bacon and cook for 5 minutes. Add the potatoes and cook for a further 2 minutes.

2. Beat the eggs with the milk and seasoning. Pour into the pan and cook for 5 minutes over a low heat. Sprinkle on the cheese and place in the oven for 10 minutes, until set and golden on top.

3. Serve hot or cold, cut into wedges, with a crisp green salad.

Chilli sausages and beans

I love the way the fat from the sausages helps to make a rich and tasty sauce. Some of the beans will burst, helping to thicken the juices.

Serves 6
Takes 1¼ hours, plus overnight soaking

400g (14oz) dried butterbeans

1 tbsp olive oil

12 pork sausages

1 red onion, peeled and finely sliced

2 garlic cloves, crushed, then peeled

2 red chillies, deseeded and chopped

1 tsp sweet smoked paprika

2 tbsp tomato purée

100ml (3½fl oz) red wine

250ml (9fl oz) beef or chicken stock, plus more if needed

1 tbsp balsamic vinegar

sea salt

freshly ground black pepper

leaves from 1 bunch of parsley, roughly chopped

1. Soak the beans overnight in cold water. The next day, drain off the water, rinse the beans and put them in a large pan. Cover with fresh water, bring to a boil and cook rapidly for 10 minutes, then reduce the heat and simmer for 40 minutes, or until the beans are soft. Drain.

2. Meanwhile, preheat the oven to 180°C/350°F/gas mark 4. Heat the oil in a large casserole pan over a medium-high heat and brown the sausages until they are a rich golden brown. Add the onion and cook for 5 minutes, then add the garlic and chilli and cook for a further minute. Stir in the paprika, tomato purée, wine, stock, vinegar and seasoning. Mix well, then stir in the cooked beans.

3. Cover with a lid and place in the oven for 45 minutes. Check while cooking and add a little extra stock if the pan is a little dry. Stir in the parsley and serve.

Chicken and pork jambalaya

This dish originates from the south of the United States and can contain a variety of ingredients, but originally it was always made with gammon or ham. Today you get very glamorous versions containing exotic seafoods, but I adhere to the humbler tradition.

Serves 6
Takes 2 hours

2kg (4lb 8oz) whole chicken

2 tbsp olive oil

400g (14oz) gammon, diced

2 garlic cloves, crushed, then peeled

2 red peppers, cored, deseeded and roughly chopped

1 onion, peeled and roughly chopped

400g (14oz) long-grain rice

115g (4oz) raisins

115g (4oz) peas

¼ tsp cayenne pepper

1 tsp sweet smoked paprika

sea salt

freshly ground black pepper

leaves from 1 bunch of flat-leaf parsley, roughly chopped

1. Place the chicken in a large saucepan and cover with water. Bring to a simmer, cover and cook for 1 hour. Check the chicken is cooked by piercing the thickest part of a thigh with a skewer; the juices should run clear. If there is any trace of pink, continue cooking for a few minutes more and check again. Allow to cool, then remove all the meat from the carcass and chop. Reserve the stock.

2. In a large saucepan, heat the oil over a medium heat and sauté the gammon for 6 minutes, then add the garlic, peppers and onion and cook for a further 4 minutes. Tip the rice into the reserved chicken stock with the raisins and simmer for 12 minutes.

3. Add the chicken, peas, cayenne, paprika and seasoning to the gammon mixture and cook for 5 minutes. Finally, mix in the cooked rice and the parsley. Check the seasoning; it should be strong and fiery, but I will leave this up to you.

Boned and rolled summer stuffed shoulder of lamb

Shoulder of lamb is good value and has a richer, sweeter flavour than the leg. Your butcher should be happy to bone the shoulder for you or, if you are feeling ambitious, you can do it yourself. You'll need a little knife to carefully make small, stroking cuts around and over the bones; it will only take you about 10 minutes.

Serves 6
Takes 2½ hours, plus 1 hour soaking

115g (4oz) dried apricots

115g (4oz) couscous

1 tbsp olive oil, plus more for the tin

1 red onion, peeled and roughly chopped

2 garlic cloves, crushed, then peeled

115g (4oz) pine nuts, toasted

leaves from 1 large bunch of parsley, roughly chopped

1 egg, beaten

sea salt

freshly ground black pepper

1.5kg (3lb 5oz) shoulder of lamb, boned weight

1. Preheat the oven to 180°C/350°F/gas mark 4. Place the apricots in a bowl and cover with boiling water. Leave to plump up for 1 hour.

2. Just cover the couscous with boiling water and fork through until soft. Heat the olive oil in a saucepan over a low-medium heat and cook the onion until soft. Add the garlic and cook for a further 2 minutes. Stir into the couscous with the pine nuts and parsley. Mix well. Drain and chop the apricots and mix into the couscous with the egg and seasoning.

3. Lay the shoulder of lamb out flat, skin side down, and fill with the stuffing, then roll and secure every 5cm (2in) with butcher's twine. Place in a lightly oiled roasting tin and cook in the oven for 1 hour 45 minutes.

4. Leave to rest for 10 minutes, then carve and serve with a tomato salad.

Pea and ham soup

When peas are abundant, make this soup and enjoy the perfect marriage of these two fresh and vibrant flavours.

Serves 6–8
Takes 2 hours

900g (2lb) smoked ham hock

25g (1oz) butter

1 onion, peeled and finely chopped

2 celery sticks, finely chopped

500g (1lb 2oz) shelled peas

sea salt

freshly ground black pepper

4 tbsp crème fraîche

1 tbsp Dijon mustard

leaves from 2 sprigs of mint, roughly chopped

1. Place the ham in a large saucepan, cover with water and bring to a boil. Cover and simmer for 1 hour. Leave to cool. When cool enough to handle, discard the skin and any gristle and strip the ham from the bone and chop; strain and reserve the stock.

2. Meanwhile melt the butter in a saucepan over a low heat and gently cook the onion and celery until soft. Add 1 litre (1¾ pints) of the ham stock and simmer for 20 minutes. Add all the peas and simmer for 8 minutes, then blend until smooth.

3. Add the ham to the soup and check the seasoning, then simmer for 5 minutes to reheat the meat. Mix together the crème fraîche and mustard, and serve the soup topped with the mustard sauce and mint.

Roast short back of smoked bacon

Tim got the idea for this recipe from one of his customers. We all love bacon and it goes so well with roasted apples and onions. Try serving this dish for the ultimate weekend brunch.

Serves 4–6
Takes 2½ hours

1 tbsp olive oil

1.5kg (3lb 5oz) back bacon, in one piece

4 onions, peeled

4 eating apples

leaves from ½ bunch of parsley, roughly chopped

leaves from ½ bunch of basil, roughly chopped

1. Preheat the oven to 190°C/375°F/gas mark 5. Lightly oil a roasting tin. Score the bacon skin, then place in the tin, skin side up. Cover with kitchen foil and cook in the oven for 30 minutes, then reduce the oven temperature to 150°C/300°F/gas mark 2 and cook for a further 1½ hours.

2. Cut the onions and apples into quarters and core the apples. Remove the foil from the tin and lift out the bacon. Increase the oven temperature to 180°C/350°F/gas mark 4.

3. Add the onions and apples to the tin and baste with the cooking juices. Return the meat to the pan and cook for a further 30 minutes. Sprinkle on the herbs and serve.

Wokked duck and greens

Duck blends so well with the spices and soy, making a lovely rich flavour. The addition of the green vegetables adds a welcome crisp crunch to the dish, and it's worthy of a dinner party starter.

Serves 2
Takes 20 minutes

1 large duck breast or 350g (12oz) leftover roast duck

1 tbsp vegetable oil

5cm (2in) fresh root ginger, peeled and finely chopped

1 garlic clove, crushed, then peeled

1 red chilli, deseeded and finely chopped

200g (7oz) Tenderstem broccoli, trimmed and florets halved lengthways

2 heads of pak choi, trimmed and halved lengthways

4 spring onions, sliced

75ml (3fl oz) chicken stock

1 tbsp soy sauce , preferably Kikkoman

1. Slice the duck breast as thinly as possible. Heat the vegetable oil in a wok over a medium-high heat and cook the duck until brown on all sides. If using leftover roast duck, shred the meat and just quickly fry in the wok.

2. Add the ginger, garlic and chilli and toss for 2 minutes. Add the broccoli, tossing frequently, then the pak choi, spring onions, stock and soy. Quickly cook for 1 minute more, then serve immediately.

Tandoori chicken wings

These wings must be eaten with your fingers as that is the only way to pick all the tasty meat from the bones. Make sure you buy free range wings from a good butcher; they are larger and have far more flavour. If children are going to be eating these wings, leave out the chilli powder.

Serves 4
Takes 45 minutes, plus marinating

pinch of saffron strands

4 garlic cloves, crushed, then peeled

juice of 1 lemon

10cm (4in) fresh root ginger, peeled and finely grated

2 tbsp garam masala

1 tsp paprika

1 tsp turmeric

½ tsp chilli powder

1 tsp ground coriander

1 tsp ground cumin

sea salt

freshly ground black pepper

16 chicken wings

1. Place the saffron in a large bowl and soak in 4 tbsp of boiling water for a few minutes, then add everything else except the chicken and mix well.

2. Cut off the small end joint of each chicken wing with a sharp knife; you can use these joints for the stock pot. Place the wings in the marinade and rub well, coating all over. Cover and place in the refrigerator overnight, or leave at room temperature for 1 hour.

3. Preheat the oven to 180°C/350°F/gas mark 4. Place the wings in 2 roasting tins and cook for 35–40 minutes until crisp and golden.

Squeaking chicken legs

Hungry mouths love this dish, and the great mix of flavours transforms
a simple roasted chicken leg into a flavour-packed surprise. Ask your local
butcher if he makes his own sausages: if so, he will usually be able to sell you
sausage meat.

Serves 4
Takes 45 minutes

600g (1lb 5oz) sausage meat

leaves from 3 sprigs of sage, finely chopped

1 small onion, peeled and finely chopped

sea salt

freshly ground black pepper

8 large chicken legs, boned

8 rashers of streaky bacon

2 tbsp olive oil

1. Preheat the oven to 180°C/350°F/gas mark 4. Put the sausage meat in a bowl with
the sage, onion and seasoning, and mix with your hands until well blended. Divide this
stuffing into 4 and use it to fill each chicken leg cavity. Wrap the bacon around the legs
to make parcels and use a cocktail stick to secure.

2. Heat the olive oil in an ovenproof pan over a medium-high heat and brown the
chicken on all sides. Transfer to the oven and cook for a further 30 minutes.

AUGUST

August on the farm

It's a pleasure to see all my sheep neatly clipped and tidy, running around the fields and moor looking fantastic. My two local shearers clipped 630 Mules in one day, then returned to finish off with 600 horned sheep and stragglers on another day. They both know what a proper day's work is all about: first thing in the morning they lay out five T-shirts, then they exchange a soiled shirt for a fresh one throughout the day to try and give themselves that extra boost to keep going. They are bent double, hauling and clipping the sheep, and say, 'Once you stop you will never start again, so we work until the last animal has been clipped and then leave to recover, eat and drink!'

My combine harvester, a real big boy's toy, has come out of the barn, the battery is being charged and Alan and I are checking it over in excited anticipation that the wheat and barley will be finishing growing, changing from green to gold, and then my days will be spent harvesting. Although I drove it over to Blansby Farm for its official service it broke down on the main road, so what was meant to be a quick job took up the rest of my day and caused a huge traffic jam around Pickering.

With all these crops growing prolifically we have major crow problems. It's maddening. They strip the ears from the barley and can decimate large patches of a field in a day. Arthur has been busy making scarecrows out of old boiler suits, stuffing them with hay, and placing bangers around the fields. I saw him the other day with a large galvanized drum on the back of the quad bike and, when I asked him what he was up to, he told me how in his last job he had learnt his lesson about laying bangers along the hedges in dry weather: once he returned to the farm to find the fire brigade there. So the bangers were going to be placed safely in drums, which will also make them louder and hopefully get rid of the crows.

It's all going a bit pear-shaped on the staffing front in London and giving me a headache. Patrice has left us to become a van driver and think about what he really wants to do with his life, as the much-anticipated salami and ham production never started.

Paulo, who originally was a porter in Moxon Street before he showed his skills in the kitchen, has been offered a job with a bakery, which is where his interests lie. Nathan, my butcher from Borough Market, has handed in his notice, as a friend of his is opening an American-style barbecue restaurant and Nathan has been asked to butcher all the meat. To top all this I have also given David three weeks off to go camper-van touring around Spain with his mum. David is my right-hand man and I really need him to help sort out the staff, but we will have to pull through it while he is on holiday. My favourite saying when it all gets a bit difficult is 'Chuffing hell'. Not sure what it means, but just saying it makes me feel a little better. Maybe I will have to move down to London for a while and settle into some work in one of the shops until we find permanent replacements, or maybe we will just make do instead, as things are pretty tight and August is usually a relatively quiet month.

> *My favourite saying when it all gets a bit difficult is 'Chuffing hell'. Not sure what it means, but just saying it makes me feel a little better.*

We are already planning ahead for Christmas. David has built a new database for all the Christmas orders and Amy is nervous, but she has been with us for a year now, so will have a better knowledge of meat with which to help customers when they're ordering.

Perry and Borut, two of our London butchers, made a trip to the farm so we could discuss and plan the butchery classes. They are now fully booked five nights a week, each for 12 enthusiastic gourmets. We feel that it's time for a change. The boys are both great on the farm and really enthusiastic, it takes Perry to a lifestyle that he has never had before, so at 6am he is in the yard looking at the pigs and then an hour later I find him walking across the fields to my Galloways and the sheep. This is especially useful, because back in the shops he can really connect with the customers and tell them about the farms and our methods. Borut, however, grew up on a pig farm in Slovenia, so he always has something to tell me about when his dad farmed their pigs.

They are great guys, and after lots of discussion we have decided to add new classes: an advanced beef class to introduce people to lesser-known cuts from the front and rear of the animal, which both require more complex butchery and cooking; and another class in response to a constant request we get for a stuffed three-bird roast. It's not something I want to sell, but a class is a good way to teach people how to do their own. We will have a partridge and guinea fowl ready and then students will be taught how to bone a large chicken, and assemble them with stuffing. The second half of this class will concentrate on carving a leg of lamb, chicken and a leg of pork.

The boys are both excited and looking forward to introducing their new classes. First of all, though, they have a holiday as there are no butchery classes this month. Scott, the butcher in Moxon Street, was very pleased when Nigella Lawson came to the shop the other day to film for her new TV series and he was the lucky butcher on duty to serve her a shoulder of pork. There must be something about his charm, as he also served fellow TV-presenter Gizzi Erskine when she was filming her show. He is one thrilled and star-struck butcher.

My pigs are breeding well and it seems as if my wish to start a new herd of Plum Pudding pigs may be happening. We should have some little ones running around in a couple of months. That will bring me immense pleasure. One of the Tamworth runts escaped the other day, I really do not know how, but he was found down at the bottom of the village. We think that he must have been out for at least two days, as he was in need of a jolly good feed.

There is never a dull day on the farm. I can never make definite plans as something always comes along and makes me have to think again, be it weather, animals, staff or breakdowns. The list is endless. One thing I do know is that I have spent so much of my life trying to produce the perfect animal that I may have forgotten to start my own family. A conscientious farmer's life is all-encompassing and relentless, but we do it because we are committed to our stock and to British farming.

This field of barley is almost ready for harvest.

Lamb tagine

Use a cheaper cut for this long, slow, gently cooked spiced tagine.
It's a perfect complete meal, as the vegetables are gently braised
with the lamb, infusing all those wonderful, exotic flavours.

Serves 4–6
Takes 2½ hours, plus at least 2 hours marinating

1kg (2lb 4oz) scrag/neck of lamb on the bone, cut into 6 pieces

1 tsp ground ginger

1 tsp ground coriander

1 tsp ground cumin

1 tsp paprika

pinch of saffron strands

pinch of dried chilli flakes

1 tbsp olive oil, plus more if needed

2 onions, peeled and finely sliced

2 garlic cloves, peeled and sliced

1 tbsp tomato purée

½ butternut squash, peeled and chopped into 5cm (2in) chunks

2 courgettes, chopped into 5cm (2in) chunks

1. Place the lamb in a bowl with the ginger, coriander, cumin, paprika, saffron and chilli flakes, and mix well to coat the meat all over. Cover, and either refrigerate overnight or leave at room temperature for a minimum of 2 hours. When ready to cook, preheat the oven to 170°C/325°F/gas mark 3.

2. Heat the olive oil over a medium heat in an ovenproof pan. Add the onions and cook until golden, then add the garlic and cook for 1 minute more. Remove and place on a plate. Add a little extra oil if needed and increase the heat to medium-high and brown the lamb on all sides. Return the onion and garlic to the pan with the tomato purée. Just cover the meat with boiling water and mix well, cover the dish, then place in the oven to cook for 1½ hours.

3. Add the butternut squash and courgette, mix well and cook for a further 30 minutes. Serve with simple, plain couscous.

Bogotá bavette of beef

My nephew spent time teaching English in Colombia and came back with all sorts of wonderful stories of the food he found there. This is one of the recipes he shared with me, which I have adapted.

Serves 6
Takes 3 hours

1 red onion, peeled and finely chopped

2 garlic cloves, crushed, then peeled

115g (4oz) mushrooms, finely chopped

2 tsp Worcestershire sauce

1 tsp grain mustard

2 tsp freshly grated horseradish

1 tsp thyme leaves

4 sprigs of parsley, finely chopped

2 bay leaves, finely chopped

sea salt

freshly ground black pepper

1kg (2lb 4oz) bavette of beef

750ml (1¼ pints) beer

25g (1oz) butter, melted

115g (4oz) breadcrumbs

1. Preheat the oven to 180°C/350°F/gas mark 4. Mix together the onion, garlic, mushrooms, Worcestershire sauce, mustard, horseradish, thyme, parsley, bay and seasoning. Lay out the beef and spread the mixture over. Roll the beef lengthways and secure with butcher's string every 5cm (2in).

2. Place the beef in a casserole, add the beer, put the pan on the hob over a medium-high heat and bring to a simmer. Cover and put in the oven for 2 hours, until the meat is tender and the liquid reduced.

3. Increase the oven temperature to 200°C/400°F/gas mark 6. Take the beef from the casserole and brush with the melted butter. Spread the breadcrumbs out on a plate and roll the beef through them, coating it generously all over. Return to the oven and cook for a further 15 minutes, until golden. Remove, keep warm and leave to rest.

4. Bring the cooking juices to a boil and reduce by half. Slice the beef and serve with the juices spooned over.

Carpaccio of beef

You really must use the best air-aged beef here. There is nowhere to hide with this dish; it shows the meat in all its true and natural glory. You can choose between sirloin, fillet or rump depending on your budget, though rump can be a little too textured for some. If possible, buy double the amount of meat you will need, as it will make carving a lot easier and leave you with steaks for the following night.

Serves 4
Takes 10 minutes, plus 1–2 hours freezing

400g (14oz) beef sirloin, fillet or rump (see above)

115g (4oz) rocket

1 lemon

4 tbsp best olive oil

sea salt

freshly ground black pepper

1. Trim the meat of any fat or sinew and place in the freezer to chill for 1–2 hours. This helps to firm the meat, making slicing easier.

2. Just before serving, slice the semi-frozen beef across the grain with a very sharp knife to make sheets of beef as thin as possible. You should be able to see light through them. Place in one layer on 4 serving plates, covering the plates all over. (You must only carve the beef just before serving, otherwise it will discolour.)

3. Top each plate with a handful of rocket, a squeeze of lemon, a drizzle of olive oil and seasoning, and serve at once.

Lasagne

A great recipe made with a mix of meats that add extra flavour to this classic dish. People of all ages love it. I think it is very important to get a golden – almost crispy – topping.

Serves 6
Takes 2 hours

1 tbsp olive oil, plus more for the dish

1 onion, peeled and finely chopped

1 carrot, peeled and finely chopped

1 celery stick, finely chopped

2 garlic cloves, crushed, then peeled

85g (3oz) bacon, finely diced

400g (14oz) minced beef

175g (6oz) minced pork

2 cans chopped tomatoes, each 400g (14 oz)

1 tbsp tomato purée

1 tbsp dried oregano

100ml (3½fl oz) red wine

sea salt

freshly ground black pepper

85g (3oz) butter

85g (3oz) plain flour

850ml (1½ pints) milk

1 bay leaf

400g (14oz) spinach lasagne, pre-cooked

115g (4oz) mozzarella or Cheddar cheese

1. Lightly oil a large, shallow ovenproof dish. Heat 1 tbsp oil in a pan over a medium heat, add the onion, carrot and celery and cook for 5 minutes, until soft. Add the garlic, bacon, beef and pork and cook until browned, stirring continually. Add the tomatoes, tomato purée, oregano, wine and seasoning and simmer gently for 45 minutes, stirring occasionally.

2. Preheat the oven to 200°C/400°F/gas mark 6. Melt the butter in a saucepan, add the flour and mix to a smooth paste. Cook for 1 minute, then remove from the heat and slowly add the milk, stirring between each addition. Add the bay leaf, return to the heat and stir until the sauce reaches a gentle boil. Remove from the heat.

3. Place one-quarter of the white sauce in the prepared dish. Top with one-third of the pasta in a single layer, then one-third of the meat sauce. Repeat until all the ingredients are used up, finishing with a layer of white sauce.

4. Slice the mozzarella or grate the Cheddar and arrange over the top, then put in the oven and cook for 45 minutes, until golden and crisp.

Roast grouse

If you must, enjoy your grouse on The Glorious 12th, or you can wait a while and the price will drop, making this an even more enjoyable meal.

Serves 2
Takes 45 minutes

sea salt

freshly ground black pepper

2 grouse

25g (1oz) butter, softened

1 tbsp olive oil

4 rashers of smoked streaky bacon

115g (4oz) watercress

1 tbsp walnut oil

½ tbsp red wine vinegar

1 Preheat the oven to 220°C/425°F/gas mark 7. Season the grouse and rub it all over with the soft butter.

2 Oil a roasting tin lightly and add the grouse. Lay the bacon over the breasts and cook in the oven for 20 minutes, or until the juices run clear when the thickest part of the flesh is pierced with a skewer, then remove and keep warm.

3 Toss the watercress in the walnut oil and vinegar. Serve the grouse with the fiery watercress salad and Bread sauce (see page 323).

Seared wood pigeon breast with blue-cheese and walnut salad

Wood pigeons have plump breasts and their meat has a great depth of flavour. They are truly wonderful cooked pink, but do slice them finely.

Serves 4
Takes 25 minutes

1 tbsp olive oil

4 skinless pigeon breasts

1 head of cos or other lettuce, washed

1 bunch of chives, snipped

85g (3oz) walnuts, roughly chopped

1 tbsp red wine vinegar

3 tbsp walnut oil

sea salt

freshly ground black pepper

115g (4oz) Roquefort cheese

1. Heat the olive oil in a frying pan over a medium-high heat and sear the breasts for 1–2 minutes on each side for pink meat and 2–3 minutes for medium. After cooking, remove from the pan and leave the meat to rest.

2. Meanwhile, make the salad. Put the salad leaves into a bowl with most of the chives, the walnuts, vinegar, walnut oil and seasoning. Toss and divide between 4 plates.

3. Using a sharp carving knife, slice the breasts as finely as possible and lie the meat across the salad. Crumble the Roquefort evenly between the plates, sprinkle over the remaining chives and serve.

Sticky duck legs braised with plums

Try this. It is truly delicious. The richness of the duck leg is offset by the tartness of the plums, while spices and chilli make the flavour sensational.

Serves 4
Takes 2¼ hours, plus overnight marinating

2 tsp five spice

2 star anise

3 tbsp soy sauce, preferably Kikkoman

1 cinnamon stick

2 red chillies, deseeded and chopped

1 tbsp demerara sugar

4 large duck legs

1 tbsp white wine vinegar

16 plums, stoned

1. Mix together the five spice, star anise, soy sauce, cinnamon, chillies and sugar in a casserole. Add the duck legs and rub all over with the marinade. Cover and leave in the refrigerator overnight.

2. The next day, preheat the oven to 200°C/400°F/gas mark 6. Place the duck legs in a roasting tin and cook for 1 hour. Now mix in the vinegar and plums, making sure that the duck legs are on top. Return to the oven, reduce the temperature to 170°C/325°F/gas mark 3 and cook for a further hour.

3. The meat should be tender and falling off the bone and the plums collapsed and soft, making a rich and sticky sauce. Serve with jasmine rice.

Accompaniments

Nothing beats a beautiful piece of meat quite simply roasted, but I do believe every good roast must have a gravy, made with the help of all those condensed rich juices that have escaped the meat while roasting. In this section, I give recipes for the classic sauces that I also find make meats sing.

It's really important to leave time to allow your roast joint to rest after cooking in order to achieve perfection. This is for two reasons: the first is that it will give you time to make the gravy; and the second is that it allows the muscles in your roast joint to relax and tenderize, and for excess juices to seep out. These can be added to your gravy for a real depth of flavour and I always tell people to keep their roast warm while it is resting. (If you have an Aga, its slow cooker is the perfect place.)

Transfer your roast to a serving platter when keeping it warm and use the roasting tray with its meat juices as a saucepan, placing it directly on the heat to make your gravy.

I use the seasons to inspire my sauces: I like to make Salsa verde in the summer to add a twist of fresh herby flavours, or I add a little Harissa for a tempting red spiced heat (for both, see page 324), or you could just enjoy a classic Mint sauce (see page 323). The choice is yours, but be inspired by these recipes and use them to add sparkling flavours that will enhance your meat.

Beef stock

The trick to a really tasty and deep brown beef stock is to roast the bones until well browned before adding them to the stock pot.

Makes 2–3 litres (3½–5¼ pints)
Takes 5 hours

2kg (4lb 8oz) beef bones

2 onions, peeled and cut into large chunks

2 carrots, peeled and cut into large chunks

2 celery sticks, cut into large chunks

3 bay leaves

4 parsley stalks

10 peppercorns

1. Put the beef bones, onions, carrots and celery in a roasting tin and place them in the oven. Turn the oven temperature to 230°c/450°F/gas mark 8 and cook for 1 hour. This browning will help to add colour to your final stock.

2. Place the roasted ingredients in a large stock pot and add the bay leaves, parsley stalks and peppercorns. Cover with 3–4 litres (5¼–7 pints) water. Bring to a boil, skim off any scum, then reduce the heat to a very gentle simmer. Partially cover with a lid and gently cook for 4 hours. It is important not to rapidly boil the stock, as this will make it cloudy.

3. Strain into a clean pan, leave to cool and set, then remove the fat from the top and discard. The beef stock is now ready for use, or you can freeze it in small tubs and use it for gravy, casseroles and soups.

Horseradish sauce

When you see a root of fresh horseradish, (it looks like a long, skinny parsnip), buy it and make this sauce. It adds fire and bite to a simple joint of roast beef, and is delicious mixed through mashed potatoes served with cold beef the next day.

Serves 6
Takes 10 minutes, plus 2 hours marinating

85g (3oz) horseradish, peeled and grated

1 tsp white wine vinegar

1 tsp English mustard

115g (4oz) crème fraîche, plus more if needed

sea salt

freshly ground black pepper

1. Tip the horseradish into a bowl, add the vinegar and mustard and blend.

2. Add the crème fraîche and seasoning and leave to infuse and improve in flavour for 2 hours before serving. Taste your sauce: if it's too hot, add extra crème fraîche.

Chicken stock

Home-made stock is a treat for every good kitchen, nothing beats the depth and freshness of flavour that will enrich anything to which it is added. Indeed, some recipes, such as Poached chicken and noodle pot (see page 260) should only ever be made with homemade stock.

Makes 2–3 litres (3½–5¼ pints)
Takes 2½ hours

4 raw chicken carcasses (if you are a good customer your butcher will give them to you)

2 onions, peeled and cut into large chunks

1 leek, well washed and cut into large chunks

2 carrots, peeled and cut into large chunks

2 celery sticks, cut into large chunks

10 peppercorns

2 bay leaves

2 sprigs of thyme

1. Place all the ingredients in a large stock pot. Cover with 3–4 litres (5¼–7 pints) water and bring to a boil. Remove any scum that comes to the top, partially cover with a lid, then gently simmer for 2 hours.

2. Strain the stock into a clean pan, leave to cool, then remove the fat from the top and discard. The stock is now ready for use, or freeze it in small tubs and use it for gravy, casseroles and soups.

Poultry giblet stock

Giblets are the gizzard, heart, liver, kidneys and neck of the bird, and sometimes you are lucky enough to have the head and feet to add to the stock pot as well. Ask your butcher for a 'long-legged chicken', and then you will get it whole, with head and feet, and can ask him to butcher it for you. If using turkey giblets, double the quantities of all the ingredients except the giblets.

Makes 600ml (1 pint)
Takes 2 hours

1 set of poultry giblets

1 carrot, peeled and cut into large chunks

1 onion, peeled and cut into large chunks

1 celery stick, cut into large chunks

1 leek, well washed and cut into large chunks

5 peppercorns

2 parsley stalks

1. Put all the ingredients in a pan, cover with 1 litre (1¾ pints) water and bring to a boil. Remove any scum that comes to the top, partially cover with a lid, then gently simmer for 1½ half hours.

2. Strain the stock into a clean pan, leave to cool, then remove the fat from the top and discard. The stock is now ready to use for gravy to accompany your roast bird.

Quince jelly

If you or a friend have a quince tree you must make this sauce. It is so very special and goes well with all roast meats.

Makes about 4 jars, 500g (1lb 2oz) each
Takes 3 hours, plus 12 hours dripping

1.8kg (4lb) quinces

preserving sugar with pectin
(see recipe below for the amount to use)

juice of 2 lemons

small knob of butter

1. Roughly chop the fruit (do not peel, core or remove the pips) and place in a heavy-based pan. Just cover with water, bring to a boil, cover and gently simmer until soft. This may take 2 hours, so check and add water if needed. When soft, set a large muslin-lined colander over a bowl, pour in the quinces and their juice and leave for 12 hours.

2. Sterilize your jars. The correct way to do this is to heat them in a moderate oven, but I put them through the dishwasher on a hot cycle. Cool.

3. Measure the juice, and for every 600ml (1 pint) add 500g (1lb 2oz) sugar. Place the liquid in a heavy-based pan with the lemon juice and stir until the sugar has dissolved. Gently bring to a steady boil for 10 minutes. Now remove a teaspoonful, place on a saucer and cool for 2 minutes. If it doesn't wrinkle when pushed with a fingertip, continue boiling and test every 3 minutes.

4. When at setting point, add the butter to the liquid to disperse the froth. Carefully pour jelly liquid into the jars and seal. Leave to cool, label and store in a cool, dark place for up to 5 months.

Redcurrant jelly

Perfect for lamb, nothing beats your own jelly, as it will be packed with fruity flavour.

Makes 8 jars, 500g (1lb 2oz) each
Takes 25 minutes, plus 1 hour dripping

2kg (4lb 8oz) redcurrants

2kg (4lb 8oz) preserving sugar with pectin

1. Place the redcurrants, stalks and all, in a heavy-based pan and gently heat and crush them with the back of a spoon to release their juices and soften. Simmer for 10 minutes. Add the sugar and bring to a rapid boil for 10 minutes, stirring frequently.

2. Set a muslin-lined colander over a large bowl. Tip in the redcurrant mixture and allow it to drip through for 1 hour. Take a teaspoonful of the jelly and place it on a saucer and cool for 2 minutes. If it doesn't wrinkle when pushed with a fingertip, continue boiling and test every 3 minutes.

3. When at setting point, pour into sterilized small jars (see left, step 2) and seal. Leave to cool, label and store in a cool, dark place until needed, for up to 5 months.

Mint sauce

Quick to make and with fresh, clean, cutting flavours to complement rich lamb.

Serves 6
Takes 10 minutes

leaves from 1 bunch of mint, finely chopped

6 tbsp red wine vinegar

2 tsp caster sugar

1. In a bowl mix together the chopped mint, vinegar and sugar.

2. Serve with roast lamb.

Bread sauce

I do believe that you either love or hate this sauce but, as I have grown older, I have learnt to enjoy its velvety texture and its creamy subtle flavours that go so well with poultry.

Serves 6
Takes 1 hour

1 small onion, one half peeled and finely chopped, the other half left unsliced

50g (2oz) butter

3 whole cloves

1 bay leaf

500ml (18fl oz) milk

pinch of ground nutmeg

115g (4oz) fresh white breadcrumbs

sea salt

freshly ground black pepper

1. Heat half the butter until it is soft in a saucepan placed over a low heat, and gently cook the chopped onion. Stud the other half of the onion with the cloves.

2. Put the bay leaf, milk, nutmeg and studded onion in the pan with the cooked onion and bring to a boil. Season and simmer for 10–15 minutes. Remove from the heat and leave to infuse for 30 minutes.

3. Take out and discard the studded onion and bay leaf. Add the breadcrumbs. Place one-third of the bread sauce into a blender and whizz, then return to the pan with the remaining butter. Stir the mixture until it is amalgamated and return to the heat to warm through. Check the seasoning, adjusting as necessary, and serve.

Salsa verde

This is really best if chopped by hand but, if you are in a rush, place the ingredients in a blender and whizz – but take care it is not overchopped and turned into a paste.

Serves 6
Takes 20 minutes

6 anchovy fillets, finely chopped

3 garlic cloves, crushed and peeled

2 tbsp capers, rinsed and finely chopped

2 tbsp gherkins, finely chopped

leaves from 1 bunch of parsley, finely chopped

leaves from 1 bunch of basil, finely chopped

leaves from 1 bunch of tarragon, finely chopped

juice of 1 lemon

2 tsp Dijon mustard

freshly ground black pepper

6 tbsp extra virgin olive oil

1. Mix together all the chopped and crushed ingredients, then mix in the lemon juice, mustard and pepper.

2. Slowly pour in the olive oil and mix to form an emulsion. You can adjust the amount of oil to your preference to give a thick or thin sauce.

3. Serve with just about everything from roast chicken to beef. It's a summery sauce, so remember to put it on the table at a barbecue.

Harissa

A hot Moroccan sauce that is not for the faint-hearted, which should always be served with Middle Eastern food. This recipe makes a jam jarful and will store in the refrigerator for up to two months.

Serves 6
Takes 25 minutes

85g (3oz) dried chillies

1 tsp ground caraway

3 garlic cloves, peeled

1 tbsp ground cumin

175g (6oz) red peppers, cored, deseeded and skins removed

sea salt

freshly ground black pepper

100ml (3½fl oz) olive oil, plus more to cover

1. Cover the chillies with boiling water and leave to soak for 15 minutes.

2. Add all the other ingredients and, using a hand-held blender, blitz to a smooth paste; adjust the consistency with water if desired.

3. This will keep in a refrigerator for up to 2 months, covered with a thin layer of olive oil.

4. Serve this 'neat' (undiluted) with grilled meat or thinned down with lemon juice and olive oil and drizzled over simply grilled fish.

Parsley sauce

A delicious sauce. Serve this sauce with my Boiled collar of ham (see page 253), to achieve complete gastronomic heaven.

Serves 6
Takes 1½ hours

500ml (18fl oz) milk

1 onion, peeled

2 cloves

2 bay leaves

50g (2oz) butter

50g (2oz) plain flour

sea salt

freshly ground black pepper

leaves from 1 bunch of parsley, finely chopped

1. Heat the milk in a saucepan over a low heat and stud the onion with the cloves. Add the onion and bay leaf to the milk just before it boils, then remove the pan from the heat and leave to infuse for 1 hour.

2. Strain the milk, melt the butter in another pan, then stir in the flour and mix to make a smooth paste. Cook for 1 minute. Remove from the heat and whisk in a small amount of the milk. Repeat until all the milk has been added. Return to the heat and bring to a gentle rolling boil, stirring constantly, for a couple of minutes.

3. Season and add the parsley, stir and serve, traditionally, with gammon or white fish.

Tomato sauce

A useful recipe that is an essential basic for all good cooks and is also as the sauce used for the Meatballs (see page 104) and Meat loaf (see page 219).

Serves 6
Takes 1 hour

1 onion, peeled and finely chopped

2 garlic cloves, crushed peeled and finely diced

3 tbsp olive oil

2 cans chopped tomatoes (each 400g)

1 red chilli, deseeded and chopped (optional)

1 tbsp red wine vinegar

2 tsp caster sugar

sea salt

freshly ground black pepper

1. Sauté the onion and garlic in the olive oil gently for 5 minutes; do not allow to brown. Add the tomatoes and chilli, if using, mix well and simmer gently for 20 minutes, stirring frequently.

2. Blend with a hand-held blender until smooth, then add the vinegar, sugar and seasoning. Return to the heat and simmer gently for a further 20 minutes, stirring frequently. If the sauce gets too thick, simply add a little water.

3. If tomatoes are in season and abundant, replace the canned tomatoes with 1kg (2lb 4oz) fresh tomatoes that have been peeled and chopped. To peel tomatoes with ease, cut a cross in their skins and plunge into boiling water for 30–40 seconds. When cool enough to handle, slip off the skins.

The very best vinaigrette

When you have a lot of guests, why not serve a very economical slow-roast shoulder of pork (see page 275) with both a green salad and new potatoes dressed with this delicious vinaigrette. To make more dressing, just double the amounts listed below.

Serves 6
Takes 15 minutes

2 tsp Dijon mustard

1 garlic clove, crushed and peeled

2 tsp caster sugar

2 tbsp white wine vinegar

6 tbsp extra virgin olive oil

sea salt

freshly ground black pepper

1. Place the mustard, garlic, sugar and vinegar in a jam jar. Put on the lid and shake until blended.

2. Add the olive oil and seasoning, replace the lid of the jam jar and shake it rapidly until the mixture is fully blended.

3. Store the dressing in the refrigerator, shaking again before use in order to re-emulsify the liquid.

Yorkshire pudding

Always use a metal container to cook Yorkshire puddings, as it will reach a higher temperature than any other material. It is also very important to pour the batter into your metal dish when it both hot and it contains hot fat.

Serves 4
Takes 35 minutes

115g (4oz) plain flour

2 eggs

300ml (½ pint) milk

sea salt

freshly ground black pepper

2 tbsp beef dripping or vegetable oil

1. Preheat the oven to 200°C/400°F/gas mark 6. In a blender, mix together the flour, egg, milk, 50ml (2fl oz) water and seasoning.

2. Heat the dripping or oil in a 23cm (9in) diameter metal cake tin or individual muffin tray. Place in the oven for 5 minutes then brush the melted dripping around the inside of the tin.

3. Put the tin back into the oven to make sure that the dripping is piping hot.

4. Carefully pour the batter into the hot tin and cook at the top of the oven for 25 minutes, until golden, puffed and crisp. Serve at once.

Roasting table

	Temperature			Cooking time		
	°C	°F	Gmk	Mins/kg	Mins/lb	Extra time
Beef: start at	220	425	7	First 20 mins cooking time		
Beef: reduce to	170	325	3	30	15	
Veal:	180	350	4	55	25	20
Lamb:	190	375	5	55	20	
Pork:	200	400	6	65	25	
Chicken:	180	350	4	40	20	20
Turkey: less than 6kg (13lb)	200	400	6	30	14	
Turkey: more than 6kg (13lb)	180	350	4	35	15	
Duck:	190	375	5	45	20	
Goose:	190	375	5	55	25 (total time)	
Guinea fowl:	190	375	5	35-40		
Pheasant:	190	375	5	35-40		
Partridge:	190	375	5	30		
Grouse:	190	375	5	25		
Quail:	190	375	5	20		
Pigeon:	190	375	5	20		
Teal:	190	375	5	20		
Mallard:	190	375	5	40		
Ham:				40	20	

Note: all the timings for the cooking of poultry are for unstuffed birds. Temperatures are calculated for a fan oven; if using a conventional oven increase the heat by 10–20°C

Kitchen tips

A Butcher's Knot

This slip knot is extremely useful when you are tying boned and stuffed loins, stuffed legs of lamb etc, as you can adjust its tension, giving a snug hold. When you are tying meat, place the roll of butcher's twine in the pocket of your apron or in a drawer to prevent the entire reel from coming in contact with raw meat.

1. Draw the end of the string away from you so that it passes under the meat, then draw it back towards you, over the top of the meat.

2. Cross the end of the string (nearest your body) under the left side of the bottom strand (attached to the roll). With your left hand, pinch the point where the strings intersect.

3. Cross the end of the string up and over the right side of the top strand, leaving a large keyhole opening.

4. Pull the end of the string under and through the keyhole. Tug the string down towards the floor, closing the knot.

4. Pull the strings away from each other in order to tighten the knot.

5. Secure with a final basic knot, making sure it is snug (but not too tight or the fibres of your meat will tear and the juices will spill).

6. Cut the end of the string that is still attached to the roll with scissors and trim as necessary.

7. Space your ties evenly, about 3 fingers apart.

N.B. if a butcher's knot defeats you, don't despair. Any knot you like, even a bow, will work as long as the meat is tied securely.

Carving a bird

A chicken is made up of dark meat, that comes from the legs and thighs, and white meat that comes from the breast. I think that the dark meat has a lot more flavour than the white. When carving, it is best to offer your guests some of each type or find out which meat the diner would prefer.

Always let a roasted bird stand and rest for 10 minutes after it comes out of the oven. Place the rested bird on a board and, using a sharp carving knife and fork, cut the skin between the leg and breast, then feel your way down to cut away the leg and thigh with the 'oyster' meat from under the bird.

Cut between the leg joint to separate the thigh and drumstick. Repeat on the other side. Cut both wings away, along with a small slice of breast meat each, to make another two pieces. Finally, carve the breast in thin slices along the length of the bird.

Turkey is carved in the same way as chicken but, due to the larger size of turkey, the meat on the thighs and legs is carved off the bone into small slices.

Duck and goose (see Michelmas goose, shown opposite) are carved in a similar manner, though most of their meat is on their breasts, with far less on their legs and thighs, so take this into consideration when plating the meat.

Achieving crispy pork crackling

The first thing you need to do is to make sure that you choose a cut of high-quality pork with a good layer of fat under the skin. (The modern hybrid pig does not have this.) Ask your butcher to score the pork skin well with a sharp knife.

There are two schools of thought on how to proceed. One is to cook your pork with a blast of high heat at the beginning of roasting. The other is to have this blast at the end – both work. Either way, a high heat is needed at some stage in order to melt off the fat and allow the skin to crunch up.

If your crackling is not crisp enough when the meat is ready to serve, don't worry. Simply cut the crackling away, return it to the oven and cook it for a further 15 minutes, while you have a gin and tonic to begin your meal. After this extra oven time, your crackling will be sure to crack like glass.

Braising and casseroling

Les in our bakery uses this great method to brown meat for casseroles. Instead of browning meat in batches in a pan on the top of the stove, he tosses it in oil and places it in a roasting tin, then simply puts it in a hot oven and roasts it until it is sealed and browned. Then he adds the vegetables and returns the dish to the oven to soften them.

The final stage is to add all the other ingredients, cover the tin with all-important baking parchment, seal it with foil, and continue to cook it in the oven.

I believe that this is a better way to cook, as the heat is far more even, the colour is deeper and it makes for a much richer sauce. If you want to go one step further, cook your dish the day before, cool it, then refrigerate overnight. Gently reheat in the oven the next day. This will give a far superior flavour and consistency to all braises and casseroles.

Curing pork

Curing pork is a traditional skill that was originally acquired through necessity, before refrigeration was widely available. Many smallholdings kept pigs and wanted to preserve the meat to feed themselves over winter, so curing was essential. The two main methods of curing are the wet cure and the dry cure. Both involve salt, sugar and spices.

Dry curing is good for sides of bacon, as the meat is thinner and the salt is able to work its way into it and start the curing process. It is important that the salt is rubbed into all the crevices and holes, as it stops bacteria forming and draws out the moisture from the pork. After curing, the meat is hung until it is needed.

Wet curing is when the meat is submerged in brine to cure (see Wet-cured ham from scratch on page 146). Many people favour wet curing, as it is both easier and gives more successful results with far less loss of precious meat than dry curing.

Once either method of curing has taken place, it is possible to go one step further and smoke the meat, which imparts flavour, though this is down to personal taste, and you will know which you prefer.

Different countries have twists that they add to their cures, such as spices, sugars, beers or wines. The list is endless and it is great fun to play around, to invent your own personal cure. Feel free to experiment with the recipe on page 146, adding your own flavourings.

The Ginger Pig — A Cast of Characters

Grange Farm
Tim Wilson: farmer

Sue Armstrong: housekeeper
Sarah Clubley: good friend and
    stockwoman
Alan Miller: stockman and farm helper
Arthur Ramage: shepherd,
    runs Grange farm stock
Ewan Ramage: apprentice shepherd
Lesley Ramage: stockwoman and gardener

Blansby Farm
Johnny Hodgson: stockman
Kevin Hodgson: pig stockman, runs
    Blansby Farm (unrelated to Johnny)

Eastmoor
Mike Cleasby: cattle stockman,
    runs Eastmoor
Richard Smith: stockman

The office at Grange Farm
Amy Fletcher: butchery-class co ordinator
    and meat-order administrator
David Harrison: operations manager and
    Tim's right hand man
Natalie Stockill: accounts
Ian Welford: accountant
Anne Wilson: co-founder

The Ginger Pig butchers
Nick Askew
Andrew Holmes
Michael Jenkins
Stephen Triffitt

The Ginger Pig bakers
John Bowes: bakery Helper
Leslie Bowes
Sandra Brown
Hester Forshaw
Julie Howe

The Ginger Pig Drivers
Christian Baker
Buggy Battulga
Darren Cottam
Andy Woolcott: transport manager

Moxon Street
Jayne Charlesworth: manager of the
    London shops and amazing co-founder
Erika Kaulokaite: butcher
Scott McCarthy: butcher
Vida Mikutiene
Arueuil Porter
Steve Smythe: butcher

Borough Market
John Baron: butcher
Thomasz Pasternak: sausage maker
Charlie Shaw: butcher

Hackney
Costin Dumitrache: butcher
Daniel Dumitrache: butcher
    (brother of Costin)
Aurelian Serban

Waterloo
Thomas Aston: butcher and shop manager
Adam Brooks: butcher

Butchery classes
Perry Bartlett: butcher
Borut Kozelj: butcher

INDEX

lamb 'Henrys' with beans 160
lamb kofta kebabs 234
lamb moussaka 274
lamb stew with capers and olives 222
lamb tagine 308
mint-crusted roast rack of lamb 232
navarin of lamb 127
regional variations 57-8
rolled and stuffed breast of lamb 255
Roman lamb fillet 186
salt marsh 57-8
seasonality 58
shoulder, cutting two joints from 70-1
slow-roast shoulder of lamb 128
spiced lamb pilaf 194
spring roast lamb with oregano 221
lambing 211
lamb's kidneys:
    lamb's kidneys in rich red-wine sauce 196
    lamb's liver with sage 183
    Lancashire hot pot 184
lasagne 312
leeks:
    boiled collar of ham
        with parsley sauce 253
    braised salmon of beef 110
    chicken stock 321
    citrus roast festive turkey 168
    poultry giblet stock 321
lemons:
    citrus roast festive turkey 168
    Italian shoulder of pork 275
    lamb kofta kebabs 234
    lemon roast guinea fowl 135
    Moroccan chicken
        with preserved lemons 281
    salsa verde 324
    sticky citrus-marinated
        pork chops 240
lentils, roast duck with Puy 187

M
Madeira, pâté, pork and 165
meat:
    on the bone 11
    cooking methods 11
    resting 319
    roasting chart 331
    selecting 11
    storing 11
meatballs in tomato sauce 104
milk:
    parsley sauce 325
    Yorkshire pudding 327
mint sauce 323
mint-crusted roast rack of lamb 232
moussaka 274
mushrooms:
    Bogotá bavette of beef 310

chicken in white wine with porcini 132
coq au vin 167
Ginger Pig beef bourguignon pie 256
lamb's kidneys in rich red-wine sauce 196
roast duck with Puy lentils 187
rolled and stuffed breast of lamb 255
sticky shin rounds with cipollini
    onions and balsamic vinegar 204
mutton 60, 139
    appearance 62
    choosing 62
    Lancashire hot pot 184
    mutton shepherd's pie 149
    slow-baked, herb-crusted leg of mutton
162

N
noodles:
    poached chicken and noodle pot 260

O
olives:
    citrus roast festive turkey 168
    lamb or hogget stew with capers
        and olives 222
    Moroccan chicken with preserved lemons
281
    olive-stuffed chicken leg 224
    Roman lamb fillet 186
    spring beef pasta 239
oregano, spring roast lamb with 221
oxtail, braised 166

P
paella, peasant rabbit 109
papaya, seared rump of beef
    with salad of bean-sprouts and 236
partridge 92
    classic roast partridge 114
pasta:
    smoked pork hock and
        parsley pasta 124
    spring beef pasta 239
pastry:
    hot water 112
    puff 179
    shortcrust 134
    suet 256
pâté:
    duck and pistachio pâté 259
    pork and Madeira pâté 165
pea and ham soup 296
peppers, braised pork with 242
pheasant 92, 93
    game pie 112-13
    pheasant pot 151
pigeon:
    game pie 112-13
    pan-roast pigeon stuffed
        with spinach 205

seared wood pigeon breast
    with blue-cheese and walnut salad 314
pigs:
    Berkshire 15, 16, 21, 157-8, 229, 267
    breeding 229
    breeds 15-17
    characteristics 21
    butchering 23
    cross-breeding 15
    Dutch Landrace 15
    fat 15
    feeding 17
    Gloucester Old Spot 15, 17, 20, 21, 229
    Large White/Yorkshire 15, 21
    litter size 16
    Lop 15, 17, 19, 21, 22
    piglets 229, 267
    Plum Pudding/Oxford 15, 16, 21, 157,
        229, 307
    Saddleback 15, 19, 20, 21
    slaughtering 22
    stages of life 18
    Tamworth 14, 15, 16, 21, 22, 120, 121,
        229, 267, 307
    Welsh 15, 21, 22
pig's liver:
    pork and Madeira pâté 165
pig's trotters:
    home-made gelatine 113
    jambon persillé 276
pilaf, spiced 194
plums, sticky duck legs braised with 316
porcini, chicken in white wine with 132
pork 15-32
    aromatic melting pork 199
    boned and rolled fennel-stuffed
        chump of pork 147
    braised pork with red peppers 242
    braised Spanish pork with muscatel
        raisins 106
    cassoulet 198
    choosing 23-4
    crispy crackling 328
    curing 330
    cuts 23-4, 26-7, 26-7
    duck and pistachio pâté 259
    fat, importance of in cooking 18
    game pie 112-13
    Ginger Pig sausage roll 179
    Hungarian pork goulash 176
    Italian shoulder of pork 275
    lasagne 312
    loin, boning, stuffing and rolling 30-1
    mid-week meat loaf with spiced
        tomato sauce 219
    Peruvian pork 217
    pork fillet with new season rhubarb 200
    pork hash 252
    pork and Madeira pâté 165
    rillettes of pork 178

Acknowledgements

With enormous thanks to all those that have been a part of the making of this amazing book. We start at the beginning with Anna Powell who conceived the idea, enticed publishers and then helped me endlessly by reading my copy and diplomatically, but firmly, advising me how to improve it. Thanks Anna. You were my sanity check, along with Michael Alcock and Francesca Barrie. Thanks to the wonderful team at Alcock and Johnson who represent Tim and myself and congratulations to Anna on the birth of her baby, Billy.

Thanks also to all at Mitchell Beazley for believing so enthusiastically and totally in this book, especially Becca Spry, for your intense guidance and drive, and Pene Parker for such handbags full of total style. We love the look that you have created, continued and confirmed as The Ginger Pig's. To our amazing photographer Kristin Perers, whose classic but individual style has transported the farm onto these pages with such care and attention, and made the food look worthy of a master's oil painting, thank you. Lucy Bannell, who organised the copy with such efficiency and super speed: amazing. Joanne Wilson who put up with all my changes and errors, and was always a total pleasure to talk to on the phone. Tracey Smith for her good humour, enthusiasm, eagle eye and total commitment, so much so that – along with Pene and Joanne – you were willing to work over weekends and until many a 'witching hour' to get things right, thank you. Our thanks also go to our production manager Katherine Hockley, without whose expertise, care and dedication, this book would not be such a thing of beauty. Last but not at all least, thanks go to Sonja Edridge, who helped me to prepare the food for photography; you were my happy, smiling and skilled tinkerbell, turning up each day with a new homemade jam for us to test. We confirm that they were scrumptious – go into business! Thank you one and all equally – we are very happy and feel that the team could not have been more committed, enthusiastic, skilled and helpful to our every request and whim.

We have to, of course, thank all The Ginger Pig farmers, stockmen, butchers, bakers, drivers, and shop staff – and not forgetting the office staff behind the scenes who make the whole thing possible. Hey guys – without you we would not have all the awards and accolades that we have won together.

Thanks also go to the discerning and knowledgeable shoppers who support The Ginger Pig and enjoy the meat and butcher's classes. We hope you enjoy this book, learn about our staff and our wonderful stock at the farm and that you will improve your meat knowledge and skills.

Last but not least, the heroes of this book are the animals. Without our stock, the business would never exist. Once again a big thank you to everyone involved in the making of this amazing and beautiful book.

Commissioning Editor | Rebecca Spry

Art Director | Pene Parker

Photographer | Kristin Perers

Design and illustration | Pene Parker

Production Manager | Katherine Hockley

Assistant designers | Freddie Villiers and Mark Kan

Project Editor | Joanne Wilson

Editorial Director | Tracey Smith

Copy-Editor | Lucy Bannell

Proofreader | Jo Murray

Indexer | Dorothy Frame

First published in 2011 by Mitchell Beazley, an imprint of Octopus Publishing Group Ltd, Endeavour House, 189 Shaftesbury Avenue, London, WC2 8JY. An Hachette UK Company. www.octopusbooks.co.uk Copyright © Octopus Publishing Group Ltd 2011 Text copyright © Tim Wilson and Fran Warde 2011

Reprinted in 2013

The authors have asserted their moral rights.

A CIP catalogue record for this book is available from the British Library.

ISBN: 978 1 84533 558 8

Colour reproduction in Singapore
Printed and bound in China